Out *of the* Shadow

Under the Sign of Nature:
Explorations in Ecocriticism

Out of the Shadow

*Ecopsychology, Story,
and Encounters
with the Land*

Rinda West

Joan—

Thanks so much
for coming to hear
about encounters with
wild nature —

Rinda West

University of Virginia Press
Charlottesville and London

University of Virginia Press
© 2007 by the Rector and Visitors of the University of Virginia
All rights reserved
Printed in the United States of America on acid-free paper
First published 2007

1 3 5 7 9 8 6 4 2

LIBRARY OF CONGRESS CATALOGING-IN-PUBLICATION DATA
West, Rinda.
Out of the shadow : ecopsychology, story, and encounters with the land /
Rinda West.
p.   cm. — (Under the sign of nature : explorations in ecocriticism)
Includes bibliographical references (p.   ) and index.
ISBN 978-0-8139-2655-1 (acid-free paper) —
ISBN 978-0-8139-2656-8 (pbk. : acid-free paper)
1. American literature—History and criticism. 2. American fiction—Indian
authors—History and criticism. 3. Human ecology in literature. 4. Nature in
literature. 5. Self in literature. 6. Nature—Psychological aspects. 7. Environmental
protection in literature. 8. Environmental ethics. 9. Ecocriticism. I. Title.
PS169.E25W47 2007
810.9'355—dc22
2007014337

To Beth and Jill

Contents

Preface

An ethic to supplement and guide the economic relation to land presupposes the existence of some mental image of land as a biotic mechanism. We can be ethical only in relation to something we can see, feel,
understand, love, or otherwise have faith in.
—Aldo Leopold, *A Sand County Almanac*

FOR A DECADE I have been volunteering in the North Branch Restoration Project, part of the Volunteer Stewardship Network of the Nature
Conservancy. Along the North Branch of the Chicago River, we practice ecological restoration on land set aside from development at the beginning of the
twentieth century but mostly unmanaged for a hundred years. The six-county
metropolitan area contains more rare and endangered species than are found
anywhere else in Illinois, and more than one third of the state's dedicated
nature preserves are located here. However, because of fire suppression, hy-
drological alteration, fragmentation, and invasive species, the original biodiversity has been replaced with a less rich mix of species; in particular, many
of the areas where we work have been overcome by European buckthorn, an
aggressive woody species that darkens the land, starving the rich variety of native plants. Working with land managers, we volunteers clear the buckthorn
and other invasive weeds, like garlic mustard; collect and plant seeds of native
plants; and participate in controlled burns. This work provides an intimacy
with the land that does not require us to leave our communities. Working in
restoration means I can experience some of nature's wildness without having
to quit my job, sell my house, and move to the Rockies.

Also for more than ten years, I have been working locally with the C. G.
Jung Institute, taking classes, undergoing analysis, and serving on the board of
directors. I first read Jung as a college junior, in a philosophy of religion class.

Answer to Job made a kind of sense to me that nothing else I'd read on religion had. Twenty years later, in a period of personal (and arguably midlife) crisis, having done enough time in the women's movement of the 1970s to have lost faith in Freud, I turned again to Jung for insight and help. I find in Jungian theory an inclusiveness, an appreciation for the feminine, and an ethical orientation that resonate with my devotion to the natural world.

During this period I also developed a course that I team taught with Terry Trobec, a biologist. Terry provided an introduction to environmental science, while I examined fictions that allow us to look at the ways different cultures have imaged nature and the human relationship with nature. As a teacher and a reader, I have felt, professed, and observed the power of stories to move people and to reframe their experience.

My observations are clearly embodied. After three turbulent antiwar years in the late 1960s as a junior faculty member at the University of Chicago, I chose to leave the university so that I could, as I put it to myself at the time, "make the revolution" with working-class students at a community college. I thus spent my career teaching at Oakton Community College, where teaching counts and language that excludes—such as that found in many scholarly debates—seems a kind of unacceptable elitism. My choices put me at the margin: academic psychology has dismissed Jung, and the fierce competition that accompanies the academic hierarchy consigns community colleges—and other teaching institutions—to the fringes, the academic ghetto. But Oakton was a good place to be a woman. I had moments of regret—moments of feeling humiliated in relation to colleagues at universities who patronized me for my choices—but I didn't have the daily experience of cutthroat departmental politics, competitive pressure, and projection of shadow that characterizes academic life for many women. In addition, Oakton was a wonderful place to work while I was raising two children, since the culture of the college supports the understanding that employees have lives as well as jobs.

After a painful divorce I began taking classes at the C. G. Jung Institute, which led me to psychoanalysis with a wonderful Jungian analyst. My own midlife experience, facilitated by reading, journaling, recording my dreams, and the talking cure, grounds my theoretical engagement with the work of Jung and the post-Jungians. Along the way my lifelong affinity for wilderness grew into a professional interest, and I discovered and began to study the renaissance in American Indian writing. My arguments in favor of restoration are based on many Sundays spent in the prairies and savannahs and on seeing the effects of these activities on ten years' worth of students who have contributed to knowledge, with their research into coyotes, riverine water quality, and the history of our watershed, and to ecological health, with their labor in restoring our campus. My interest in American Indian writing first developed as I taught novels that allowed me and my students to examine various ways of understanding being human in relationship to the rest of nature. I was also personally drawn to the philosophies and religious orientations of Plains Indian cultures, and I have participated in two wilderness solo experiences modeled on the vision quest, one organized for "women whose lives are in transition" by a group of feminist women in Colorado and one organized by the Jung Institute of Evanston and patterned not only on traditional Lakota lines but also on the tradition of withdrawal to the wilderness characteristic of much Western thought.

Thus, the three strands of this study have braided for me over a decade: natural areas restoration and a growing commitment to what Aldo Leopold articulated as the land ethic; an interrogation of the varieties of representation of nature in stories; and an exploration of Jungian theory and practice, particularly the ideas of shadow and individuation.

To write from nature is to practice a kind of postcolonial criticism. This is so in part because Western discourse has historically conflated nature and natives; both are "savage," to be tamed, domesticated, and put to use. However useful this identification was to colonial power, it also reflected, unintentionally, the way many traditional cultures identify with the natural world they inhabit. Therefore, in the search for alternative stories of humans in nature, I have foregrounded American Indian fictions. But the case goes beyond identification with the natural world. Postcolonial writers, and others who imagine themselves into ecosystems, subvert the assumptions, epistemologies, conventions, and ethics of the discourse of normative science and commercial culture. To do so, they may appropriate the language and forms of that discourse, recasting them so they can carry the burden of a place, its relationships and interactions. Thus, the novel, which is linear, heroic, and inscribed, comes to contain the cyclical, enmeshed, community-centered, and often oral way of ecological seeing. In some respects these novels are like dreams, in that they remind us that some part of us is not doomed simply to linear time. The whole of a life is present and alive in dream, and the whole community gets constellated and restored there too.

Many friends and colleagues have provided encouragement and helpful feedback on drafts, in particular Jill Anderson, Mandy Cooper, Terry Davis, Hollace Graff, Mike Kabakoff, Marilee McGowan, Mary Mittler, Laurel

Ross, and Richard Storinger. I'm grateful to the Jungian analysts who read all or parts of the manuscript, including Fred Gustafson, Catharine Jones, Jane Kamerling, Daniel Lindley, Dennis Merritt, Lee Roloff, and Murray Stein.

My students have contributed many insights to this process, and I would especially like to acknowledge Jonathan Lahn and Scott Santoyo. Parts of the book have formed the basis for papers I have given at the conferences of the International Association of Jungian Scholars, the Native American Literature Symposium, and the Association for the Study of Literature and the Environment; many colleagues in the latter organization have been encouraging and helpful, particularly David Brande and David Williams. Parts of the book have appeared in *Spring Journal*, and an early sketch of some ideas on restoration and the work of Louise Erdrich surfaced in a 2001 article in *Michigan Quarterly Review*.

I am grateful to Boyd Zenner and Carol Sickman-Garner at the University of Virginia Press and to Scott Slovic and John Tallmadge for helpful suggestions along the way. I also want to express my gratitude to Trisha Collins, Judy Kroll, and Gretchen Schneider for unfailing humor and efficiency in responding to my many library requests, and to Beth Anderson, Liz Scholom, and Monica Schulter for help checking quotations.

Out *of the* Shadow

1

Toward a Land Ethic

Nature and Shadow

It is inconceivable to me that an ethical relation to land can exist
without love, respect, and admiration for land and a high regard for
its value. By value, I of course mean something far broader than mere
economic value; I mean value in the philosophical sense.
—Aldo Leopold, *A Sand County Almanac*

We Americans need now more than ever before—and indeed more
than we know—to imagine who and what we are with respect to the
earth and the sky. I am talking about an act of the imagination, essentially, and the concept of an American land ethic.
—N. Scott Momaday, *The Man Made of Words*

INTRODUCTION

THE BOY IN LINE behind me just couldn't stand still. "I love it here," he
said to me. "It's so pretty, and it smells so good. I just wish we could go
to the vegetable garden. But my teacher said there wasn't time." We were in the
cafeteria at the Chicago Botanic Garden. There were a lot of school groups,
as there usually are in the spring, and I asked him if his parents could bring
him back. "I don't think they know where it is," he said. He told me he lives
with his dad on the south side. He didn't think his dad had ever been to the
Garden. I asked him if he had any place to plant a tomato, and his face lit up
again. "My grandpa has a garden," he said. "He grows tomatoes." They had
been giving away seedlings in the fruit and vegetable garden, so I gave him
mine. It came with instructions on how to grow the tomato and recipes as

well. I watched him go sit with some classmates and read the instruction sheet.

This boy, like most people today, lives far from places where things grow wild. Even at age nine his life is fast and stressful. The Chicago Botanic Garden offers this child a chance to run around among flowers and trees. It's not wild nature, but it tells an ancient story of how people have tended plants and fostered both beauty and abundance. When I see children at the Garden, from toddlers to young teens, running, laughing, bending over to marvel, I often think of how different they look at the mall, where their faces are bland with boredom or tight with desire. Every day children—and adults, of course—hear stories of war, layoffs, bills, catastrophes, corruption, followed by ads for electronic toys, new drugs, and snazzy cars. In this environment it's easy to sink into fantasies that technology will solve energy shortages, to believe that the loss of species is trivial, or simply not to think. Today is all that matters, the TV croons. Anyway, it's more fun to watch reality shows than to worry about real places we'll never go and real people we don't know. The stories we hear most often, both rapid-fire narratives of the latest disaster and accounts of consumer satisfaction, alienate all of us from nature and from our own sympathetic responses. But alternative narratives that imagine a different relationship between humans and the land are beginning to flourish, stories about connection, community, and personal well-being. Some of these stories are being told in novels written in the last thirty years or so. As these new fictions attract readers, they enter the culture and offer hope for changing consciousness about nature, humans, and the relationship between the two.

This book traces a story of hope that emerges from the damage that has been done to people, cultures, and the land by an attitude of conquest. I begin by looking at two nineteenth-century stories of adventure and exploration that illustrate how the Western attitude toward nature helped to rationalize the conquest of land and the people who lived on it. I then turn to two novels of precolonial life that reveal the worldviews of people living as members of the natural community. The greatest part of my study, however, consists of an examination of contemporary novels that speak to processes of healing, to ecological, psychological, and cultural restoration. When supplemented with an immediate experience of the land, stories about people who find new ways to live with nature, with others, and with themselves can help to reframe alienating old ideas. I group these contemporary novels around three different kinds of places, each of which is associated with a different emphasis in the conservation movement: wilderness areas, rural sites, and land in the process of being restored to a preindustrial condition.

The first novels center on a wilderness sojourn, which in many cultures accompanies a rite of passage into adulthood. Wilderness exposes people to a reality beyond the social world they know. In such novels wilderness experiences inspire young characters to look past the limiting roles constructed for them by their culture. It also opens them to experiences that they cannot explain rationally. In this way it fosters imagination, receptivity, emotional connection, and intuition—all ways of knowing that have been discouraged by the school system and the organization of culture. The experience of wilderness on a personal level underlines the urgency of protecting wilderness politically.

The second group centers on a return "home" to places that have not lost their traditional quality. Characters confront changes that occur in midlife, when public identity begins to wear thin or crack, and people are granted an opportunity to reinhabit potentials they may have left behind. In these novels characters turn from the city to the land, often as the result of a breakdown or trauma. All these works feature characters with dead or absent mothers, who have suppressed their ability to feel. Their turn to the land enables them to reclaim their capacity to love and suggests a movement toward personal integration. These fictions shed light on the bioregional movement, or the thrust toward "reinhabitation," which aims to educate people about their local watershed and promote sustainable living as a way to resolve the alienation between human and nature.

The final group of novels expands the focus to embrace the geographic and cultural community. While these novels' individual characters undergo a variety of personal changes, their weight as a whole is on the restoration of vitality to the culture in the place. They thus include many possible ways of being human in the world. These novels enact the movement toward natural areas restoration, a strategy that engages a community in restoring land to the complexity and self-directing wildness that have been compromised by development.

In all these cases the crucial step involves characters' acknowledging what C. G. Jung called the shadow—the repressed, often frightening and shameful elements of the psyche. Confronting and absorbing these parts of the self into consciousness allow characters to admit the ways they have been projecting their own wild nature onto others, to withdraw these projections, and to learn to practice restraint. When this is accomplished, other potentials that had to be repressed for the characters to survive in their family and culture of origin—positive energies that can serve to enhance psychological, social, and natural life—begin to surface, and the characters are able to live more whole-heartedly.

My work rests on two key premises. The first is that human actions toward the natural world arise from assumptions about nature and the place of humans in nature that are deeply ingrained. These assumptions, which are usually not made explicit, are encoded in a variety of stories, from myths of origin to advertisements for toothpaste. In particular, ideas about the relationship between humans and the rest of nature underlie most literary fictions. When readers are exposed to fictions in which the relationship between humans and the land is very different from the customary one, they begin to see that attitudes they had assumed were universal are not true everywhere, and alternative beliefs and behavior may become more attractive.

The second premise is that assumptions about external nature often reflect the attitude of an individual or a culture toward the animal part of human life—the instincts, the body, the unconscious. Western culture has been dominated by the idea that humans are superior to the rest of nature and raised above our "animal" being by reason or spirit or divine ordination. This separation and sense of superiority lead people to see nature as something very different from humans, making it a "resource" to be exploited for human benefit rather than a community of which we are a part. One consequence is the ecological crisis we now face. Another is a rigid divide between consciousness and the unconscious, a condition that fosters emotional alienation and psychological poverty, cutting people off from intrapsychic resources such as dream and imagination.

The ecological crisis and the current epidemic of addiction, depression, and hopelessness go hand in hand. I believe it's possible to create a new feedback loop that can begin to ease both these sources of distress. Increasing intimacy with nature can soothe stress, and increasing openness to psychological complexity can foster empathy with others, including nonhuman others. If we are to change the current condition, however, we need, among other things, new stories that will reframe old assumptions and provide hope.

CONSERVATION, WISDOM, AND THE LAND

In *A Sand County Almanac*, published just after his death in 1949, the conservation philosopher Aldo Leopold argues that seeing land only in economic terms leads to its degradation. In this context he articulates a "land ethic." "A thing is right," he argues, "when it tends to preserve the integrity, stability, and beauty of the biotic community. It is wrong when it tends otherwise." Refusing to separate humans from nature, Leopold maintains that we must extend the idea of "community" to include the nonhuman—forces, both living and energic, with which we share the planet, "soils, waters, plants, and animals, or collectively: the land."[1] Thus, what ecologists call the ecosystem, Leopold calls "community," a term suggestive of a continuum that includes humans and extrahuman nature. In its inclusiveness this ethic echoes the relationship with place practiced by most American Indian people for millennia before colonization. In placing humans within, instead of above, the biological community, Leopold recalls the ethic of relationship articulated by Vine Deloria Jr., of the Standing Rock Sioux.

A leading American Indian scholar, Deloria goes beyond Leopold in linking ethical behavior in relation to the land with psychological maturity:

> The living universe requires mutual respect among its members, and this suggests that a strong sense of individual identity and self is a dominant characteristic of the world as we know it. The willingness of entities to allow others to fulfill themselves, and the refusal of any entity to intrude thoughtlessly on another, must be the operative principle of this universe. Consequently, self-knowledge and self-discipline are high values of behavior. Only by allowing innovation by every entity can the universe move forward and create the future.[2]

Deloria's ethic mandates mindfulness and respect because it extends a sense of identity to entities beyond the human. In valuing individual, cultural, and biological diversity, this ethic promotes the possibility of novelty of idea and natural adaptation, and hence of change.

Leopold bases his argument for a land ethic on the interdependency of all life, which he illustrates with the image of a biotic pyramid composed of trophic—or feeding—levels. Soil, with its rich mixture of animal, vegetable, and mineral matter, nourishes plants, which provide, through photosynthesis, the food energy for everything else. Insects and herbivores feed on the plants, birds and fish on the insects, and so on up to the large carnivores. At each level up we find fewer and fewer individuals, since the energy transferred to the consumer is only about 10 percent of the energy required to produce and sustain the meal. Hence the pyramid, on which, Leopold observes, "man shares an intermediate layer with the bears, raccoons, and squirrels which eat both meat and vegetables." This land pyramid is more a "tangle of chains" than a chain of command, and "man is one of thousands of accretions to [its] height and complexity." We cannot live or thrive without healthy and abundant layers "below" us. Understanding the interdependence of the pyramid's elements allows us to see that "land . . . is not merely soil; it is a fountain of energy, flowing through a circuit of soils, plants, and animals. Food chains are the living channels which conduct energy upward; death and decay return it to the soil."[3] Interdependence and energy flow implicate humans in a system in which we are not at the top, not the rulers, the purpose for creation, but rather one element, albeit one whose mind permits us an impact that may have unforeseen effects. "The land," in Leopold's use of the term, implies this energy circuit; it is not just soil or geography but a whole interdependent system of life. Leopold points out that the plants and animals native to a place have evolved there to make fullest use of its particular structure of soil, water, climate, other plants, and animals; in this way evolution has favored diversification. Such complex interdependency permits energy to circulate.

Deloria finds in the traditional wisdom of "the old Indians" a very similar understanding of the relationships among beings that determine energy flow. In the American Indian approach to science, knowledge—as well as loyalty and love—comes from long-term observation of a unique mountainside, or arroyo, or grove. Such intimate knowledge is also moral. Its purpose is not to abstract general principles but "to find the proper road along which . . . to walk."[4] Thus, in this traditional worldview the relationship with the land is a religious one, and what humans seek is not control of other entities but rather knowledge of how to live morally in relationship with them in order to preserve the energy flow for all.

When humans interfere in nature's energy circuits, they alter the world in simple or unimaginably far-reaching ways. Leopold writes about how the eradication of wolves led to deer overpopulation and the defoliation of mountainsides. Based on his experiences, he believed that people need to learn to "think like a mountain" so they can take into consideration the long-term consequences of present actions.[5] For example, recent research into trophic cascades elaborates on the ways that changes at one trophic level have huge and unforeseen consequences at seemingly unrelated levels. When corporate headquarters move from cities to farmland or exurbs, often they must build retention ponds to protect themselves from potential flooding. The presence of liquid water in winter attracts large populations of geese, who feed on the lush lawns favored by corporate aesthetics. Goose feces join the fertilizers used to maintain those lawns and then drain into the water table, causing eutrophication, or excess phosphorus in the water, which induces algal blooms. When the algae die, aerobic bacteria feed on them, depleting oxygen in the rivers and lakes and killing fish. This example suggests how quickly natural systems can be changed by human choices, and it indicates how much we still have to learn about the world.

Leopold's vision remains radical today, especially considering that humans have not been able to extend compassion to other humans very successfully, much less to other species. When people live isolated from the land or from people of other races or religions, it's hard for them to develop respect and fellow-feeling. People don't change their fundamental ideas without some profound motivating experience. Aldo Leopold wrote: "An ethic to supplement and guide the economic relation to land presupposes the existence of some mental image of land as a biotic mechanism. *We can be ethical only in relation to something we can see, feel, understand, love, or otherwise have faith in.*"[6] Leopold here underlines two crucial parts of an ethic: it requires experience *and* explanation, practice and theory. Time spent in nature is not enough to generate a new ethic, but neither is story or theory alone sufficient. Change will require that large numbers of people have opportunities to spend time with the land: in urban garden plots and greenways; school programs that teach about and immerse children in nature; corporate headquarters that replace stretches of sod with native plantings and engage employees in restoration of biological diversity; community-supported agriculture that brings volunteers to the farm; restoration projects in city parks; and science education that takes young people to the field to observe, hypothesize, experiment, and reflect. But people also need a new vision of the world that will reframe both our sense of ourselves and our ways of living with the land. When people imagine that a clean environment requires nothing but sacrifice, they see no reason to give up their cars or McDonald's just so a darter snail or a mahogany tree can survive. A new ethic needs to address what humans can gain from living more sustainably. Deloria links the land ethic with psychological growth by stressing the personal values of self-knowledge and self-discipline. Growing conscious of nature can foster self-knowledge and ease alienation, thus rewarding people for practicing a land ethic.

ECOPSYCHOLOGY: KNOWING OUR PLACE (ON THE PYRAMID)

Leopold's image of the biotic pyramid suggests that humans' place in nature is dramatically different from what most people grow up believing. Where *do* humans fit in? And how does ecological practice flow from a person's, or a culture's, beliefs about their situation in relation to the rest of creation?

Among people concerned about the contemporary ecological crisis, a number of theories exist about the causes of the Western divide between humans and the rest of nature. Lynn White Jr. argues that the roots of the ecological problem go back to Genesis, where nature is given as bounty to God's children, to do with as they choose. At the same time the natural world is seen as God's handiwork; it is man's task and joy to steward it. Paul Shepard indicts agriculture as the source of division. Following Vico, Robert Pogue Harrison traces the destruction of forests to early humans' apprehension of sky gods. Jonathan Bate suggests that the longing for a lost "golden age" is as old as civilization itself and that communion with nature was lost when people gathered together in cities to promote survival. In *The Death of Nature*, Carolyn Merchant argues that most Europeans in the period before the Enlightenment believed nature to be animate, resisting such extractive activities as mining as violations of Mother Earth. With the Enlightenment came a new belief that humans are radically different from other animals by virtue of the power of thought. Francis Bacon and Rene Descartes pioneered the scientific method, which assumes an inanimate planet from which the human thinker can distance him- or herself through abstract thought.[7]

Other strains of thought have continued to see spirit in nature, despite the dominant dualism. The English romantics and the American transcendentalists believed nature to be innocent, imbued with spirit, and saw humans, likewise, as in essence good. Many traditional thinkers have understood humans as a part of nature, responsible by virtue of our consciousness, but not superior to animals, plants, and minerals, who are also animate.

Different theories about the place of humans in the natural order have resulted in different ideas about the roles of nature and culture in the formation of human thought and behavior. In literary studies the evidence of nearly three thousand years' worth of written texts suggests that the social forces of history, class, gender, and culture have a resounding influence on the development of character. Jane Austen's women are not Jane Smiley's. However, the same literary history also bears witness to a number of themes that recur across cultures, representing common human experiences, suggesting that something in our biological makeup inclines humans to respond in similar ways. Jane Smiley's women are not, after all, so different from Chaucer's. There is debate today in literary studies about the extent to which we can speak of a human nature. Most theory that clusters around the term *post-*

modernism starts from the premise that culture has the decisive influence on human experience: one cannot locate essential characteristics, because everything is traceable to the particulars of history, class, gender, and race. Such theory has been important in challenging assumptions about, say, women's "place" or "nature," or the notion that Western values are universal, a posture that has helped to maintain a conservative power structure.

Some, however, like the ecocritic Glen A. Love, argue that literary studies needs to attend to the work going on in departments of ecology and evolutionary biology. Love criticizes "nature skeptical" theorists, who believe that the mind is a blank slate, that "human behavior . . . is strongly influenced by genetic orientations that underlie and modify, or are modified by, cultural influences."[8] Donna Haraway, a feminist biologist and professor of the history of consciousness, links biology and culture in her notion that humans are cyborgs, hybrid creatures that are part animal and part technology, both a physical/historical body and a political attitude or consciousness that interacts with information networks, some of which have been developed with human technical knowhow.[9]

Leopold's trophic pyramid is an image that also illustrates a psychological configuration common in Western culture. In spite of changes in thinking among scientists and intellectuals, most people still see humans as the apex of the pyramid. The psyche constructed by this worldview imagines the rational ego, or intellect, as the end point of development, the command center of the brain. In this familiar model the ego "controls" the impulses that are "beneath" it. One way of exercising such control is to deny the existence, or the autonomy, of drives or images arising from the unconscious. The ego constructs a relatively impermeable boundary between itself and the rest of the psyche, which remains mostly unconscious. In this way the ego maintains its self-image as the whole of psyche. It then ignores or discounts information that comes through any pathway but that of the senses, trivializing dreams, fantasies, and physical symptoms. As Jerome Bernstein remarks, one characteristic of the Western ego is that "much of what might fall into the nonrational realm is perceived as irrational, that is 'counter-rational,' and plays into a phobic abhorrence" of, for example, information received through intuition or emotion, or an acute sensitivity to the plight of animals.[10]

The unconscious in humans is often associated with instinct, and the attempt to conquer instinct and impulse has produced a kind of feedback loop. What we conquer we tend to see as inferior, so gradually both instinct and the fantasizing, dreaming, and intuitive parts of the mind have taken on negative associations. As Western culture embraced the scientific and industrial revolutions, the habits of mind associated with myth and religion, the search for meaning and transcendence, became suspect. What could not be demonstrated lost value, and the mythic mode of thought no longer complemented the logical. In cultures as male centered as those of Western Europe, the Middle East, and the United States, intuition and receptivity were assumed to be "female" qualities and were devalued and denied.

The cultural habit of splitting or denying certain traits has also bolstered the conquest of nature. For expanding European empires the superior attitude toward nature was part of the racism that justified colonial conquests of native people. Fear of nature and native people fed the desire to conquer and subdue them, just as greed led to their exploitation or destruction. Both the European "scramble for Africa" and the American "winning of the West" took place at the height of Victorian denial of sexuality and repression of instinctual energy. Those who prided themselves on being civilized projected their own instinctuality onto the people they feared, justifying conquest by calling both nature and natives "savage," "untamed," "lazy," or "wild." The rhetoric of imperial ventures as missions to convert the pagans and civilize the savages implicated the white victors in a hypocrisy that required that they suppress what they had seen and replace it with a "truth" they had constructed. One consequence for the conquerors was a feeling of alienation from their own "natural" selves. Because they identified nature, women, and native people with instinct, passion, violence, idleness, and dreaming, they had to deny these parts of themselves and assert the primacy of commerce and practical reason.[11] Most people today who live in Western countries have inherited this disconnect. Theodore Roszak, who popularized the term *ecopsychology*, argues, "Our sense of being split off from an 'outer' world where we find no companionable response has everything to do with our obsessive need to conquer and subjugate."[12]

Just as the pyramid offers an image of the Western psyche, however, Aldo Leopold's energy pyramid shows that humans are not independent of other species for survival, nor are we alone at the summit: we are one species among many, mutually dependent for survival. Similarly, in psychological life the ego is not all there is to the mind, nor is reason the only source of information. The ego is not independent of the mammalian brain, it is not in sole control, and it may not even be the high point of the psyche. The theoretical work of Carl Jung, the Swiss psychologist who split with Freud over the nature of the unconscious, and that of post-Jungians like James Hillman, Andrew Samuels, and Susan Rowland, provides a way to think about the effects of both nature and culture on the individual psyche. Freud focused on the first half of life, on the causes of neurosis, and on the individual's development of a persona adjusted to culture and environment. Jung focused on the second half of life, on the deconstruction of the persona, and on the growth of consciousness. His concepts of the shadow, the Self, the archetypes, and individuation are particularly useful in looking at literary representations of both human relationships with the natural world and human "nature." Although some postmodernist critics dismiss Jung's idea of the collective unconscious and the archetypes as essentialist and Eurocentric, I see it as a way of acknowledging the power of our biological history and of talking about powerful tendencies to respond in certain ways to situations common in human life.[13]

In addition, the unconscious, as Jung thought of it as "nature," provides a means of apprehending the human continuity with all life. Where reason proposes that humans are separate from nature and struggles for control, the unconscious intuits the connections among humans and those between humans and other beings. For Jung the goal is neither to "conquer" nature (to mine the unconscious until its power is sapped) nor to submit to the unconscious and simply live instinctually. Rather it is to work toward a balance, making nature conscious and learning to deal ethically with instincts and drives. In the novels I study here, connecting with the land appears to be a way also to come to know human "nature," our unconscious life, including both frightening and enriching energies, and our connections with other beings. As Theodore Roszak argues, "The bridge we need to find our way back to a significant sense of connectedness with nature may lie in that shadowed quarter of the mind we have for so long regarded as 'irrational,' even 'crazy.'"[14] The path to wholeness or integration requires that individuals acknowledge their complicity in the frightening and shameful aspects of nonhuman nature as well.

JUNG AND ECOPSYCHOLOGY

For Jung the goal is to live what he called the symbolic life.[15] By this he meant a life guided and enriched by the language of the psyche, revealed in dreams, fantasies, myths, and art. To live the symbolic life entails attending to the images presented by the unconscious, living in the knowledge that ego-consciousness is only a part of the entire personality. Thus, ego is accompanied and eased in its loneliness by its relation to a larger psyche that is the source of great energy. This geography of the soul mirrors the experience of the human in nature: like ego in psyche humans are part of the natural world, neither its purpose nor its conqueror. For Jung the unconscious had a compensating and prospective function. That is, ego-consciousness is limited, and the unconscious compensates for the ego's limits by presenting information the ego does not know. Moreover, unconscious imagery is interesting and important because it suggests directions in which the ego must go in order to grow toward wholeness. Jung broke from Freud over Freud's insistence that the unconscious is primarily sexual in content and that its messages are useful mainly to understand past traumas. Jung believed the psyche includes, in addition to the sexual, impulses that propel a person toward meaning. Living a symbolic life increases meaningfulness and moderates isolation.

Jung proposed two components of the unconscious: the personal and the collective. The collective unconscious is "a hypothesis ... [that] would establish the continuity between the human psyche and the rest of organic nature."[16] It is made up of archetypes, or patterns of behavior and response, that represent "nature"—the human predisposition, because of evolution and genetics, to certain structures of experience and behavior that are triggered by either biological development (e.g., puberty, aging) or environmental stimuli (e.g., the parent, the object of sexual desire). The archetypes are different from the images through which they are known; archetypes are dynamic tendencies to organize experience according to patterns. Jung said of them: "The term ... 'archetype' ... coincides with the biological concept of the 'pattern of behaviour.' In no sense is it a question of inherited ideas, but of inherited instinctive impulses and forms that can be observed in all living creatures."[17] In an ecopsychological context this idea is interesting because it suggests creative as well as destructive elements to instinct. Instinct propels animals to behave in certain patterned ways, as we see in mating flights, territorial struggles, nesting, imprinting, and other phenomena. Archetypes link humans to our evolutionary history and remind us that we are not so different from the rest of the world. Roszak even proposes the existence of an "ecological unconscious" that serves as "a resource for restoring us to environmental harmony."[18]

Jung used the image of a riverbed to elaborate on the idea of archetypes: "Archetypes are like riverbeds which dry up when the water deserts them, but which it can find again at any time. An archetype is like an old watercourse along which the water of life has flowed for centuries, digging a deep channel for itself."[19] The water in this image is psychic energy. As an individual passes through different stages of life, libido ebbs and flows in archetypal channels. The channels, or archetypes, are not themselves images or ideas, but simply patterns. Images of these archetypal patterns can be found across cultures. The instinctual nature of the patterns explains why certain experiences and story types move people deeply.

The notion of archetypes suggests that instinctual energy is organized into recognizable patterns of behavior and feeling that are stimulated by events or persons. When an individual comes into contact with a person or situation that arouses the archetype, emotions and perceptions organize themselves around a powerful, highly charged, instinctual center. These emotions are then associated with subsequent occasions when the archetype is called into play. The Jungian analyst and theorist Antony Stevens uses the example of the mother-child bond. The archetype of the mother becomes constellated in the infant by the mother's presence; the archetype of the child constellates for the mother when she holds her infant: "each constitutes the perceptual field responsible for *evoking the archetype* in the other."[20]

The general structure of archetypes may be common, but they manifest differently in each life in particular ways. Jung called these specific instances personal complexes, which are the way individuals experience the archetypes. He used the word *constellate* to suggest the way feelings organize themselves around particular centers. Complexes become constellated in charged moments when an event triggers the original feelings. Because of the instinctual core, an emotion may be so intense as to feel like possession, as the complex exerts its power over consciousness, or it may feel like regression. Phenomena such as falling in love come from archetypal impulses, and the feeling of being possessed or "crazy in love" testifies to the command that archetypes can exercise. Especially people who think of themselves as highly rational can be astonished at the power of archetypal forces.

The theory of archetypes helps to explain the power and tenacity of personal complexes. As a person's experiences accumulate, archetypal energy organizes memories around highly charged centers that may appear almost as destinies, internal voices, or separate personalities. Jung believed such dissociation was entirely normal. These "secondary selves" appear in dreams, trance, and imagination as figures such as the anima and animus and the shadow. Through this process "personal life becomes grafted, so to speak, onto the collective history of the species."[21] Culture, history, and politics certainly shape human experiences in very different ways, but the relatively short evolutionary history of humans suggests that we are not far removed from the instinctual drives of our common ancestors.

THE SHADOW

Jung was clear that humans individually and collectively have developed consciousness as a means of containing instinct and freeing ourselves from its hold. However, the side effect of that increasing freedom is the shadow. Jung identified shadow as the archetype that has "the most disturbing influence on the ego."[22] As an individual becomes conscious, or develops an ego (what Jung calls an "ego complex," suggesting the charged emotions linked to the sense of self), he or she also constructs a shadow, where rejected and repressed potentials reside—impulses and potentials unacceptable in the family, religion, culture, and historical period. The individual's shadow resembles Freud's unconscious, but in Jung's thought it is not all negative, nor does it constitute the whole of the unconscious. Positive qualities may occupy a person's shadow, such as artistic abilities or athletic talents that were not developed or approved in the family of origin. The taste for certain foods, the desire for ease, or the longing for self-expression may be forbidden and thus come to occupy shadow. Love of nature may be discouraged or untended, so that the individual feels frightened of animals, insects, or unfamiliar environments.

Like the construction of ego, the construction of culture engenders shadow: some beliefs and behaviors must be suppressed, and these make up the unconscious, repressed, and denied shadow of the culture. Early in evolutionary history people must have understood that survival required suppressing impulses to kill members of the clan. As cultures developed, taboos became more elaborate, requiring individuals to conform to complicated codes of desire and behavior. These moral codes carry emotional charges, have the force of divine sanction, and are enforced by collective power. They promote behaviors that improve survival and punish those that endanger it. The collective shadow of the Christian world is personified as the devil; even today some people speak of being possessed by the devil. Some elements of collective shadow will only be triggered in an individual when that person is in a group situation, such as a lynching, a riot, or an orgy. Some aspects of a collective shadow may not disturb members of the group but still be obvious and even offensive to those outside the group. Marie-Louise von Franz offers the example of a group of scholars who spend an evening in spirited intellectual discussion and do not notice the lack of emotional contact: "If all have the same problem, it feels wonderful!"[23]

To become conscious of one's shadow takes considerable effort and entails, as Jung says, "recognizing the dark aspects of the personality as present and real." Shadow evokes powerful feelings of guilt and shame. Rather than acknowledging painful shadow contents as its own, the ego projects them onto others or acts them out as everything from guilty pleasures to violent outbursts. The parent strikes the child because she "asked for it," and the boss screams at the worker because he's "lazy." The most resistant shadow contents tend to be those that are projected, the cause of the emotion seeming to lie in the other person. "The effect of projection," according to Jung, "is to isolate the subject from his environment, since instead of a real relation to it there is now only an illusory one. Projections change the world into the replica of one's own unknown face. In the last analysis, therefore, they lead to an autoerotic or autistic condition in which one dreams a world whose reality remains forever unattainable."[24] Thus, shadow projections divide people from one another and from nature itself.

Metaphors in common use reveal the association of nature with psychological distress: feeling flooded or swamped, being lost in the woods, weaseling out of an obligation, pigging out, bugging someone, and so on. All these represent projections of troublesome human emotions onto nature. They suggest a link between self-loathing and a willingness to dissociate oneself from the natural world. If you want to glimpse your shadow, examine closely those people you most immediately despise or those places from which you recoil. In the loaded and emotive language of both Joseph Conrad and Francis Parkman, for example, we see evidence of the projection of shadow onto both nature and native people. The belief that the jungle is "menacing" or the prairie "empty" justifies their conquest, just as labeling native people "savage" and "primitive" rationalizes their enslavement and devastation.

Repressed impulses do not vanish. A shadow instinct toward violent behavior can be socially indulged if the shadow is projected onto the Other, justifying a righteous war. In nineteenth-century European culture, sex was consigned to shadow, its danger often projected by men onto women; this gave sex great power, leading Freud to believe it the fundamental drive. And just as individuals can become more conscious about their own instinctual drives, enabling them to become more ethical in restraining antisocial impulses, cultures too can release certain material from its confinement in shadow and become more conscious, capable of better behavior. Freud's work has dissolved some of the denial of sexuality, freeing individuals to a greater erotic enjoyment while asking of them more conscious ethical standards for sexual conduct. (Obviously, higher standards do not guarantee better behavior.) Similarly, in the last half century, the United States has made progress in withdrawing some shadow projections from people of color and releasing their talents and energies into the culture.

Whatever forces may be forming human conduct, consciousness provides the possibility of acknowledging them and responding with an ethical way of behaving. These cultural examples suggest how acknowledging shadow energies as one's own and withdrawing their projections from another release energy. A biologically based understanding of archetypes does not condemn humans to a biologically constrained existence; moreover, the possibility that certain structures of response are biologically based does not undermine the power of consciousness to shape the specifics of a life or of culture to change in response to greater consciousness. If men and women are different—and recent research suggests something more like a continuum than a binary switch—that does not mean that women should perform clerical work rather than brain surgery any more than it means that men must join the army to act out their territoriality. New understanding of the capacities of both sexes can become encoded in cultural practices and written into law. Jung called self-development an *opus contra naturam*: consciousness, as it absorbs its own "nature," makes ethical choices about how to act on that knowledge. Without consciousness there is no freedom from the compulsion of instinct. But without access to the unconscious, the ego lacks energy; the personality becomes sterile and, as Jung said, "autistic."

JUNG'S IDEAS OF THE SELF

Jung posits a model of mind in which, in the course of development, the ego differentiates itself from the whole of psyche, which Jung calls the Self. Jung's apprehension of the totality he called the Self is often confusing, since he also used the word to mean the psyche's tendency toward self-correction and wholeness, as well as its tendency to produce images and symbols of God, the hero, the transcendent. In both these capacities the Self indicates a sense of purpose, order, and hope in psychic life. The way Jungians talk about the Self suggests a kind of wisdom in the DNA. This language reveals Jung's penchant for what may seem to be a paradox—the Self is both center and whole—that derives from his commitment to holding opposites in tension. Marie-Louise von Franz calls the Self "an inner guiding factor that is different from the conscious personality and that can be grasped only through the investigation of one's own dreams. These show it to be the regulating center that brings about a constant extension and maturing of the personality. . . . How far it develops depends on whether or not the ego is willing to listen to the messages of the Self."[25]

From the idea of the Self emerges one of the most important characteristics of Jung's thought, a characteristic that distinguishes it from Freud's. Jung believed that "everything unconscious aspires to the condition of consciousness, and that this aspiration possesses a fundamentally *religious* intention."[26] At times in Jung's work, it seems that the Self is the intrapsychic manifestation of God, and at other times it appears that God is the projected image of the Self. It helps me to think of an atom: the Self is both the nucleus and the entire atom, abuzz with electrons in varying states of motion and balance. If one thinks of an atom as both matter and energy, the inevitable imprecision in defining the Self becomes more understandable. If one lets go of asking "Is God within or without?" one can see the Self as a way of speaking about the human drive to find meaning and the human experience of numinosity.

Because people find in extrahuman nature energies that are both frightening and transfiguring, the religious response to the nature around us can provide insight regarding the kindred "nature" within. According to William Willeford, a Jungian analyst and professor of literature, the "human urge to find and create meaning is not derivative but primary, and . . . feeling and imagination are necessary to some of the deepest kinds of meaning."[27] This "urge to find and create meaning" is a part of human "nature." The Self also communicates to the ego in dreams, fantasy, and active imagination, providing images that compensate for the limitations of consciousness and in that way suggesting directions in which the psyche needs to move in order to manifest potentials or correct imbalances in its journey toward wholeness. This Jung saw as the prospective function of the Self.

INDIVIDUATION

Messages from the Self, whether they come in dreams, cultural symbols, or religious experiences, do not automatically drive the growth of consciousness; growth requires work. Jung believed that the task of life is to bring to conscious use the potentials that were spun off into shadow or that never made it into consciousness. He called this process of increasing wholeness or integration "individuation," which entails reconciliation of consciousness and instinct or, on a larger scale, of culture and nature. Individuation is distinct from individualism, which involves the assumption that we can make it on our own without help from (or responsibility to) anything larger—community, family, society, deity, the unconscious. Jung saw individuation as the goal of the second half of life, a process of increasing recognition of shadow, integration of neglected potentials, and restraint of repressed drives that represents a movement toward wholeness. The process of individuation provides a way to think about changes that need to take place in the culture in order to achieve a consciousness dedicated to living sustainably.

Individuation most often begins in midlife, and the first step is usually an encounter with shadow. This may occur in a number of ways: recurrent nightmares may bring the shadow into consciousness; anger or envy may consume a person's energy; addiction may reach a crisis; boredom and loss of libido may lead to severe depression or simply feeling stuck. This encounter is sometimes experienced as a process of breakdown, or deconstruction, in which one has to give up old ideas about the self, particularly heroic ideas, and accept one's flawed, mutable, physical, unappealing, and shameful aspects. In this process a person may enter a liminal space in which old adjustments no longer work but there is no sign of a new outlook. Countless writers testify to the humiliating quality of the experience of confronting shadow. It involves understanding that qualities one had ascribed to Others are really one's own. Such recognition feels shameful, and it can be overpowering. But once a person has begun to acknowledge embarrassing, even repugnant, parts of his or her nature, it becomes possible for that person to withdraw projections and reclaim other parts of the personality that had been abandoned in the course of developing a persona. A process of reintegration can begin.

Confronting the shadow requires what practitioners of analytic psychology call a *temenos*, or container, where the painful experience can be sheltered, the difficulty honored. Twelve-step programs, for example, recognize that addiction is a form of possession by shadow that can be overcome by the acknowledgment that the ego is "powerless" and needs the assistance of a "power greater than ourselves"; meetings provide a community and a container for telling and retelling painful stories. In this process cultural and personal shadow can be held, acknowledged, and gradually absorbed into consciousness.

Psychological transformation depends upon the ego's recognition that it is only part of the whole, that "the images of the unconscious are not produced by consciousness, but have a reality and spontaneity of their own."[28] The ego has to acknowledge the autonomy of the unconscious in order to begin to bring into consciousness some of its images, and with them some of its vast energy. This allows the ego a relationship to the unconscious in which it is neither the master (the inflation of ego is hubris) nor the slave (psychosis). Ego and the unconscious must exist together not as opposites but in a relationship of tension, an agon. As James Hillman, a leading post-Jungian theorist, puts it, "we are composed of agonies not polarities."[29] The ego, especially in Western culture, often resists the suggestion that there is more to psyche than itself. However, we do not will our dreams into being any more than we will the oak to bear acorns. The ego is only part of a complex flow of psychic energy.

Jung called the capacity for self-healing the *transcendent function*, "a function based on real and 'imaginary,' or rational and irrational, data, thus bridging the yawning gulf between conscious and unconscious. It is a natural process, a manifestation of the energy that springs from the tension of opposites, and it consists in a sequence of fantasy-occurrences which appear spontaneously in dreams and visions."[30] In opening oneself to consciousness of the products of the psyche, such as dreams, symptoms, and projections, one can find ways to go beyond the ego-driven impulse to divide, deny, and act out. In conflicts the transcendent function presents the ego with an opportunity not to solve but to move through what may appear to be mutually exclusive alternatives. According to Antony Stevens: "One has to become aware of both *poles* of every conflict and endure, in full consciousness, the tension created between them; then, some radical shift occurs which leads to their transcendence. This comes about through the power of the unconscious to create a new symbolical synthesis out of the conflicting propensities."[31] The transcendent function involves a dialogue between the conscious ego and the symbols and projections of the Self; its goal is to bring about a new consciousness of the larger nature that makes up psyche. Consciousness of the power and fertility of psyche lets the individual find a way to flow past what had seemed insoluble.

The transcendent function serves individuation and frees space for alternative ways of knowing the self and the world. Both Jung and James Hillman maintain that the psyche (Hillman prefers the term *soul*) is multiple, not unitary. Many "persons" occupy psyche, and Hillman even argues that individuals are part of psyche, rather than the other way around: "We are part of the soul, rather than the soul being our possession. To do soul-work, then, one must work in relation to the world."[32] The ego complex, which is itself culturally inflected, casts in shadow the multiplicity of the psyche. As a person works with dream or active imagination, he or she may be able to eclipse the light of ego briefly in order to become aware of the many perspectives within, fostering a more ethical attitude to those "Others" previously scorned. Mary Watkins points out that the focus of these approaches to psychological healing is "the *larger whole* of which each individual self is but a part. . . . Our well-being as selves is seen to be dependent on the well-being of the material and natural world, as well as on the social world."[33] Individual and community psychological growth, that is, has to take place intentionally in a historical context and actively in the world. Thus, the aims of psychological growth are entirely compatible with a land ethic and are consonant with the maturity that Vine Deloria Jr. advocates.

ECOPSYCHOLOGY AND THE POST-JUNGIANS

Since Jung's death in 1963, a number of developments in Jungian psychology have extended his ideas. Of these the two I find most relevant are the work of the archetypal psychologists, including James Hillman, and the political ideas put forward by Andrew Samuels. Hillman comments that his patients' complaints—"distortions of communication, the sense of harassment and alienation, the deprivation of intimacy with the immediate environment, the feelings of false values and inner worthlessness"—reflect disease in the world itself; "to place neurosis and psychopathology solely in personal reality is a delusional repression of what is actually, realistically, being experienced."[34] Peter Bishop, in *The Greening of Psychology*, adds: "We are drawn to recognize the soul of the world primarily through ecological breakdown, our fears about the dangers that lurk in things—the food we eat, the air we breathe, and so on. Our soul-sicknesses are caused by the loss of connection with an animated world."[35]

Andrew Samuels argues that "the tasks of depth psychologists who seek to engage with the political are to locate the enormous psychic energy that is presently locked up in collective and subjective self-disgust, and to try to release the energy so that it becomes available for political renewal." Samuels speaks of "resacralizing" experience by honoring the irrational and the numinous, reconnecting with "a feeling level that we sense once existed but we find has vanished from the modern world," in order to release that energy.[36] Such energy comes from many sources and can be known in various ways. According to Gary Snyder, "grandparents, place, grammar, pets, friends, lovers, children, tools, the poems and songs we remember, are what we *think with*."[37] I would add that we also "think with" dreams, fantasies, habits, and the local soil under our fingernails. All these are pathways to reconnect with the land, with ourselves, and with each other in a feeling way.

ECOPSYCHOLOGY AND HEALING

Today what is "natural" about humans often occupies shadow, from body odor to mortality. Commodity culture urges us to shape our bodies to impossible ideals and to hone our minds to the edge required by corporate life. This alienation from nature—and human "nature"—has a number of consequences psychologically. Several ecopsychologists, including Chellis Glendinning, Paul Shepard, and Ralph Metzner, argue that separation from nature contributes to neurosis, addiction, and violence in contemporary culture. Richard Louv has identified what he calls "nature-deficit disorder" in children deprived of free play in nature. Thomas Berry even argues that people in the West have become "autistic" in relation to nature.[38] In the developed world distress is widespread in such forms as addictions, child abuse, massive consumer debt, and the persistence of what Thoreau called "lives of quiet desperation." The culture itself exhibits signs of psychological rigidity and adolescent values, and racism, sexism, homophobia, and ageism continue to saturate public life. Many people live in fear, whether realistic fear of gun violence or a fear that has been stirred up by media hype. In the face of hopelessness about the possibilities of change, social fragmentation, and a persistent ideology of individualism, civic life crumbles. Among people who are the principal victims of colonialism, the loss of culture, language, community, and land has led to powerlessness, rage, and frustration. The carrot of integration into mainstream culture rewards a few, while the stick of police action, poverty, environmental insult, and legal injustice leaves many people weakened in their ability to resist. Self-hatred and shame ensue. The internal emptiness that feeds a competitive consumer culture is mirrored in the despair of those it excludes. Both drain hope and erode compassion.

When environmentalists focus primarily on the damage humans have done to the planet, the result is guilt. This enlarges the shadow. Theodore Roszak argues that appeals to guilt will succeed only in the very short term in altering behavior and ideas. Andrew Samuels makes a similar point, criticizing the environmental movement's "unrelenting litany of humanity's destructiveness," which can lead to self-disgust and depression.[39] Instead, the environmental movement needs to proclaim the joy, richness, and personal growth found in connection with nature. A relationship with a place can foster psychological healing, while activism on behalf of the land promotes both community and personal fulfillment. In the period since Rachel Carson wrote *Silent Spring*, there have been significant successes in environmental political action. Green political ideas, particularly in Europe, reach large numbers of people with an alternative vision. In the United States the conservation movement has had significant success in protecting habitats via the Endangered Species Act, and environmental legislation has led to cleaner air and water. At the same time more and more people visit national parks, garden, bird, hike, ski, hunt, and fish. The personal satisfaction found in a significant relationship to the natural world can help to sustain and augment green movements. Such pleasures complement activism, sustain individuals in long struggles, and appeal to people who are seeking meaning in their lives. They are much more sustainable than guilt.

What most interests me is the extent to which people seek and value a vision beyond getting and spending. Jung's concept of the Self expresses the tendency of the psyche to seek meaning and desire growth. This has in the past found expression both in religion and in a sense of the sublime in nature. Just as the wildness and otherness of nature may connect humans with unconscious forces, the sublime beauty of nature may stimulate the ability to transcend the ego.[40] According to Hillman, individuation, or soul-making, "does not seek a way out of or beyond the world toward redemption or mystical transcendence. . . . The curative or salvational vision of archetypal psychology focuses upon the soul in the world which is also the soul of the world."[41] In equating the soul in the world with the soul of the world, Hillman locates unconscious human "nature" in the realm of extrahuman nature. Thus, soul-making has a similar goal intrapsychically as does a reorientation toward Leopold's land ethic: it opens the human will to forces greater than itself, incorporating into the circle of compassion what had been banished. Moreover, it makes human consciousness responsible, as cocreator, for the health of both psyche and world. We are one species, albeit a very powerful one. But we are not alone, and we need a diverse, sometimes violent, sometimes sheltering, sometimes fruitful nature in order to exist.

In the novels I study here, characters who are able to connect with the natural world in a receptive way are more likely to come to acknowledge their shadow sides, enter a process of individuation, and develop a more integrated life in community. These stories offer alternatives to the worldview most common today. They address what to me are key questions: How can a relationship with nature foster ethical growth, and how can stories reinforce an ethical commitment to nature? How does an individual come to transcend the assumptions built into his or her culture and develop what the Chickasaw poet and novelist Linda Hogan calls an "ecology of mind"?[42]

LITERARY THEORY

In the last thirty years, academic literary study has been engaged with the ideas of poststructuralist philosophers, who have questioned many of the assumptions of Western culture. Perhaps poststructuralism's central contribution to my thinking is its analysis of the ways Western thought has divided virtually everything into opposing categories and then prioritized one of these terms. This dualism comes to us in the familiar mind/matter, day/night, thought/feeling, reason/imagination, and of course culture/nature. While previous thinkers imagined these oppositions to be natural, poststructuralists have argued that they are projections of the minds of the observers, who take a fundamental experience of self/other and expand it to embrace other familiar experiences of difference, such as male/female, life/death, presence/absence, and so on, extending to the "like" term ascendancy over the "other" term. In making the case that these dichotomies are not inherent in things, poststructuralists call into question the basic value judgments of Western thought. Clearly, such questioning is fruitful for environmentalists, who point out the ways that humans are implicated in the web of nature. The enterprise poststructuralists propose has been termed "deconstruction," which is intended not as an inversion of previous binaries but rather as a way to reconceive phenomena to allow multiple possibilities and many centers of value. The goal, in other words, is not to invert hierarchies but to deconstruct them, to dislodge the habits of thought that have served colonialism and inequality.[43] In a provocative study, *Jung and the Postmodern*, Christopher Hauke argues that Jung's work "challenges the splitting tendency of modernity: the splitting of the 'rational' and 'irrational,' the splitting of the social, collective norm and individual, subjective experience, the splitting of the Human and the Natural, of mind and matter, and perhaps, above all, the splitting of the conscious and unconscious psyche itself."[44] In its resistance to dualism on an individual as well as a cultural basis, Jung's thought provides an alternative "both-and" way of rethinking dilemmas. In addition, Jung's idea of the transcendent function (see chapter 5) suggests that the psyche has ways of moving past contradictions.

The idea of "nature" itself has been examined by many critics in an effort to deconstruct the dualism of nature and culture. Raymond Williams calls *nature* "perhaps the most complex word in the language."[45] Theories of the social construction of nature suggest that virtually all of what we today think of as "nature" or "the land" is the product of human design, from the drained fens of England to the deserts of what was once the Fertile Crescent. Even those cultures that never industrialized shaped the land to their purposes in many ways—for example, in their uses of fire or their irrigation practices. But "social construction" also suggests that for most people in industrialized countries, both the understanding and the experience of nature are shaped by cultural ideas. Our ideas about what to expect when we venture into wilderness shape the ways we experience the wild.[46] Some theorists go so far as to suggest that we cannot know anything meaningful about what is "out there."

In the postmodernist project the Enlightenment model of the disembodied knower has given way to a new understanding that all knowledge is situated. Humans do not have access to pure objectivity and cannot pretend to simulate a disinterested "eye of God." The scientific enterprise to create replicable data now acknowledges that hypotheses grow from a specific historical, geographical, and even gender location, as Donna Haraway has demonstrated. The embodied observer is understood, even if not always acknowledged, as part of any study. The interpretation of data about the natural world produces ideas that are affected by the behavior or presence of the observer, and scientists now speak of "the story that the data tell." *Story*, then, becomes a term that suggests the embedding of ideas in the details of a narrative that acknowledges the situation of the storyteller. As such, *story* recognizes the contingency of any conclusions. This idea is particularly well suited to the development of an understanding of ecology, where one of the central principles is the notion that deeply complex systems elude our certainty. Haraway develops a notion of knowledge that implies a *relationship* between knower and known. She locates the object of knowledge both outward and inward, acknowledging that thinking and talking about nature are enmeshed in thinking, talking about, and constructing ourselves. Haraway calls for "an account of radical historical contingency for all knowledge claims and knowing subjects, a critical practice for recognizing our own 'semiotic technologies' for making meanings, *and* a no-nonsense commitment to faithful accounts of a 'real' world."[47] This model of human subjectivity and knowledge requires a provisional, embodied, and narrative account of the world. While some poststructuralist thinkers locate themselves in the discourse analysis that insists that we can know only text,

ecologists, nature writers, and ecocritics look more toward a negotiation between the limited observer and a world that surely exists out there.[48]

Poststructuralism also questions both the notion of a stable, unitary Subject, or sense of identity, and the possibility of objective knowledge. The heroic
individualism of the British and American past has come to seem the fiction
of the white, male, privileged thinkers and writers whose power rested in part
on the assumption that their particular experience was the same as all experience, the life of Man. Many forces have contributed to deconstructing this
idea, including the feminist and anticolonialist movements, psychoanalytic
theory, and the work of Marxist thinkers. Subjectivity used to be imagined
as organic and universal; now it is seen as constructed of a matrix of forces
that include race, gender, class, history, culture, genetics, religion, and family.
Moreover, subjectivity is understood to be unstable and subject to change and
even dissolution.

The identity promoted by advanced capitalism—individualistic, competitive, materialistic, mistrustful, and insecure—is radically alienated both from
nature and from natural sources of energy, connection, nourishment, information, amusement, satisfaction, and compassion. Describing the psychological
condition of contemporary culture, Mary Watkins writes: "We stimulate our
productivity through self-criticism, self-doubt, and a fear of failure on the one
hand, and an exaggerated sense of self-importance on the other. Well-being
becomes tacitly concerned with the regulation of this oscillation, rather than
with seeing through it to the structure of selfhood with which one is in com-
pliance and drawing it into question."[49] Consider the relationship with the
body: popular culture presents images of young, beautiful, thin people, the
message, both overt and covert, that control must be exercised over the body.
Yet Americans have never been fatter. The domination of the fast-food mar-
ket and the oscillation Watkins mentions—which results in retreats into food
as a form of medicating emptiness—have produced an epidemic of shame in
relation to the body, its needs and functions, its health, its aging. The body is
a possession, and the drive for its perfection fuels eating disorders and feeds
envy. If most people feel bad about their bodies, how can they care about the
world?

ECOCRITICISM

Ecological literary criticism, or ecocriticism, grew in influence during the
1990s as large numbers of students in the United States brought their envi-

ronmental concerns into their English classes. Cheryll Glotfelty, one of the originators of ecocriticism, explains that "ecocriticism takes as its subject the interconnections between nature and culture, specifically the cultural artifacts of language and literature. . . . It negotiates between the human and the non-human."[50] Ecocritics look at nature as it is represented in literary texts—the myths and metaphors the text creates or references and the attitudes toward the land it reflects or fosters. They replace what ecocritic William Howarth calls "the conviction . . . that experience is mind-centered and free of reference to actualities of space and time" with the belief that knowledge is situated not just historically but geographically.[51] They often turn to insights from feminist criticism, seeing parallels between the exploitation, marginalization, and silencing of women and treatment of the land. "Ecology insists that we pay attention not to the way things have meaning for us, but to the way the rest of the world—the nonhuman part—exists apart from us and our languages," according to SueEllen Campbell, a leading ecocritic.[52] While most ecocritics acknowledge that much of our experience of nature is mediated and socially constructed, they also believe that experiences in nature can be transformative both emotionally and politically. If ecosystems matter, then humans have to find ways to think, as Aldo Leopold says, like a mountain, to transcend the limitations of human time, and space, and ego. Ecocriticism contributes to this by celebrating intimacy with nature and acknowledging our power to destroy it—or to preserve it. Moreover, many ecocritics are themselves also environmental activists, and they propose that criticism needs to be wedded to practice to be effective. Often, nature-oriented literature is taught in interdisciplinary contexts. The critic Glen Love advocates even greater reciprocity between ecocriticism and the biological sciences, drawing on the work of the biologist E. O. Wilson, particularly on Wilson's idea of "biophilia," an innate love for nature.

Recently, several books have been published that address a limitation in much ecocriticism that is centered on nonfiction nature writing. Specifically, under the rubric of "expanding the boundaries" of ecocriticism, or "greening" literary studies, scholars like Patrick Murphy, Karla Armbruster, and Kathleen R. Wallace are looking at poetry, novels, plays, films, and theoretical work that were not originally imagined as "nature writing" with an eye to exploring the ways such texts enrich our understanding of the relationship between humans and our planetary habitat.[53]

ECOFEMINISM AND POSTCOLONIAL CRITICISM

Since my goal is to explore alternative stories about nature, many of the texts I examine come from writers from traditional cultures, mostly American Indian, and from women. Both, of course, have been the victims of shadow projection on the part of Western commercial and colonial culture. Their emerging literatures allow readers to question the assumptions behind these projections and to see the world in different ways.

Edward Said used the term *orientalism* to describe "the corporate institution for dealing with the Orient—dealing with it by making statements about it, authorizing views of it, describing it, by teaching it, settling it: ruling over it: Orientalism as a Western style for dominating, restructuring, and having authority over the Orient." The dynamics of European domination of the Orient, which Said calls the source of the "deepest and most recurring images of the Other" for Europe, resemble closely the processes of imperial construction of both traditional North American and African Others.[54] In the centers of "civilization," the alien inhabitants of new colonies are named, studied, psychologized, romanticized, or vilified, and codified into law, their conquest rationalized along with the taking of their land and its "resources." This is all most Western people know of the people and the cultures to whom they are bringing "progress." Said's pioneering work is a cornerstone of what has become the study of postcolonial literatures, the emergent writings of formerly (and, in the case of American Indian literatures, currently) colonized people. These writings offer alternative versions of history, philosophy, psychology, and biology.

In *The Empire Writes Back*, Bill Ashcroft, Gareth Griffiths, and Helen Tiffin define postcolonial literatures as those that "emerged in their present form out of the experience of colonization and asserted themselves by foregrounding the tension with the imperial power, and by emphasizing their differences from the assumptions of the imperial centre."[55] One central difference of such literature has to do with the place of humans in relation to those with whom we share the planet. All the theories I mentioned earlier, about the origins of the divorce between humans and nature, have limited themselves to Western history, philosophy, culture, and institutions. An examination of the history, philosophy, and culture of indigenous people, however, suggests that this alienation from nature is not inevitable. The nations of the Americas lived for millennia in a sustainable relationship with their ecosystems, largely as a result of a way of understanding themselves and the world that is radically different from that of the West. In the absence of a nature-culture dualism, indigenous people also developed a geography of psyche that valued states of mind and ways of knowing that for Western people are mostly unconscious or undervalued. Seeing "nature" differently, they also saw themselves differently.

Because of their direct, daily experience of the shadow of American prosperity and self-righteousness, American Indian writers cannot ignore the political realities of the current culture. Perhaps because of the centrality in American Indian culture of the trickster, these writers focus not only on the colonial devastation of their land, their languages, and their lives but also on what the Anishinaabe novelist and critic Gerald Vizenor calls "survivance."[56] The American Indian novels that have appeared since N. Scott Momaday won the Pulitzer Prize for *House Made of Dawn* in 1969 have provided many new ways to imagine living joyously as part of the natural world. These literatures cannot be accurately described as "postcolonial," however, since American Indian people are still living in a colonial situation.[57]

In the literatures of indigenous cultures, we see represented a worldview that nourishes a developing land ethic. The environmental movement needs to look to the traditional values, practices, and beliefs of people who have long inhabited North America for ideas and inspiration, and to work on issues of social justice as part of a program of environmental sustainability. However, there is a crucial caution here: as Linda Tuhiwai Smith, a Maori theorist, writes, "It appals us that the West can desire, extract and claim ownership of our ways of knowing, our imagery, the things we create and produce, and then simultaneously reject the people who created and developed those ideas and seek to deny them further opportunities to be creators of their own culture and own nations."[58] Acting in the name of the land goes hand in hand with advocating for the rights of indigenous people and restoring their land to its traditional relationships. There is no environmental justice without human justice.

THE POWER OF FICTION

Gary Snyder says, "*Books are our grandparents!*"[59] Even in the Internet age, people still read, and reading novels provides the stillness, the opportunity for reflection and critical thinking, and the imaginative space to rethink the world. Especially in the Internet age, when cyberspace seems to replace physical geography, novels with place at their center remind us that we really do still live just here. Jonathan Bate argues, in his ecocritical book *The Song of the Earth*, that art "may create for the mind the same kind of re-creational space that a park creates for the body."[60] For many people reading is itself a kind of ritual that slows one down and helps remedy overstimulation. The ecocritic Scott Slovic writes about nature writers' attention to consciousness and their work in inscribing "watchfulness" and inspiring "awakening"; it seems to me that reading and writing are reciprocal in this respect. If "watchfulness is enhanced by the process of writing," reading encourages a kind of introspective attention, a movement of mind from words to images to personal memories and associations.[61] Ink on paper yields to imagined voices, forests, wolves. The stillness of the book allows the mind to connect the storied action with related experiences, so that what happens to imaginary strangers can lead to insights about real problems, both personal and political. The Jungian literary critic Susan Rowland remarks: "The structure of reading literary texts is a mode permeable to unconscious forces. . . . Reading . . . reformulates the subject."[62] Stories connect our solitary minds with the imagined thoughts of others, ease our loneliness, give us mirrors, and extend our capacity to commiserate. Reading imaginative accounts of people who find other ways to live may also open the psychological space necessary to the empathy that a land ethic requires.

BEYOND INSTRUMENTAL REASON

As science took form with Bacon and his followers, nature lost its animation; it became "dead," a resource for our exploitation. The scientific method that has dominated Western thought has focused on experimentation, replicability, and objectivity. In collecting data, scientists have attempted to take themselves, their subjectivity, and their location out of the picture. From this developed a state of mind that imagines that "objective truth" is possible and that looks to manipulate the world to achieve its ends. The social critics Theodor Adorno and Max Horkheimer called this "instrumental reason," the belief that rational planning and cost-benefit analyses offer the superior, perhaps even the only path to improving human society, and that ethics and aesthetics are secondary. In this view Western technology demonstrates the superiority of Western ideas and provides the yardstick by which to measure everything. In practice this view has made nature a resource, commercialized culture, reduced meaning to quantifiable units, and sanctioned efficiency above social justice. Adorno and Horkheimer focused attention on the destructive social and spiritual consequences of the Enlightenment in its exclusive reliance on instrumental reason, seeing it as a kind of "disenchantment of the world" and the "extirpation of animism," which produces alienation from a nature rendered inanimate.[63]

Traditional literatures and cultures offer alternatives to this exclusive rule of reason. Vine Deloria Jr. argues that "Indians consider their own individual experiences, the accumulated wisdom of the community that has been gathered by previous generations, their dreams, visions, and prophecies, and any information received from birds, animals, and plants as data that must be arranged, evaluated, and understood as a unified body of knowledge."[64] This does not mean that only the subjective counts, but that incorporating information gathered from subjective experience enriches the outcome. Since the goal in traditional contexts is not domination but finding a basis on which to craft a moral course, no knowledge is separate from ethics. But since the relationship between the individual and the land is one of love, aesthetics also enter, as what is right is also what is beautiful. Finally, the relationship between humans and the land is religious, expressed in the language of celebration and prayer, which both asserts and creates the relationship.

Jung also criticized the modernist tendency to exalt instrumental reason, pointing out structures of power that have implicated themselves in subjective experience. In particular, Jung criticized the "masculinist" values that underlie modern culture and the exclusion of "feminine" values from the public arena. On the achievements and limitations of rationality, Jung wrote: "At the time of the Renaissance ... the newly won rational and intellectual stability of the human mind ... managed to ... penetrate further and further into the depths of nature. . . . The more successful the penetration and advance of the new scientific spirit proved to be, the more the latter—as is usually the case with the victor—became the prisoner of the world it had conquered."[65] Jung's use of the verb *penetrate* here suggests how this instrumental rationality served masculinist goals of conquest and hierarchy. Jung saw contemporary culture as excessively masculine, extraverted, and overly rational, and he believed that the interest in the unconscious represented in the flowering of psychologies was part of a general psychic compensation for the limitations of the culture.

One need not fall back into dualism and proclaim the superiority of traditional ways of knowing. Both reason and intuition contribute to wisdom. In particular, critical reason, the capacity to develop hypotheses and test them against evidence, is essential in both personal and community life. Reason provides the means to learn from information offered from all sources. As mentioned earlier, Jung used the term *individuation* to indicate a process by which a person reclaims lost potentials, differentiates him- or herself from the mass mind, and absorbs into consciousness dangerous shadow tendencies so that they can be restrained. Vine Deloria Jr. calls this "maturity," which he defines as "the ability to reflect on the ordinary things of life and discover both their real meaning and the proper way to understand them when they appear in our lives."[66]

Individuation/maturity and political commitment to the land and to those humans who have been exploited as Other are mutually reinforcing processes. Experience with extrahuman nature can itself be an aid in the process, and individuation can become a powerful ally of the movements for social justice and environmental integrity. The land provides a powerful image that focuses desire and in that way encourages change; the biologically diverse, stochastic, and autonomous forces of nature permit a mirroring of a personal existence that does not flow in the channels dug by consumer capitalism. Experiencing nature can liberate energy to protect, preserve, and restore the land, and attending to the multiple voices of psyche can inspire a person to defend the rights of other people to justice, a sustainable economy, health, education, shelter, and food.

THE ARGUMENT AND ORGANIZATION OF THIS STUDY

To bring a land ethic into practice requires the psychological work of individuation and maturity. Both demand conscious engagement with nature and an acknowledgment of shadow. Ecopsychological growth both nourishes and grows from social movements for environmental justice, wilderness protection, reinhabitation of the land, and natural areas restoration. In the novels I explore, characters who are open to other ways of knowing, and who undertake the work of individuation, have a richer interior life and a deeper relationship with both the land and other humans. I believe these fictions can provide images of hope that may inspire readers to question assumptions and persist in their own struggles, both personal and ecological. Donna Haraway documents differences among the scientific accounts, or "stories," of observers of the same langur monkeys to suggest that science, no less than other fields, embraces contests over meanings.[67] I believe literature can be a site for significant engagements with outgrown ideas and that for many people stories provide the emotional dimension that provokes reflection and stimulates change.

In the next chapter I explore the experience of shadow in Joseph Conrad's *Heart of Darkness* and Francis Parkman's *The Oregon Trail*. In chapter 3 I contrast these stories with indigenous versions of history in which a more intimate relation with the land produces a different psychology. In both Chinua Achebe's *Things Fall Apart* and James Welch's *Fools Crow*, cultural rituals mediate between the human and the land, and dream, trance, myth, and story suggest a richer integration of ego and the unconscious.

In chapter 4 I survey contemporary environmental ethics and ecopsychology, including a summary of three trends in conservation ethics in the United States today: wilderness protection, bioregionalism, and natural areas restoration. These form the basis for the next three chapters, which group recent novels around the places they explore: wild land, traditional sites of "home," and restored communities. These books offer images of resistance, hope, and other ways of living. They build on one another developmentally, presenting characters in different life stages interacting with the human and natural communities. Chapter 5 considers Marilynne Robinson's *Housekeeping* and Margaret Atwood's *Surfacing*, novels in which youthful characters have significant and transformative encounters with wilderness. It also explores the Jungian ideas of the transcendent function and the symbolic life. Chapter 6 explores the archetype of the Mother as it plays out in the land and in the psyche, examining the process of individuation in N. Scott Momaday's *The Ancient Child*, Leslie Marmon Silko's *Ceremony*, and Barbara Kingsolver's *Animal Dreams*, stories of midlife homecomings, where living with the land and the local community becomes a means to personal psychological health. Chapter 7 takes up the trickster archetype in the Anishinaabe novels of Louise Erdrich, finding in the community that persists throughout her saga images of restoration of land, culture, community, and individual well-being. The afterword suggests new directions for further research.

2

The Colonial Shadow

Conrad and Parkman

Alienation from the unconscious and from its historical conditions
spells rootlessness. . . . That is the danger that lies in wait for the conqueror of foreign lands, and for every individual who . . . loses touch
with the dark, maternal, earthy ground of his being.
—C. G. Jung, "Civilization in Transition"

EARLY IN *HEART OF DARKNESS*, Joseph Conrad's narrator, Marlow,
speaks of jungle grass growing through the ribs of his predecessor, "tall
enough to hide his bones."[1] Like an image in a dream, this captures the rich
and ambivalent experience of nature in much modern Western thought: nature is mindless, indifferent to the life and death of individual humans, stupidly fertile, a force we can exploit and harness to our own ends or one that
will defeat us. But nature is also hopeful, renewing, improvisational; even
when we pave or poison the earth, it finds ways to recover. In this chapter I
examine the Western beliefs about nature that are revealed in *Heart of Darkness* and *The Oregon Trail*. I suggest that in the minds of colonialists, anxieties
about nature and fears of native people became confused with their greed for
ivory, rubber, and land, and that their projection of shadow onto nature and
natives rationalized their brutal attempts to conquer African and American
Indian people and their lands.

Published in 1899, *Heart of Darkness* grew from Conrad's work on a steam-
boat in the Congo in 1890, during the tenure of King Leopold II of Belgium.
Leopold wished to conquer the native population, harness them for labor,
and strip the continent of its ivory and rubber. Under his rule an estimated
half of the Congo's population died. Worked to death, starved, their hands

cut off, whipped, held hostage, shot, and tortured, the African people suffered unthinkably. *Heart of Darkness* recoils from the brutalities Conrad witnessed in Africa, but it is principally a psychological, not a political, novel, exploring the psychological dynamics that enabled civilized Europeans to devise or participate in such a horror.

While Leopold's practices eventually attracted international criticism, assumptions very similar to his guided imperial policies and practices throughout the world. In the United States colonialism had different ends, but the results were every bit as horrific for the native population. Like Africans, Native Americans were dispossessed of land, killed in battle, starved, and subjected to rape and other forms of torture. Since settlers in North America were not, for the most part, looking to use natives as labor, there was even less concern for the survival of native Americans than there was for Africans.

Written for popular audiences, *Heart of Darkness* and *The Oregon Trail* explained, mediated, and mapped the new and foreign territory for those who remained at home. The understanding available to Conrad and Francis Parkman was limited by their class, their race, their moment in history. They in turn provided images for readers that simplified and objectified the Other. Edward Said remarks that what matters to Conrad's readers is not what happens to the natives but "how Marlow makes sense of everything, for without his deliberately fashioned narrative there is no history worth telling."[2] The European *mission civilatrice* and the American ideal of the frontier rationalized practices of imperial conquest. Today, we can see how these narratives also expose the underside of the conquerors' sense of themselves as superior. In addition, we glimpse the psychological cost to the conquerors of splitting off the shadow side.

THE SHADOW

The shadow is the archetype imaged in the evil twin, the double, the dark side, Darth Vader. It is the truth about ourselves that we cannot see or admit. Ego, or the consciousness of oneself as an "I," emerges in infancy and develops as the growing child learns which of his or her unique capacities, desires, and fears is acceptable in the family, culture, and time in which he or she was born. These acceptable parts of the individual's psyche become incorporated into ego, and all those that are unacceptable—dangerous, shameful, or simply irrelevant—get consigned to shadow. The ego of an individual is a product of historical, cultural, and familial values and ideas about the world. As ego develops, all the child's potentials that don't fit the mold constellate to form the shadow. Thus, ego, or consciousness, and shadow, which is unconscious, are complementary and developmental. Because it is usually personified, the shadow functions as an internal Other, a shameful second self. For this reason we often come to know our shadow through those we most irrationally despise. In dreams shadow usually appears as a person of the same sex who carries an ominous or repulsive charge.

Jungians like to use the Greek myth of Procrustes, a robber who put his victims on an iron bed. If they were too tall for it, he chopped off the excess; if too short, he stretched them till they fit. In order to become civilized, people suppress some parts of their own nature and exaggerate or inflate others. Clearly, civilizations cannot function without forbidding certain behaviors, such as murder, incest, and theft. But shadow is greater than simply dangerous potentials. When families assign rigid gender roles, for example, each gender may consign to shadow its own potential to develop qualities that would expose it to ridicule or punishment. In a culture that considers instrumental reason the only reliable way of knowing, people may repress or ignore their intuitive, expressive, and sensory insights. Thus, while the ego consolidates itself and shapes itself to social norms by amputating or stretching parts of itself, what's repressed is not gone.

Shadow holds frightening instinctual forces, as well as parts of the psyche the ego believes are dangerous to its adaptation to its environment. Because these potentials are denied, they take on the power of unconscious energies and become contaminated by shame and fear. These parts of the personality don't disappear (any more than the water that is drained from farmland or the toxins spewed in industrial processes can go "away"); they only disappear from consciousness. For ecopsychology the concept of shadow explains how people have come to feel fear and contempt for our habitat, since Western culture encourages people to deny their own animal being. Repression blocks the possibility of change or conscious choice. Repressing knowledge of brutality and greed does not prevent people from behaving badly, but it does allow them to deny responsibility for what they do and project the fault onto the object of their rage. Often others know parts of ourselves that we deny, just as people downstream receive the effluent from what we dump. Parts of what Jung calls the cultural shadow—qualities a culture suppresses, denies, or ignores—are clear to those outside the culture.

The imperial conquerors' image of themselves as the great civilizers required that they deny their own brutal impulses. They projected these dangerous qualities onto those they were brutalizing, casting Africans and Indians, along with their land, as "savage" (and also, given that these were exploiters imbued with the virtue of work, "indolent"). Abdul R. JanMohamed calls this projection the "racial pathetic fallacy . . . the ascription of moral character to race and environment and, therefore, ultimately to nature."[3] Today, the legacy of these conquests remains in shadow for most Europeans and their American cousins. How could civilized Europeans sanction such barbarism? And how could they forget it? Both *Heart of Darkness* and *The Oregon Trail* expose the psychological dynamics of conquest. In both cases the invaders believed themselves possessed of higher culture, intelligence, and virtue. Conflating native people and the land they inhabited, they split from consciousness their own viciousness, greed, power lust, and cruelty, projecting these qualities onto the people and places they overran and thereby rationalizing their conquest. As Ward Churchill argues, "the overwhelming preponderance of writing concerning the American Indian during the U.S. expansion was designed to create an image allowing conquest 'for the Indians' own good,' to effect 'betterment' and 'progress.'"[4] Today, this history is mostly forgotten or ignored, but its traces remain in the shadow of the settlers. Conquest required severe psychological alienation and splitting on the part of the conquering people, which now, together with estrangement from the land, forms one basis for widespread isolation and depression.

HEART OF DARKNESS

Conrad wrote in two fields: popular adventure discourse and psychological fiction. His psychological discourse is cloaked, even coded, like psyche itself. Also shrouded is an anti-imperialist message potentially offensive to the readers of *Blackwood's Magazine*. This double coding suggests Conrad's respect for the images produced by psyche, which are not discursive. It may have allowed him to publish an account that excoriates the brutal practices of imperialism when a more direct exposé would not have been printed. However, this tactic makes Conrad vulnerable to criticism for racism, most notably from Chinua Achebe, who remarks, "*Heart of Darkness* projects the image of Africa as 'the other world,' the antithesis of Europe and therefore of civilization, a place where man's vaunted intelligence and refinement are finally mocked by triumphant bestiality."[5] Fredric Jameson criticizes Conrad for his "muffled" representation of the human labor that sustains the enterprise, pointing out the "impressionistic strategy of modernism whose function is to derealize the content and make it available for consumption on some purely aesthetic level."[6] The "content" Conrad derealizes is not just labor, but nature and native people, making them either objects of adventure or images of psychic journeying, not subjects in their own right. For the most part, they are blank screens onto which he can project his own shadow.

Language, Shadow, and Ego

In *Heart of Darkness* Conrad's narrative language, with its great sweeps of "incomprehensibles" and its brooding gloom, acts out the problem of shadow. To express the horror of shadow, Conrad needs vague and emotionally charged language, fraught with the shame of repressed material, as we see in passages like the one where he describes the experiences of the Roman bureaucrat assigned to pagan Britain: "All that mysterious life of the wilderness that stirs in the forest, in the jungles, in the hearts of wild men. There's no initiation either into such mysteries. He has to live in the midst of the incomprehensible which is also detestable. And it has a fascination, too, that goes to work upon him. The fascination of the abomination—you know. Imagine the growing regrets, the longing to escape, the powerless disgust, the surrender—the hate."[7] Disgust, surrender, and hate are emotions we associate with powerful experiences of shame; the words "incomprehensible," "detestable," and "abomination" also suggest the power and the unconscious qualities of shadow. Marlow cannot make his responses any more precise because they come from the shadow, from the unconscious. For this reason his narrative remains elusive and allusive, showing the reader not a map of Africa, but rather a geography of Marlow's psyche.

The jungle Marlow explores assumes a voracious female quality, its menace provoking a shudder of fear of the *vagina dentata* that ate the flesh off Marlow's predecessor's ribs and then grew grass "tall enough to hide his bones." As they steam up the river, "the great wall of vegetation, an exuberant and tangled mass of trunks, branches, leaves, boughs, festoons, motionless in the moonlight, was like a rioting invasion of soundless life, a rolling wave of plants piled up, crested, ready to topple over the creek to sweep every little man of us out of his little existence."[8] Shadow projection is obvious here, with Marlow experiencing the native plants as an "invasion." There is also a Dionysian quality to Conrad's jungle—its wild fertility, its intoxicating suffocation. Coming from a Europe celebrated for its manicured lawns and domesticated nature, Marlow responds with revulsion.

Since he is traveling on the river, Marlow's response to the jungle cannot be ascribed to its capacity to obstruct his mission. Its menace is more symbolic and psychological than practical. Conrad's language frequently suggests that Marlow's experience resembles a dream, "remembered with wonder amongst the overwhelming realities of this strange world of plants and water and silence. . . . It was the stillness of an implacable force brooding over an inscrutable intention. It looked at you with a vengeful aspect."[9] The silence of the jungle invites projection: a "vengeful aspect," an "inscrutable intention." In truth, jungles are loud: morning and evening, birds, frogs, and insects make enough noise that human voices in the jungle may not be heard. At midday this noise quiets down somewhat, but falling leaves and branches, even quite small ones, make significant startling sounds, so much so that it's easy to image human footsteps when all that's afoot are falling leaves. Monkeys in the canopy screech or disturb branches, birds flying through the forest call and shake tree limbs, small rodents and lizards on the forest floor disturb the duff. What's astonishing about walking through a jungle is not its quiet but its noise. But Marlow cannot understand the language of the jungle any more than he can comprehend that of the people who live there.[10] His is the language of ego, so he sees the jungle as an ominous power, "inscrutable."

Marlow is a man of words, a storyteller. Any quality that challenges this sense of himself also occupies shadow. He remarks that the life of the jungle is "soundless." He characterizes the "wall of matted vegetation standing higher than the wall of a temple" as "great, expectant, mute."[11] Marlow would like to project the powerlessness he associates with lack of speech onto the jungle, but he worries that it may instead be menacing. Its silence thwarts and unnerves him.

The native people of Africa are not silent, but they cannot speak to Marlow. Rounding a bend in the river, the ship encounters "a burst of yells, a whirl of black limbs, a mass of hands clapping, of feet stamping, of bodies swaying, of eyes rolling . . . a black and incomprehensible frenzy."[12] Like the "exuberant" trunks of African trees, the people of Africa are passionate but incomprehensible. They appear to be dancing or engaging in ritual. But Marlow responds to the natives as he responds to nature: with fear and fascination. Conrad's language underscores the otherness of the natives. Nowhere in this passage, or in most of the others in which Marlow confronts natives, do we see words like *men* or *people*. Rather, the natives are "limbs," "hands clapping . . . feet stamping." The language disembodies the Africans; dissection renders them harmless.

In his response to the Africans' language, Marlow enacts the European imperial assumption that native people do not speak. Tveztan Todorov quotes from Columbus's journal of October 12, 1492: "If it please Our Lord, at the moment of my departure I shall take from this place six of them to Your Highnesses, so that they may learn to speak."[13] Differences of language in Europe are the norm, yet, encountering different languages in colonial contexts, Europeans assumed the Other could only babble. Thus, Marlow cannot receive any information from either the people of Africa or the land.

Conrad shows us Marlow in the act of delineating his own shadow as he shores up his ego. As Marlow travels up the Congo, the wilderness becomes even more frightening: "Going up that river was like traveling back to the earliest beginnings of the world, when vegetation rioted on the earth and the big trees were kings." Ceaselessly, Mother Africa gives birth to a jungle where the vegetation "riots" as if it knows the intentions of the colonizers. The emotive language here suggests that rebellious emotions occupy Marlow's shadow, which he must counteract with "a deliberate belief." To what he recognizes in himself as irrational—perhaps even the potential for rebellion against the horrors he sees in the imperial venture—he responds with speech, with a carefully reasoned, constructed idea: "An appeal to me in this fiendish row—is there? Very well. I hear, I admit, but I have a voice too, and for good or evil mine is the speech that cannot be silenced."[14] In the threatening nature of this final comment, Conrad locates Marlow with the conquerors. He will stifle his own feelings with speech and work, which anchor him in the ego. Work keeps him busy. Speech locates him in a recognizably rational, European sphere; buttresses him against slipping into the muck of shadow; and separates him from the natives whose distant kinship he cannot allow himself to experience. He imposes his language, his names, his maps, his cultural practices, his institutions on a land and a people whom he sees as either empty or threatening. In the process he composes a persona for himself that is noble, pioneering, missionary, rational, and cultured, even if he cannot articulate his "deliberate belief."

Kurtz offers Marlow a glimpse of his own shadow. Kurtz, who "presented himself as a voice," stands distinct from the silence of nature and the row of the natives. En route Marlow has taken succor in his fantasies of talking with Kurtz, whose promise is "his words—the gift of expression, the bewildering, the illuminating . . . the pulsating stream of light or the deceitful flow from the heart of an impenetrable darkness."[15] Earlier in the narrative Marlow has remarked on many occasions on the sham that is the Company, with its mannequin accountant and its rapacious petty bureaucrats. He understands that if speech sets him apart from the Africans, speech, too, can be treacherous. Nonetheless, since he is a man of words, he seeks his likeness in Kurtz.

Kurtz fascinates Marlow because he's civilized. Marlow expects to meet not the monster Kurtz, but the Kurtz promised by all the buzz, the "prodigy . . . an emissary of pity, and science and progress." Because he has identified Kurtz with language, Marlow expects self-control, logic, and reason. What he finds instead is the lustful, greedy, brutal shadow of Western enterprise. Pride has allowed Kurtz to accept idolatry; greed has made him the most productive procurer of ivory on the Congo; laziness has left his outpost "decaying . . . half buried in the high grass." Brutality has led him to conclude his Treatise with the scrawled notation, "Exterminate all the brutes."[16]

Language, then, is no bulwark against shadow. If a civilized, articulate, even brilliant man can become this raving skeleton, then what can save Marlow from a similar fate? He has only work—which he identifies with dedication to an Idea, to a task or value beyond the frail and undefended ego—to keep him from his fear of going mad. Even this, even the deliberate belief, is vague at best, limited by his own participation in the lies his culture requires. The restraint with which Marlow is so preoccupied appears as the equivalent of a strong superego, a personal *mission civilatrice* aimed at keeping his own savage impulses from driving him to madness.[17]

Wilderness and the Self

Kurtz's descent into madness seems to have been caused by a combination of greed, power lust, isolation, and a culture of violence. In his growling rapacity and entitlement, and in his death's-head emaciation, Kurtz exposes the truth of European enterprise in Africa. The real-life ivory and rubber barons on whom his character is based cut off hands, displayed severed heads, and cooked people alive, as Adam Hochschild recounts in *King Leopold's Ghost*. In *Heart of Darkness*, however, the particular form of Kurtz's evil is said to have grown from his immersion in the wilderness: "The wilderness had patted him on the head, and behold, it was like a ball—an ivory ball; it had caressed him and—lo!—he had withered; it had taken him, loved him, embraced him, got into his veins, consumed his flesh, and sealed his soul to its own by the inconceivable ceremonies of some devilish initiation. He was its spoiled and pampered favourite." It would be somehow easier to understand if loneliness, ambition, or lust had so reduced Kurtz, but Conrad is specific: the *wilderness* has done all this.[18]

While the wilderness provides a convenient scapegoat for the psychological damage caused by unlimited power, the unavoidable suggestion is that Kurtz has identified with the jungle, felt himself its equal. Marlow has earlier likened the jungle to an implacable force, an inscrutable intention, the heart of darkness. Its fertility is part of its menace. The journey is clearly inward, the unmapped jungle a pathway to the unconscious. To identify with this unconscious is a form of inflation, what the Jungian theorist Edward Edinger calls a "Yahweh complex." Edinger defines inflation as "the attitude and the state which accompanies the identification of the ego with the Self. It is a state in which something small (the ego) has arrogated to itself the qualities of something larger (the Self) and hence is blown up beyond the limits of its proper size."[19] The Self in Jung's work refers to the whole of psyche, suggesting an energy that propels growth toward wholeness. Because the Self is much larger than the ego, intuition of the Self feels like a mystical or transcendent experience. Thus, the Self is the source of images and symbols of God, the hero, the divine Other. It provides a sense of purpose, order, and hope in psychic life. For the ego to identify with the Self is to suffer a bloated pride, and Kurtz's brutal and cadaverous person is the shadow image of the inflation implicit in European imperialism. As such, Kurtz is terrifying to Marlow, who may be apprehending his own complicity in this venture.

Marlow interrupts his narrative around this point to remind his audience, and perhaps himself, that they owe their sanity to "solid pavement" and "kind neighbors," "the butcher and the policeman," and the "holy terror of scandal and gallows and lunatic asylums."[20] These social referents also provide a humbling sense of the individual's limits in relation to larger powers. In the jungle Marlow laments the absence of external restraints. Language, in Marlow's view, acts as a civilizing force, just as the presence of others who are like oneself restrains brutish instincts. In the wilderness Marlow finds nothing but silence, vast brooding incomprehensibles, and Others. Stationed among silent plants and incoherent natives, Kurtz, his own voice filling the mute wilderness, is seduced into a willingness to believe himself its equal.

Ego and Shadow, Language and Lies

Marlow appears to equate language with civilization, restraint, and reason. But he also knows the dark side of language, its capacity to inflate, to distort, to deceive. The vicious and stupid practices of the Company all wear the fine dress of elevated rhetoric, and the most vile greed parades as "benevolent enterprise" and "fostering care." Like the Company's chief accountant in his starched collar and cuffs, the Company's public image glistens with European civility. But it is a lie, and Marlow says he hates a lie. Still, when Kurtz says to him, "I am lying here in the dark waiting for death," Marlow, the good Victorian, replies "Oh, nonsense!"[21] Marlow will not offer Kurtz the comfort of acknowledging his death; like sex, "brutal instincts," and greed, death is unspeakable. Most readers focus on Marlow's later lie to Kurtz's Intended, but I believe that this casual lie, unheralded in the narration, is just as important.

In many places in the text, Conrad links lies and civilization, civilization and women, women and lies. Women live in a world fabricated of lies, which, according to Marlow, have "a taint of death, a flavour of mortality," that makes even the city sepulchral.[22] Civilization is a lie, but the wilderness claims men's sanity. It's no wonder that Marlow loves the sea. If Kurtz represents the hidden and frightening knowledge of the barbarity of Western imperialism, Marlow's lie suggests that suppressing this truth is the price we pay to control forgotten and brutal instincts. Kurtz's rhetoric and Marlow's storytelling define civilization: a series of inflations, evasions, and lies necessary to conquer and restrain the terrifying passions at the heart of the human animal, as well as the anarchic fecundity of the natural world.

But language also preserves memory, leaves traces that can't be extinguished as easily as the jungle swallows adventurers. Language is the medium of consciousness, the "self" we have wrested from impulse. It creates ego consciousness and at the same moment banishes the instincts to shadow. If language makes reason possible, and reason enables us to make tools, build shelters, work together, and shape stories, surely these capacities repay us for the burial of our instinctive selves, the loss of innocence. If, to preserve any history of our sojourn on this planet, we must have language, then perhaps its ability to instruct us about the past outweighs its capacity to lie. Civilization is the project of language, the purview of women, an artifice to protect us from our own obliteration. Marlow opts for civilization, even if it is a lie.

But civilization in this narrative, like language, is exclusively European, and *these* lies shield Marlow from understanding the effect of his shadow projections on their objects, the people and land of Africa. He knows the European mission is founded on lies, but he does not understand the extent to which European language, and the shadow constructed by European culture, are instruments of conquest and exploitation, based on the denial of subject status and of language to the conquered people and land.[23] The rights to a voice, to legal representation, to political power, have historically been denied to conquered people, and the land has only recently acquired legal advocates. The qualities of language Marlow finds most disturbing—its rhetorical capacity to lie, to misrepresent, to inflate—are exactly the properties of European languages that, according to Todorov, enabled the Spanish to conquer the native people of Central America. Because of the disconnection between language and the condition it names—the slippage between signifier and signified—European languages are well suited to the tasks of conquest and control, lying to the domestic audience about the rapacity of empire and proclaiming to the conquered that their condition is natural.[24] By contrast, in traditional cultures words have power over the world and are tied to specific objects and places. Language exists in relation to the natural world and is not the exclusive tool of humans. Because words have the power to conjure the things, events, or conditions they name, it is much more difficult to lie.[25]

Shadow and Lies

Central to the challenge of living in an ethical way in relation to both nature and other people is the ability to acknowledge one's own shadow. Lying, in *Heart of Darkness*, has to do with denial, that is, with shadow. Marlow's acquiescence to the lie is a form of forgetting that afflicts most Westerners. It is easier and safer not to oppose official actions, convenient to forget the suffering and dispossession that made possible a comfortable lifestyle. Adam Hochschild calls this "the politics of forgetting," the act not "of erasure, but of turning things upside down, the strange reversal of the victimizer mentally converting himself to victim."[26] This act condemns history to shadow and makes it difficult to learn from the past. Chinua Achebe has criticized Conrad for the racism at the heart of his story, and feminist critics of *Heart of Darkness* have pointed out that the starched collars of the *mission civilatrice* depend on silencing the laundress. Marlow cannot acknowledge that shadow, and "hence a gap opens in the text between the imperial oppression visible to Marlow when it sends native *men* to the grove of death, and the masculine oppression that remains invisible to him because it seems 'natural.'"[27] Although he understands some of the ways the Company has abused the natives, he still cannot grasp that they have a culture of their own. This is true of Africa's people and of the African land, which Marlow has utterly silenced within the confines of his narrative. So nature, natives, and women evoke projection because they evoke emotions Marlow cannot acknowledge as his own. Marlow imagines the magnificent African woman who grieves Kurtz's departure as an icon of "the whole sorrowful land, the immense wilderness, the colossal body of the fecund and mysterious life," composed of parts of himself he finds troubling.[28] Here at last is a woman who does not live in a world fabricated of lies, but Marlow fears her too. He fears the lie, and he fears the truth. He needs to control her in part because he needs to control himself.

Nature and the Unconscious

What's most fascinating to me about Conrad is not what he misunderstands about native cultures but what he understands about the association of wild nature with unconscious forces. In *Heart of Darkness* the unconscious threatens humans—Kurtz acting as the object lesson—with inflation or immolation or both. Nature and natives evoke for Marlow almost exclusively frightening associations; in their mute or savage riot, they appeal to instincts long since leashed by commercial European cultures. Peter Bishop calls wildernesses "frontiers of an imagining of extremes. As unambiguous shrines of natural beauty, they are also contemporary entrances to the underworld."[29] In representing the mad soul of Kurtz, Conrad confronts Marlow with an image of a shameful, fascinating, dangerous, and at least recognizable part of himself. He recoils from it, but he knows it. However, in looking into the jungle, Conrad himself meets a power he cannot name, can barely represent.

Conrad images the power of the unconscious/wilderness in relation to the puny ego in a number of places in *Heart of Darkness*. The "boiler wallowing in the grass" and the "undersized railway truck lying there on its back with its wheels in the air" suggest how the wilderness, as a figure for the irrational, persistent fertility of nature, dwarfs and turns to helpless beasts the artifacts humans import.[30] As the jungle overwhelms Marlow, the Self towers over ego. The text at least suggests that these are not simply verbal relationships: the experience of wilderness stimulates an apprehension of the unconscious. Had Marlow risked significant contact with the African people, and thus been able to establish a different relationship with the African land, he might have been able to withdraw some of his projections and come to see in the relation of the adventurer to the land an image of the situation of the ego in the psyche. He might have learned some humility, some compassion. He might have been able to acknowledge to Kurtz his impending death or explain to his Intended the nature of his disease. Had he dealt with his own shadow, he might have been able to stand up to the evil he witnessed.

Marlow cannot transcend the limits constructed for him by his culture. Perhaps in acknowledging to his shipmates that he lied to protect Kurtz's image, he comes close to acknowledging his personal shadow. But he has nowhere to take his new consciousness, other than the story he tells. That story implies that the menace, riot, and indolence of both nature and natives in

Africa are qualities projected onto them by Western greed. But Marlow has gained no real knowledge of either Africans or Africa. His lie represents complicity in colonialism, turning away from shadow, repressing it again. So he shores up his ego and lives in a splendid (Buddhalike) isolation.

According to the Jungian analyst Antony Stevens, "The encounter with the shadow is invariably experienced as a *mortification*; humiliating, despicable parts of oneself have to be confronted and integrated; the feelings of guilt and worthlessness have to be suffered, taken on and worked through."[31] Marlow barely acknowledges a "distant kinship." He cannot work through his likeness to Kurtz or withdraw his projections from the natives and the natural world enough to see and hear them. Nonetheless, he identifies a key element of dealing with shadow, at least as long as he's in the jungle: restraint. Confronted with shadow, he maintains his sanity and protects himself from danger by the practice of restraint. Unlike Kurtz, he does not give in to unspeakable urges. In Kurtz, however, Conrad recognizes the potential for such a turn to the midlife passage.[32] Marlow ends the narrative in a state of ego-isolation. Telling the story in the dark to his nameless auditors, he claims no enlightenment. While one must confront shadow in order to go through an individuation process, simply encountering shadow is not enough.

The people who benefit economically from the conquest of nature continue to suffer from the quarantining of psychic energy, its exploitation for enterprise, and ultimately its desiccation. In acquiescing to the lie, Marlow turns away from both the horror and the power. Marlow represents, then, a version of the modern ego: alienated, at sea, without a sense of place, disenchanted with religion, repelled by inflation, ironic, frightened of passion, and investing the task at hand with a sense of purpose in order to keep from going mad. He can neither accept European imperialism nor escape it. But he can tell its story and, in doing so, expose the collective shadow to readers who may be able to use the narrative as an aid to their own enlightenment.

THE OREGON TRAIL *AND THE AESTHETIC RESPONSE TO NATURE*

The novelist and critic Louis Owens writes: "Seen from the stock Euramerican perspective, frontier is the cutting edge of civilization. Beyond the frontier is the incomprehensible 'other.' To inhabit that frontier is to somehow accommodate a radical alterity, the internalization of which leads dangerously in the direction of psychic disintegration or schizophrenia."[33] Inhabiting frontier, Owens implies, is like encountering the unconscious. From the "stock Euramerican perspective," this is very dangerous. Owens distinguishes frontier, which remains unmapped and liminal, from territory, safely enclosed by Euramerican names, laws, and barbed wire. In these terms both *Heart of Darkness* and *The Oregon Trail* are frontier stories. *Heart of Darkness* develops the European notion that Africa makes men wild, in part because it is liminal space. However, the Charlie Marlow who tells the story on the *Nellie* remarks that the map has now been filled in with "rivers and lakes and names," and his story itself, climaxing in his lie to Kurtz's Intended, provides the metanarrative that psychologizes Africa, transforming it into the object of Marlow's projections.[34] Thus, *Heart of Darkness* is itself part of the territory. Although Francis Parkman enters the frontier, camps with Indians, speaks and dines and travels with them, he keeps himself in control by never really encountering the Other. In both *Heart of Darkness* and *The Oregon Trail*, the narrative adventure/encounter becomes part of the stockade, a bolt in the fence stretched around territory. In neither text does an encounter with the Other in nature, humans, or psyche lead to a transformative experience.

Coming from Boston, Parkman would have been familiar with the tradition that identified Indians with an authentic Americanness, a lineage that ran from the Boston Tea Party through secret societies like Tammany and the Red Men. While the meanings of the identities performed through impersonating Indians had altered, European Americans' willingness to act out Indianness depended on their belief in the absence of actual Indian persons. By 1828 a "full-blown ideology of the vanishing Indian" had arisen. "Propagandists shifted the cause-and-effect of Indian disappearance from Jacksonian policy to Indians themselves, who were simply living out their destiny," according to Philip Deloria.[35]

Gerald Vizenor calls Parkman "one of the masters of manifest manners and the simulations of savagism."[36] Vizenor's term *manifest manners* links culture with the ideology that rationalizes conquest. In characterizing Parkman's accounts of the native people he met as "simulations," Vizenor points to Parkman's role in constructing a racist ideology about American Indians. However, *simulations* also suggests the way Parkman's focus remains on the surface, whether he is looking at people or at the land. Compelled by images, Parkman's work shows how such objectification leads easily to violence. Parkman is distinctly uninterested in culture or psychology, his principal terms of judgment *ugly* and *beautiful*. This is a text in which readers today may encounter elements of their own shadow—at least I did. Because we live in the age of the image, Parkman's response to the grand adventure he undertook can still surprise us with recognition.

Framing Indians

A rich kid from out east, Parkman set out in the spring of 1846 for a season of adventure in the Western wilderness of the United States, determined to study "the manners and character of Indians in their primitive state . . . to sketch those features of their wild and picturesque life which fell . . . under his own eye."[37] In *The Oregon Trail* he narrates his experiences in a prose vivid with detailed pictures of the land and its people. Parkman's account displays an aesthetic appreciation that has long characterized the Euramerican response to nature and that continues to motivate many ecotourists, adventure travelers, and environmentalists. At the same time Parkman's inability to go past surfaces suggests a psychological disposition to see difference as *the* meaningful information. His accounts of the native people he meets helped shaped the worldview that condoned their displacement and massacre.

Rarely does Parkman refer to Indians using any other general noun than *savage:* "For half a mile before us and half a mile behind, the prairie was covered far and wide with the moving throng of savages." While sometimes youth and stature may win his praise, more often he speaks of "squalid savages" and "hags," "old women ugly as Macbeth's witches." His frequent descriptions of the natives as "childish," "brutish," "treacherous," and "rapacious," as well as his injunctions to the reader to "trust not an Indian," to "let your rifle be ever in your hand," argue that for Parkman *savage* carried both personal and cultural shadow.[38] He had himself just finished Harvard Law School, where he no doubt had any personal uncivilized edges smoothed off. *Childish* is a term to be feared if you are a young adult. And perhaps there weren't as many lawyer jokes then as now, but *brutish, treacherous,* and *rapacious* are terms from which a young attorney might wish to distance himself.

Although he never revised his racist viewpoint, Parkman held it in tension with his experience of Indian hospitality, honor, generosity, and courage. He describes the Dacotah people among whom he lived as "wild democrats of the prairie." He notes that the Ogillallah preserved distinctions of "rank and place," but that "wealth has no part in determining such distinctions."[39] On a number of occasions, Parkman sits in the circle of elders as they decide on a course of action, so he sees democracy in practice and observes the efficiency and coordination required to move a village of several hundred inhabitants from one hunting area to another.

Aesthetics and Ethics

Where Marlow feels threatened by nature's muteness and the natives' incomprehensible tongue, Parkman seems above threat, amused, like a father watching the antics of his children or pets. Indeed, Parkman several times likens Indians to animals; some of his worst racism has the intensity of the personal shadow. Speaking of a shaman, Parkman muses on "the old conjurer, who with his hard, emaciated face and gaunt ribs was perched aloft like a turkey-buzzard, among the dead branches of an old tree, constantly on the look-out for enemies. He would have made a capital shot. A rifle bullet, skillfully planted, would have brought him tumbling to the ground. Sure, I thought, there could be no more harm in shooting such a hideous old villain, to see how ugly he would look when he was dead, than in shooting the detestable vulture which he resembled."[40] Parkman fantasizes about shooting the man *to see how ugly he would look.* He sees these people as images, the focus of his aesthetic gaze, objects rather than subjects. They are as silent to him as the jungle is to Marlow.

On several occasions Parkman remarks on how *picturesque* the village looks: "But when the sun was just resting above the broken peaks, and the purple mountains threw their prolonged shadows for miles over the prairie; when our grim old tree, lighted by the horizontal rays, assumed an aspect of peaceful repose . . . ; and when the whole landscape, of swelling plains and scattered groves, was softened into a tranquil beauty; then our encampment presented a striking spectacle."[41] Even in its intense-emotion-recollected-in-tranquility quality, this description is romantic, echoing the English landscape movement of the early nineteenth century in its preference for the wild and craggy. Like the landscapers, though, Parkman prefers his wild designed rather than free, his picturesque composed and softened, not natural. Parkman's aestheticism also draws him to the native people he meets, but it does not serve them. The aesthete appropriates people, turning them into objects for his pleasure—consumer goods, almost. This reduction strips them of power, flattens them, and renders them mute and malleable. As is apparent in the passage describing the shaman in the tree, when the object of the gaze fails to please, it can evoke an almost casual hostility.

Aesthetics and Shadow

Parkman's aesthetic sense also governs his response to both animals and the land. He seems drawn to animals' heedless occupation of their own territory, their beauty, their independence, even their domestic arrangements. For some of them, such as the grizzly bear, he holds great respect, and he admires the beauty of others. His attitude toward animals is strikingly revealing of his projected shadow, in both its romantic and its destructive aspects:

> Yet wild as they were, these mountains were thickly peopled.... I recol-
> lected the danger of becoming lost in such a place, and therefore I fixed my
> eye upon one of the tallest pinnacles of the opposite mountain. It rose sheer
> upright from the woods below, and by an extraordinary freak of nature, sus-
> tained aloft on its very summit a large loose rock. Such a landmark could
> never be mistaken, and feeling once more secure, I began again to move for-
> ward. A white wolf jumped up from among some bushes, and leaped clum-
> sily away; but he stopped for a moment, and turned back his keen eye and his
> grim bristling muzzle. I longed ...

I interrupt here to repeat my earlier point that a reader today can from time to time encounter personal shadow in Parkman's story. Here is one such place. What does Parkman long for here? He feels secure and confident. The moun-tains are beautiful, "peopled" with graceful animals. It is perfectly still.

What he longs for is "to take his scalp and carry it back with me, as an ap-propriate trophy of the Black Hills."[42] Parkman's use of the word *scalp* here suggests that he sees the wolf as at least as human as an Indian. A trapper would long for the pelt, but Parkman is not a trapper, and he's looking not for wealth, but a trophy. He wants to consume the wolf the way an aesthete does—by taking its image and making it into an object. The passage makes clear the equation of nature and native people in Parkman's mind—and his sense of entitlement over both.

As I recoil from Parkman's mind at this passage, I think of my own long-ings for some token to remind me of my visits to wild country. A consumer ethic penetrates consciousness, conferring a sense of entitlement that contin-ues to render protected lands vulnerable to tourist shock. This passage makes me glad for souvenir stands where I can purchase T-shirts instead of steal-ing volcanic rock or native plants. But at the same time, these very souvenir stands can persuade people that they are environmentally sensitive because they wear a shirt that says they love Yosemite. Purchasing the object stands in for political action.

Parkman seems to joust with his shadow most consciously in relation to animals. When he hunts buffalo, near the end of his adventure, he hunts both for food and for sport. At one point he remarks, "'You are too ugly to live,' thought I; and aiming at the ugliest [buffalo], I shot three of them in succession."[43] This obsession with ugliness strikes me as the mark not only of the aesthete but also of the aristocrat. In an America that proclaims itself free of class snobbery, taste is one of the ways members of the ruling class express their superiority. Focusing his contempt on the buffalo, Parkman can voice and act out the class struggle without exposing himself. His aesthetics form a narrative that justifies his brutality.

Seeing others as images enables this brutality and thoughtlessness. Although he declares he is hunting for food, he and his companions take only the "fattest and choicest parts" of the meat, abandoning the rest for the wolves.[44] In this behavior, it strikes me, Parkman exhibits some of the worst traits of American individualism. Such self-interest, heedless of the consequences of actions, leads to what Garrett Hardin calls the tragedy of the commons: the depletion of our common wealth of land, food, and clean air and water as the result of an accumulation of individual decisions, each of which seems inconsequential to the person making it. Parkman catalogs the uses to which the Dacotah put all the parts of the buffalo, but for him, an "American," only the choicest meat matters.

I find another passage even more chilling, probably because it evokes some shadow for me. Here, Parkman is traveling alone a distance of eighteen miles from Fort Laramie to the camp where his companions await him. He spots an antelope:

It approached within a hundred yards, arched its graceful neck, and gazed intently. I leveled at the white spot on its chest, and was about to fire, when it started off, ran first to one side and then to the other, like a vessel tacking against a wind, and at last stretched away at full speed. Then it stopped again, looked curiously behind it, and trotted up as before; but not so boldly, for it soon paused and stood gazing at me. I fired; it leaped upward and fell upon its tracks. Measuring the distance, I found it two hundred and four paces. When I stood by his side, the antelope turned his expiring eye upward. It was like a beautiful woman's, dark and rich. "Fortunate that I am in a hurry," thought I; "I might be troubled with remorse, if I had time for it."[45]

Here, the internal conflict is sharp: Parkman feels sympathy for the creature *because of its beauty*, but his errand is too important for him to take the time for remorse. This passage draws me up short, not because it seems in-

conceivable but because it is so familiar. I recognize in it a million similar ex-
cuses for insensitivity: busyness, responsibility, stress. In both these passages
Parkman's response to death is not that of the hunter—certainly not that of
the traditional hunter who expresses his gratitude to the animal for giving its
life. Parkman's response is chilling because it is so casual. Even in cases where
he can identify with the animal or see its beauty, he acts on the belief that the
animal's death does not count. As the aesthete distances himself from the
object of his view, he also silences a part of himself that has the capacity to
respond to the suffering—and hence to the ethical claims—of the Other.

Aesthetics and the Self

In most of the passages where he paints a landscape, Parkman is an observer,
separated from the scene he describes, appreciating it from a distance. Once,
however, landscape and recollection blend, giving us an insight into Parkman's
mind. Something impels him to enter a narrow defile where "all within seemed
darkness and mystery. . . . The genius of the place exercised a strange influence
upon my mind. Its faculties were stimulated into extraordinary activity, and
as I passed along, many half-forgotten incidents, and the images of persons
and things far distant, rose rapidly before me, with surprising distinctness. In
that perilous wilderness, eight hundred miles removed beyond the faintest
vestige of civilization, the scenes of another hemisphere, the seat of ancient
refinement passed me, more like a succession of vivid paintings than any mere
dreams of the fancy."[46] Parkman here comes close to a feeling of awe; the place
evokes in him a response that finds value beyond the beautiful. Throughout
The Oregon Trail description is literal. The occasional simile—"green undula-
tions, like motionless swells of the ocean"—or use of personification—"mel-
ancholy trees"—suggests a literary consciousness, but Parkman's strength as
an observer also constitutes his limitation as a participant. Here, by contrast,
something in the place—the genius of the place—carries him along. In this
mountain defile Parkman finds "darkness and mystery." He is "determined to
explore the mystery to the bottom," and here for once his exploration does not
dissipate the mystery. He acknowledges the experience of being gripped by
something larger than himself and details the recollections to which the genius of the place leads him: Saint Peter's on Easter, Mount Etna, the Passion-
ist convent, and the glaciers of the Splugen. These four places—two interior
scenes of religious life and two exterior scenes of natural magnificence—seem
to share associations of death and birth or rebirth. Etna, in its resting beauty,
sends "wreaths of mild-white smoke against the soft sky," but its "inky mantle

of clouds" suggests the threat that rests, quiescent, beneath the sleeping volcano. The glaciers of the Splugen give birth to the Rhine, which, "bursting from the bowels of its native mountain," yields to a peaceful and life-sustaining course further down in the "little valley of Andeer." From the deathly "gloomy vaulted passages" of the convent, Parkman remembers sneaking glances at the decay of ancient Rome; his young, rebellious gesture denies the death-in-life of the stern monks, robed in black. Saint Peter's on the evening of Easter presents an image of radiant triumph over death. All of these images suggest that what happens for Parkman in the mountains is an apprehension of the sacred, an encounter with the Self.[47]

Like his shadow projections, Parkman's experience of the Self is culturally inflected. What I read in this passage is literally what Parkman says is there: the action of the genius of the place on his mind. It reflects an openness that is unusual in this narrative, an openness to the kind of life energy in nature that awed Conrad. It is qualitatively different from Parkman's usual posture of detachment. Here, the mountains are not just a picture for him to observe. They lead him to a profound experience of transcendence. This is what drew Emerson and Thoreau to nature and what draws many people today—the possibility of losing oneself in a place, of finding release and renewal in the experience of one's own smallness and the vastness of nature.

In Edward Edinger's terms openness to nature can facilitate the formation of the ego-Self axis. This term suggests an appropriate relationship between the ego, the conscious "I" that is only a part of psyche, and the Self, both the totality of psyche and the source of numinous energies. When a person develops a sturdy ego-Self axis, the ego feels a proper humility, recognizing its relative powerlessness. At the same time, however, the ego-Self axis provides the ego access to some of the energy of the Self and thus to a renewed sense of well-being and purpose. Only in humility can the ego safely relate to the Self. The experience of being in wild nature can stimulate this state of mind, because the individual cannot help but understand his or her smallness in relation to nature's vastness. The individual is part of nature, but nature is much greater than the finite being. This is the only place in *The Oregon Trail* where Parkman seems to receive nature without defenses.

Parkman shares a stance—that of the adventurer, the travel writer, the observer—with Conrad's Marlow and with the many ethnographers who followed him into Indian Country. Parkman prized the beauty of the mountains and the prairies and the generosity and dignity of the Indians. He lacked Conrad's intuitive understanding of the power of nature and the feeling tone of shadow, but we can see in Parkman's work a pull to the wild, along with curiosity, even perhaps a longing for something more than he could find in the genteel drawing rooms and libraries of Boston. Like Conrad, Parkman reveals both the affinities to nature embedded in Western culture and this culture's divorce from the animated planet.

Both Conrad and Parkman give us images of the shadow that Western culture has cast onto nature and native people, but only the voices of those people can express what that shadow has obscured. Reading their stories allows everyone, whether indigenous or settler, to remember the history that has been suppressed, to settle into and live with the knowledge of the blood under our very feet. This is a politics of remembering. Moreover, Western culture has constructed one way of looking at nature, while African and American Indian cultures understood nature quite differently. Listening to the voices of African and American Indian people, a reader brought up in a Western context can discover other ways of naming and of knowing.

3

Out of the Shadow

Things Fall Apart *and* Fools Crow

H EART OF DARKNESS and *The Oregon Trail* demonstrate how Western powers justified conquest by projecting shadow onto the victims and onto the land, soon to be turned from a sacred presence into a commercial "resource." Both depict a period of transition, observed by writers who saw themselves as adventurers rather than conquerors. After they left came a series of changes in the law, enforced by the military and mediated by missionaries. The land fell into European or American ownership; the native people lost their livelihood and fell under the rule of traders, settlers, missionaries, teachers, and bureaucrats who took their language, labor, culture, and homes. The land was farmed, mined, logged, and paved. A century or so later, stories and memories had been so erased or distorted that even the descendents of the conquered people often did not know their own history. But recently, writers from colonized cultures have begun rewriting colonization narratives from their own point of view. In these we find represented people living intimately in their natural habitat, at home in the world of plants, animals, and spirit. These narratives explode the ideology of savagery perpetuated by even the most enlightened Western explorers and expose the shadow projected onto natives and nature. Both Chinua Achebe's *Things Fall Apart* and James Welch's *Fools Crow* aim to reclaim the history of their people as part of the process of nation building. Both reframe the theft of land, culture, and history now encoded into law and recorded as manifest destiny, placing the Western reader at the margin, where he or she may feel confronted by unfamiliar language and images that challenge the conventional Eurocentric way of knowing.

The Igbo culture of *Things Fall Apart* and the Blackfeet culture of *Fools*

Crow were oral. Without written records these cultures depended on stories to transmit history, values, practical information, and wisdom. Their stories, whether traditional ones handed down from generation to generation or those invented in the present, were social. Storytelling was a community activity, and everyone participated. Listening was as important as speaking, and the storyteller depended on the imaginative participation of the audience.

Novels representing these cultures are, therefore, hybrid constructions. Although they are written and read largely in private, they share features of the oral culture: the prominence of stories; a recursive, nonlinear plot construction; and a refusal of translation or explanation. Both Achebe and Welch use features of the oral culture to generate for the reader an experience of a different epistemology; a different subjectivity; a different relationship to the unconscious, to nature, and to community. Where written language permits a high degree of dissembling, and words can be used to manipulate the audience, oral cultures assume truthtelling and the power of language to conjure an imaginative reality. To name a particular place, animal, plant, or person serves to evoke its presence and thus imposes a moral responsibility on the storyteller to respect the entity named. Both Achebe and Welch use words from the native culture, forcing Western readers to enter the indigenous space. The presence of these untranslated words disturbs the reader's assumption that standard written English represents the "normal" way of understanding. Further, the early parts of both novels take a nonlinear, inclusive narrative form, telling many stories that are not all hooked to a plot thrust. This narrative openness recognizes the webs of relationship that characterize indigenous cultural ways: others in the community need to be respected, their stories attended to. Both Achebe and Welch thus foreground the differences between their traditional cultures and contemporary mass culture and at the same time create the means for the reader to share, at least briefly, other life experiences.[1] Both texts also insist on what Louis Owens calls "the informing role of the past within the present, a role signified by the presence of . . . myth and history reflected in both form and content."[2]

Both Achebe and Welch have also written novels representing Igbo or Blackfeet people after conquest. In these a reader can find the marginalization, the chaotic life experience, the divorce from nature, and the reduction in ego that are often characteristic of people living under colonialism. *Things Fall Apart* and *Fools Crow*, however, explore the experience of preconquest life. In witnessing these cultures without the projection of the Western shadow, the reader cannot avoid realizing that European characterizations of indigenous people are wrong. In this way the reader begins to recognize the projection, coming to understand that invasion and conquest expressed vicious and savage elements of the conquerors themselves. Confronting the shadow of Western imperialism can distress contemporary readers—an important part of any process of change. As mentioned earlier, however, acknowledging shadow can liberate energy that has been repressed.

When the ego maintains itself by asserting its difference from the natural and human Other, a split in consciousness results. This can lead to projection, and it can also result in a personified interior Other, an "evil twin" of whom one is ashamed. This divorce from elements of the psyche requires considerable energy to maintain and results in feelings of self-distrust and desiccation. The West has no monopoly on this human instinct to protect the clan and the ego by vilifying outsiders. However, the contents of shadow are different in the West than in the traditional cultures represented by Achebe and Welch. In reading their novels, Western-educated readers can apprehend ways of living in the world that do not involve dissociation from nature and that reveal considerable openness to sources of information, such as dream and vision, that Western culture generally discounts or disregards. Such readers can see, moreover, that other cultures view as shameful qualities such as individualism and personal ambition, which are cherished in the West. Retrieving shadow for Western readers, then, may include gaining access to inner sources of wisdom, including dream, ritual, and an intimacy with the natural world. Moreover, acknowledging and withdrawing shadow projections may result in greater compassion for the internal Other.

Finally, both *Things Fall Apart* and *Fools Crow* use similar narrative strategies. Each tells an intimate story of daily life preconquest. These episodes lead readers to understand the economics, family structure, political life, values, stories, practical wisdom, and ritual life of the culture. In both cases the story of one man offers the occasion for the smaller stories woven through the narrative. Okonkwo and Fools Crow both represent their cultures, though in different ways, and each becomes implicated in the defeat of his people. In both cases history, as Western culture understands it, is imposed on a ritual way of understanding time as the cycling of seasons, planting, hunting, harvest, ceremony. In many ways the novels reveal the central importance of ritual, myth, and story in knitting together humans in a community and linking humans with the other-than-human world.

THINGS FALL APART *AND THE EUROPEAN SHADOW*

Chinua Achebe weaves the story of Okonkwo, a figure of near mythic proportions, "tall and huge," into the fabric of a novel written to give the lie to Western depictions of Africa.[3] The nine villages of Umuofia share with other Igbo villages a life rooted in tradition and the ancestors, existing in harmony with the natural cycles of the year.[4] Achebe organizes the first part of the novel around incidents that illustrate tribal life, many of them involving rituals and celebrations. Each is a self-contained story, and the connections among them are not made explicit. For a willing reader *Things Fall Apart* offers a chance to encounter the unknown, and reading it can feel like dreaming.

Rituals and Daily Life
Rituals in the novel fulfill social, political, judicial, religious, and ecological functions. They derive from the clan's wisdom and regenerate its primary values. The ritual of the kola nut precedes all social interaction; the village gathers ritually to debate whether to go to war, to settle lawsuits, to cheer on wrestlers; rituals surround planting and harvest, as well as relations with the ancestors. Collective ritual life is governed both by the *egwugwu*, the living representatives of the ancestors, and by the priestesses of the earth and of the oracle.

Ritual is closely linked to the land. Like farmers everywhere, Umuofians study nature closely. Many of their rituals are directed at ensuring the land's fertility, but the awesome power of nature evokes their reverence for the Oracle of the Hills and the Caves, Agbala. People come to consult the oracle when misfortune, conflict, or uncertainty plagues them. Agbala represents a tremendous numinosity associated with the earth's dark interior:

> The way into the shrine was a round hole at the side of a hill, just a little bigger than the round opening into a henhouse. Worshippers and those who came to seek knowledge from the god crawled on their belly through the hole and found themselves in a dark, endless space in the presence of Agbala. No one had ever beheld Agbala, except his priestess. But no one who had ever crawled into his awful shrine had come out without the fear of his power. His priestess stood by the sacred fire which she built in the heart of the cave and proclaimed the will of the god. The fire did not burn with a

flame. The glowing logs only served to light up vaguely the dark figure of the priestess.[5]

Imagine the emotional condition of the petitioner, who must abase him- or herself to crawl through a hole in the earth and enter a "dark, endless space." Contrast this with the heady awe of standing in a great, Gothic cathedral. There, light and space, soaring heights, and the rich colors of stained glass invite the spirit to ascend. Here, the petitioner returns to his earthy origins in a ritual that manifests a reverberating interiority. Entering the womb of all life, enveloped by a great power, the worshipper receives the wisdom of the earth and the ancestors through the agency of the priestess.

An extended incident involving the oracle occurs near the middle of the novel, when the priestess of Agbala comes to Okonkwo's compound to take his sick daughter Ezinma to the oracle. Her mother, terrified, races after, and the incident ends when the child's mother realizes that Okonkwo too has followed his daughter. The incident deepens our experience of the culture of the tribe, but it does not drive a linear narrative. We are left to infer that the visit to the oracle connects somehow to Ezinma's cure, but Achebe offers no discursive explanation. In many ways the incident reads like a dream, with symbols we can't quite decipher. M. Vera Bührmann, a South African psychiatrist, notes the following about Xhosa rituals: "No living ritual is meaningless; the efficacy is often difficult to *understand*, but when one is an involved participant, one can *experience* its power to transform and make whole. The healing power of these rituals to a large extent remains a mystery, no matter how much we try to conceptualise it and to fit it into a mould of our own making."[6] At least within this narrative, the ritual works.

As in many traditional societies, Umuofians practice a place-based religious life. Ritual celebrations begin with the beating of drums in the *ilo*, the village playground, "which was as old as the village itself." The drums call the villagers to assemble, and in their rhythm they set the life-clock of the clan: "Their sound was no longer a separate thing from the living village. It was like the pulsation of its heart. It throbbed in the air, in the sunshine, and even in the trees, and filled the village with excitement."[7] This ritual drumming, in effect, unites the people and the place into a single organism, expressing and regenerating their unity. This earth-centered religion helps account for the Umuofians' low-impact agriculture. Fields can be only as large as will allow a family to work them, and they can spread no further than a distance that will make it possible for a person to get there, work, and get home in one day.

Wole Soyinka, the Nigerian Nobel Prize winner, writes, "Where society lives in a close inter-relation with Nature, regulates its existence by natural phenomena within the observable processes of continuity—ebb and tide, waxing and waning of the moon, rain and drought, planting and harvest—the highest moral order is seen as that which guarantees a parallel continuity of the species." He calls this the "metaphysics of the irreducible: knowledge of birth and death as the human cycle; the wind as a moving, felling, cleansing, destroying, winnowing force; the duality of the knife as blood-letter and creative implement; earth and sun as life-sustaining verities, and so on. These serve as matrices within which mores, personal relationships, even communal economics are formulated and reviewed."[8]

One of the most important rituals in the novel is that of the *egwugwu*, figures of the ancestors. These figures appear during the annual ceremony in honor of the earth deity and also whenever an issue comes to trial. The *egwugwu* carry out the justice of Umuofia in the tradition of the ancestors in order to prevent intratribal resentments or conflicts. As spirits of the ancestors, the *egwugwu* emerged from the earth, masked and speaking an esoteric language. "It was a terrifying spectacle," and the people addressed them in tones of reverence and awe, befitting the spirits of the nine sons of the founder of the clan, each representing one of the nine villages of Umuofia.[9] Bührmann comments on the centrality of the role of the ancestors in the Xhosa people's belief system, identifying two kinds of ancestors—those known personally to the family and honored in shrines in the family compound, where they seem to share in everyday life, and those who are "not known by their faces." These latter "are powerful and awesome and live under the water and in the forest. On account of their numinosity, they cannot be approached or consulted without special precautions being taken."[10] The *egwugwu* carry this awesome energy for the Umuofians; through this ritual the tribe resurrects its emotional ties and regenerates the original unity that diminishes the importance of individual rivalries. Ritualized reverence for the ancestors acts as a kind of cultural memory, linking the particular present with the timeless traditions of the clan. Paul Shepherd remarks that masked rituals reveal "humankind's central means of reconciliation with a world of changes."[11] In the Umuofian ceremony the *egwugwu* give faces to the tribe's traditions and ensure continuity in clan life. The ritual allows the people to navigate ambiguity and to accommodate history within a social structure set down in the distant past. In this light the desecration of an *egwugwu* near the end of the novel represents the tragic severing of tribal unity and memory.

Ritual and Shadow

Achebe gathers both the virtues and the shadow of the culture into the character of Okonkwo. He is represented as physically imposing; mythically skilled in wrestling, the premier sport of the culture; and driven by ambition to distance himself from his lazy father, Unoka, and achieve the highest ranks of the clan. The story of Okonkwo has the feel of a classical tragedy, the downfall of a great, and flawed, leader.

Ritual protects the clan by acknowledging and containing shadow. We see this partially through Okonkwo's infractions of ritual practices. During the Week of Peace, for example, the narrator tells us, Okonkwo beats his wife to discipline her. Ezeani, priest of Ani, visits him, saying: "You know as well as I do that our forefathers ordained that before we plant any crops in the earth we should observe a week in which a man does not say a harsh word to his neighbor. We live in peace with our fellows to honor our great goddess of the earth without whose blessing our crops will not grow. You have committed a great evil. . . . The evil you have done can ruin the whole clan. The earth goddess whom you have insulted may refuse to give us her increase, and we shall all perish."[12] The Week of Peace expresses in ritual the need to restrain impulse and curb aggression in order to keep the human and natural worlds in balance. When Okonkwo cannot control his temper, his violation of the ritual jeopardizes the community, causing imbalance among all the cosmic forces. As Wole Soyinka remarks, "A breakdown in moral order implies, in the African world-view, a rupture in the body of Nature just like the physical malfunctioning of one man."[13] Both the earth's fertility and the harmony of the clan are necessary to survival, and a threat to one is a threat to the other. The Week of Peace serves an ecological as well as a community function: planting before the time is right can endanger the harvest or exhaust the earth, so the ritual of peace serves to keep humans' restlessness in check, maintaining balance not only within the human community but also between humans and the land. Just as ritual can connect individuals with larger sources of energy, as may have been the case in the scene with Ezinma, it can also express the limits imposed on an individual's will by both the necessities of community life and the rhythms of nature. Ritual thus provides a container to make available to the individual and the community energies that transcend the rational, ensuring that humans do not identify with these energies and become inflated, as Kurtz did.

Umuofia also assigns a particular location to its cultural shadow: the Evil

Forest is "alive with sinister forces and powers of darkness."[14] Any forest is an object of some fear in Umuofia, uncleared ground, beyond the human, akin to the dark forests of Grimm fairy tales.[15] Forests in general represent known fears, but the Evil Forest contains greater terrors, amorphous anxieties, and abominations. When Okonkwo's father, Unoka, dies, he cannot be buried because his death is the result of a "swelling which was an abomination to the earth goddess. . . . He was carried to the Evil Forest and left there to die." Twins are abandoned in the Evil Forest, as are the *efulefu*, "worthless, empty men . . . the excrement of the clan."[16] Clan leaders instruct Christian missionaries to locate their places of worship there, since the people believe no one can survive in the Evil Forest. There, the missionaries attract exactly those individuals who occupy Umuofia's cultural shadow. Achebe himself is the son of a convert, and his first teaching assignment was in a Christian school—the ironically named Merchants of Light School, built in just such an evil forest, "the dumping ground for several corpses . . . [where] potent fetish objects had been deposited."[17] Because he has the advantage of distance, Achebe can see cultural shadow that is invisible to his characters. His narrative attributes significant responsibility for the fall of Umuofia to the missionaries' ability to divide the clan, which is a result of the clan's ignorance of its own shadow. However, it's worth noting that one of the *egwugwu* is Evil Forest. Like the rehabilitated Furies in Aeschylus, Evil Forest is the voice of justice and "natural restitution for social disharmony."[18] Although the Umuofians are able to acknowledge and honor some shadow forces in this way, incorporating them into the rituals of justice and the geography of the clan, shadow remains in some crucial ways unconscious.

Ritual, Time, and Place

Ritual contains shadow and promotes mindfulness. It celebrates and orders the responsibility humans share with nature for fertility and the preservation of habitat. Two theories of ritual illuminate elements of Igbo life in *Things Fall Apart*. Mircea Eliade's work on the rituals and myths of "archaic" or traditional people suggests ways ritual bound people to the natural forces of their habitat and created community cohesion. Wole Soyinka's reflections on the role of ritual and myth in Yoruba culture suggest the power of ritual in navigating psychological life.

In *The Myth of the Eternal Return*, Eliade develops a theory of ritual cultures, arguing that for traditional people what's real, or ontologically significant, is not the unique historical action but rather the gesture repeated from divinely fashioned archetypes. He uses the word *archetypes* not in the sense attached to it by Jung, evoking patterns resident in the collective unconscious, but rather in a Platonic sense, referring to paradigms or exemplary models. The actions of "gods, civilizing heroes, or mythical ancestors" give rituals their form, but they also make any action performed after their pattern into a ritual. In this world "every responsible activity in pursuit of a definite end is . . . a ritual" and therefore not only sacred but also necessary to the continuation of the universe. Thus, a hunt undertaken in the pattern passed on by the ancestors, a childbirth undergone in the manner of the original mother, a crop planted with prayers to the corn goddess, a meal served after the model of the gods—all these have meaning because they are repetitions of the original acts. Ritual gives significance to daily life and connects the individual with an ordered, cyclical, and transcendent reality that Eliade calls cosmos. Ritual transforms the particular space and time of the ceremony into the place and moment of the original act, so that ritual repetition re-creates time and regenerates place.[19]

Not only does ritual rejuvenate the bonds between people and place, but it also makes the people cocreators. When they revere their ancestors, Umuofians reestablish the nine villages; when they celebrate the Week of Peace before they plant a new crop, they participate in the fertility of the land. In ritual the participant steps out of linear time, out of history, and into a new beginning. Just as the annual cycle of the seasons ensures the regeneration of life on earth, the annual cycle of ritual events brings about the regular regeneration of the individual and the community, and reverence for the ancestors provides a man continued influence even after his death.

Eliade distinguishes ritual consciousness from historical consciousness, which maintains an ironic distance between the individual and the ritual performance. Likewise, Achebe, as a modern writer, faces the problem of representing a culture with a cyclical and ritual consciousness in a fundamentally historical form, that of the narrative. The moment that he captures in the novel sits at the boundary of a change from ritual to historical consciousness, imposed on the Umuofians by their colonizers, who bring with them the historical sense that their actions constitute "progress." Achebe's response to this challenge is to embed the story of Okonkwo, who sets himself apart from others in his tribe by his ambition, within an account of the ritual life and traditions of the clan. Achebe provides his contemporary reader with an experience of traditional Igbo culture in the first two thirds of the novel, where the pace of the writing imitates the leisurely, ordered rhythm of life.

With the story of Okonkwo, however, a linear, tragic motif intrudes, just as the imposition of British authority is about to disrupt Igbo life. Achebe's attention to Okonkwo's psychology suggests that Okonkwo's pride is a danger, prophesying the fate that is about to overtake Umuofia.

Culture and Myth

Wole Soyinka's account of the myths and rituals of Yoruba culture illuminates the relationship between Okonkwo and his culture. In Yoruba culture there are four worlds—of the living, of the ancestors, of the unborn, and the "dark continuum of transition where occurs the inter-transmutation of essence-ideal and materiality." This recognition in African metaphysics of a liminal or chthonic space, a place of change, corresponds with the unconscious, where energy takes shape. This is the arena in which ritual has power, and it accounts for the efficacy of ritual to reconfigure psychological reality. Thus, when Ogbala carries Ezinma to the oracle, she is performing a ritual that constellates in all the participants this world of change where reality can be transformed. Soyinka notes that "the act of hubris or its opposite—weakness, excessive passivity or inertia—leads to a disruption of balances within nature and this in turn triggers off compensating energies."[20] Okonkwo's overcompensation for the weakness of his father suggests an imbalance in psychological nature that becomes connected to a disharmony with external nature. It is specifically an imbalance between father and son, which threatens continuity.

In some ways Okonkwo stands in relation to Umuofia as Kurtz does to Europe: an overdeveloped ambition renders each vulnerable to energies from the unconscious that have gained in power because of the one-sided conscious orientation. Soyinka points out that, like humans, Yoruba gods have flaws, such as self-indulgence and hubris. Acting out these flaws requires that the gods pay penance and compensation to their human victims. The Igbo moral world is close to that of the Yoruba; Okonkwo, as a man of near-mythic stature, suffers excesses, challenges his *chi*, and behaves as though he is larger than life. After his first transgression he makes compensation through his exile, but in the end, colonial conquest aborts his capacity to atone to his clan for his excess. In his banishment Okonkwo resembles Ogun, "the embodiment of . . . the Promethean instinct in man, constantly at the service of society for its full self-realisation." Okonkwo suffers, as Ogun does, from the "experience of dissolution and re-integration" in his motherland.[21] He would lead his society back to wholeness by killing the soldier who comes to break up the village meeting. However, the power of the colonial law has terrified Umuofia, missionaries have divided the clan, and so Okonkwo cannot regenerate his people. He has no choice but to kill himself and suffer the ultimate banishment to the Evil Forest.[22]

Shadow and Sacrifice

Rituals form containers that can acknowledge and restrain forces that would be dangerous to the balance between humans and habitat if they ran free. Rituals transform personal shadow contents into larger cultural forms, allowing individuals to express dangerous impulses without acting them out. In this context the killing of Ikemefuna deserves more than a passing reference.

When one of its members murders a Umuofian woman, a neighboring village sends a youth, Ikemefuna, to Umuofia in order to avoid a war. He comes to live in Okonkwo's compound and is absorbed into the family. His integration into Umuofian life expresses its "feminine" inclusiveness, and Okonkwo becomes genuinely fond of the boy. After three years the Oracle of the Hills and Caves declares it is time for the clan to sacrifice Ikemefuna. The oldest man in the area comes to Okonkwo to break the news and to instruct Okonkwo specifically to take no part in the killing, because the boy regards him as a father. Okonkwo, however, will not listen and insists on participating. For the other men on the expedition, this is ritual, but for Ikemefuna and Okonkwo it is personal. Okonkwo retreats to the rear of the procession, but when the first blow fails to kill Ikemefuna, and Okonkwo hears him cry out, "My father, they have killed me," Okonkwo runs toward him. Ashamed of his own tender feelings, Okonkwo kills the boy rather than be seen as "weak" like his father.[23]

This scene illustrates the way the shadow works. Tenderness is part of Okonkwo's shadow. As a strong man he sees himself as fearless. But his fear of being seen as soft is deep and irrational. Because this fear is unconscious, it appears with intense force. Fear thus possesses him, and Okonkwo does what he *knows* he should not do. Okonkwo's acting out his shadow contaminates the impersonal ritual, dragging it out of a cultural cosmos into personal history.

Afterward, Okonkwo taunts his friend Obierika that he stayed home out of fear, disobedience, or squeamishness, projecting his own shadow. Obierika replies: "If I were you I would have stayed at home. What you have done will not please the Earth. It is the kind of action for which the goddess wipes out whole families."[24] The fate Obierika pronounces for Okonkwo proves accurate and deadly: later in the narrative the memory of Ikemefuna's murder drives Okonkwo's estranged son, Nwoye, into the camp of the missionaries, dividing Okonkwo's family as the missionaries divided the people. Okonkwo kills Ikemefuna because he has become possessed by his shadow—"dazed with fear"—at the moment of decision. He can't act rationally because he can't acknowledge his vulnerability or even his affection. Soyinka points out that the Yoruba origin story incorporates such a psychic division: the primogenitor of god and man was attended by a slave, Atunda. Atunda rolls a huge boulder on to the god, shattering him into fragments that hurtle into the abyss.[25] This origin story itself suggests something about the nature of consciousness, which appears to be whole but can at any moment fragment through the action of some enslaved element.

The image of ritual human sacrifice predictably disturbs Western readers, but this is an example of what Tzvetan Todorov calls the culture of sacrifice. Writing about the conquest of the Americas, Todorov contrasts Western European and American Indian cultures as cultures of massacre and cultures of sacrifice. Ikemefuna is first sacrificed by his own people to avert war. In cultures of sacrifice, or "religious murder," the victim is carefully chosen and publicly sacrificed, usually in a ritual manner. One child is sacrificed to protect many others from the devastation of a war of revenge. Christianity, too, is based on an original sacrifice; indeed, *sacrifice* means "to make sacred."

In cultures of massacre, by contrast, "massacre is . . . intimately linked to colonial wars waged far from the metropolitan country. The more remote and alien the victims, the better: they are exterminated without remorse, more or less identified with animals."[26] Adam Hochschild documents the brutality of European explorers and merchants in *King Leopold's Ghost*, and Conrad implies that Kurtz was such a killer. Thus, we can contrast the sacrifice of Ikemefuna with the practice of Kurtz. As Todorov remarks of the Spanish perpetrators of massacre in the New World: "Far from the central government, far from royal law, all prohibitions give way, the social link, already loosened, snaps, revealing not a primitive nature, the beast sleeping in each of us, but a modern being, one with a great future in fact, restrained by no morality and inflicting death because and when he pleases."[27] Ritual sacrifice, like the "cannibalism" Marlow claims to have witnessed, was a practice seized upon by Western powers to distract people from recognizing the far more destructive effects of their own deadly path.[28]

Abdul JanMohamed reads Okonkwo's story in the context of the Igbos' "attempts to realize simultaneously their aristocratic and democratic ideals."[29] Okonkwo's overreliance on the aristocratic virtues of ambition and pride blind him to the more democratic virtues of his father and his culture. Likewise, he is deaf to the counsel of Obierika and numb to the sensitivity of Nwoye. His refusal to show emotion estranges him from others and leads him to challenge his *chi*. This constitutes alienation from himself, his ancestors, and his culture. So ironically, in striving to excel in Umuofia, Okonkwo estranges himself. He embraces the aristocratic part of Umuofian culture as his identity and casts the democratic, artistic, and "feminine" qualities into shadow. This accounts in part for the ways that Okonkwo seems a very Western character, driven and self-absorbed. JanMohamed argues that when Okonkwo is sent into exile in his motherland, the clan offers him a "retreat into and possible modification by the feminine principle." However, Okonkwo maintains his exclusive allegiance to virile values, refusing the opportunity offered by the withdrawal into shadow. JanMohamed goes on to propose that "the invading culture penetrates Igboland through the acquiescence of the feminine, flexible, and adaptable elements of Igbo society," elements that constitute shadow for Okonkwo. Nwoye, in turn, is alienated from his culture because of the sacrifice of Ikemefuna, whom he had come to love. JanMohamed claims that the "opposition and imbalance in society, embodied by father and son, cause it to fall apart under the impact of Western imperialism."[30] This line of argument preserves the agency of Igbo culture, privileging it above the imperialists' guns, missionaries, and civil servants. We will see this attitude again in *Fools Crow*, where Welch uses a central story of the Blackfeet people to suggest that the culture contained the seeds of its own conquest. According to Lori Burlingame, such "retroactive prophecy" offers "empowerment through self-responsibility and cultural awareness and reconnection."[31] This approach to history implies that reviving conquered cultures requires them to acknowledge shadow.

In *Things Fall Apart* Achebe reanimates the role of ritual as a means of mediating between humans and the creative and frightening powers of nature and the unconscious. Ritual makes it possible for humans to enter into relationship with these energies, and culture provides a context in which the acknowledgment and restraint of such energies constitutes a central reality of social life. The rituals, myths, and stories of the Blackfeet people likewise provide a window into their consciousness.

FOOLS CROW: *OTHER WAYS OF KNOWING*

For individuals living in cultures that have been conquered or colonized, the language, stories, and religious traditions of the clan or nation have been forced into shadow by the practices of the conquerors. Ngugi wa Thiong'o, the Kikuyu writer and critic, argues: "Colonialism imposed its control of the social production of wealth through military conquest and subsequent political dictatorship. But its most important area of domination was the mental universe of the colonised, the control, through culture, of how people perceived themselves and their relationship to the world.... To control a people's culture is to control their tools of self-definition in relationship to others."[32] For Achebe and James Welch, writing a novel that reinscribes history is part of a deliberate process of bringing what has been forced into shadow to light, releasing the energy contained there.

The problem faced by writers of suppressed histories is how to create a text that is both authentic and hopeful so that the story itself becomes a means of revitalizing the culture. If a story is true to history, how can it be hopeful? One strategy is to saturate the reader in the values of the preconquest culture, thereby revivifying it. Like Achebe, James Welch needed to reappropriate history and revoice the silenced. Moreover, Welch needed to connect the particular narrative of *Fools Crow* with both the historical process of colonization and the phenomenon of the American Indian Renaissance, the flowering of writing by American Indians that has occurred in the last fifty years or so. Like Louise Erdrich's *Tracks*, another novel that reinscribes history, *Fools Crow* exists intertextually, even though the events it represents precede the texts that provide its context. Welch is an intellectual, a writer, publishing in a mainstream house, but he's also Blackfeet. The writer is himself an embodied contradiction, and so is the text. *Fools Crow* represents a refusal to be silenced, to be vanished.

Writing not from the margins of Western culture but from the center of Blackfeet land, Welch reconstructs a mythic world. Speeches, stories, and songs assume a prominence appropriate to their cultural place in Blackfeet culture. The novel shapes itself principally around the experience of White Man's Dog, a young man of the Pikuni band of Lone Eaters, part of the Blackfeet Nation, who later assumes the name Fools Crow. The novel's point of view shifts often enough to construct the recounted events as the story of the people and not simply that of one man. Throughout, Welch gives voice to the traditional values of his culture. Thus, myth performs a function much like that of ritual in *Things Fall Apart*, exploring the meanings of experiences and providing the means to pass values from generation to generation. Myth and story map the relationship of the people to the world. Moreover, in oral cultures the human voice is one of the sounds of nature, story and song joining the human with the rest of the world.

Welch translates Blackfeet names for animals literally, so buffalo are "black-horns." Months are "the moon of the burnt grass" or "first thunder moon." Places are "the Backbone of the World" or "Woman Don't Walk Butte." He uses English to indicate what writers including Leslie Marmon Silko and David Abram have also suggested—that traditional names contain stories and vital information that connect the people to the place. William Cronon underscores this idea with his description of the ecological habits of nam-ing practiced by New England Indians, who gave places names that indi-cated what plants could be gathered in that location, where shellfish could be collected, where beaver dams could be found, and so on: "The purpose of such names was to turn the landscape into a map which, if studied carefully, literally gave a village's inhabitants the information they needed to sustain themselves."[33] Arnold Krupat calls what Welch does "anti-imperial transla-tion." Whereas a translation distorts the language of traditional people to fit the language of the colonizer (or simply imposes the terms of the colonizer on the geography and tongues of the colonized), anti-imperial translation "seeks to disrupt the habitual desire of [the colonial] audience to use the text as an occasion to know *about* the Other." According to Krupat, "The language [Native writers] offer . . . derives at least in part from other forms of practice, and to comprehend it might just require, however briefly, that we attempt to imagine living other forms of life."[34]

Often, the Western-oriented historical worldview sees oral cultures as oc-cupying a stage in the development of written transmission. This opinion serves the interests of conquest. Oral cultures are not deficient or immature; they represent an alternative way to locate humans in the world, one that takes embodiedness as its starting point. Gerald Vizenor argues that "the no-tion, in the literature of dominance, that the oral advances to the written, is a colonial reduction of natural sound, heard stories, and the tease of shadows in tribal remembrance."[35] Thus, "oral" elements of *Fools Crow* buttress its overt representation of the ecological and psychological experience of the Pikuni band of Blackfeet.

Like Achebe, Welch overlays a picture of daily life with the story of an individual. Unlike Okonkwo, however, Fools Crow has no tragic flaw. He functions as an exemplar of his culture, and while other characters, as Louis Owens notes, act out of idiosyncratic impulse, Fools Crow's role as emblem precludes his having a fully developed shadow.[36] Welch chooses instead to create the shadow figures of Fast Horse and Owl Child to suggest undevel-oped qualities of Pikuni culture. The novel details Fools Crow's subjectivity, allowing him inner conflicts, ambivalence, and occasional lapses from propriety, as well as growing wisdom, humility, reverence, and access to non-ego-based ways of knowing. He is our threshold into Pikuni consciousness.

As in *Things Fall Apart*, the world we see in *Fools Crow* includes both events thrust on it by the white invasion of the land and events that grow organically from the life of the Pikunis. The novel's balance between externally imposed and internal, organic actions gives it a character that is both political and mythic. It's the latter quality that I want to explore in detail, since myth is what keeps dread at bay: the culture is lost, but not irretrievably; the relationship with place, self, and community that allowed the Blackfeet to live intimately with nature persists through stories. In particular, alternative ways of knowing are enacted in the novel through the power of animal helpers, dreams, ceremonies, and stories. Most of Western culture has cast into shadow the ways of knowing practiced by traditional people like the Blackfeet. Welch's exploration of these ways of knowing allows us to experience states of mind that Western culture has disowned or discounted.

Dream, Power Animals, and Song

In *Fools Crow* a dream is not simply a subjective experience. The problem of dreams occupies the beginning of the narrative, when both Fast Horse and White Man's Dog have power dreams. Not every dream is a big dream; some simply worry over events of the day or represent real people in habitual occupations. But a big dream represents spiritual characters or occurs repeatedly, carrying an urgency that makes it more than personal.[37]

On the way to the Crow camp, Fast Horse has a powerful dream in which Cold Maker comes to tell him that the horse raid will only be successful if they remove a rock that has fallen over a spring on Woman Don't Walk Butte. When Fast Horse tells his dream, he translates it from the private to the communal. It requires a response, and the raiders interrupt their journey to pursue it. Puffed up at his big dream, Fast Horse brags that Cold Maker has chosen him for this important message. But they cannot locate the spring. Yellow Kidney, the leader of the raid, prays for guidance and decides to continue the raid, but with extra caution. When they reach the Crow camp, Yellow Kidney steals down to seize a prize horse from his enemy. However, he is exposed when Fast Horse rides into the camp, shouting boasts.

Unlike Fast Horse, White Man's Dog keeps his dream private, withholding vital information. He dreams, several times, of a lodge in an enemy camp filled with naked white-faced girls, who carry an erotic charge. White Man's

Dog's failure to share his dream also exposes Yellow Kidney to danger. In the Crow encampment Yellow Kidney initially escapes detection when the watch is roused by ducking into a lodge filled with young people who have smallpox. In the dark he cannot tell that they are diseased, however, and in the heat of the moment, he has sex with one of the girls. As a result, he contracts smallpox. When the Crows capture him, they cut off his fingers and send him out in the snowy night as a warning to the Blackfeet.

The story of White Man's Dog's dream illustrates both the social quality of dreams and the way Welch uses them to characterize Pikuni culture. When he hears Yellow Kidney's account of his suffering, White Man's Dog feels gnawingly responsible for the older man's condition. He confides his feelings of guilt to his father, and Rides-at-the-Door responds: "It is true that you should have told Yellow Kidney about your dream, and it might be true that he would have turned back. But I believe that it would have been too late. Already the world was out of balance. You were too close to the Crow camps to see reason and so you proceeded, knowing the risks. No, do not blame yourself. At most, you made an error in judgment. I'm afraid your friend, Fast Horse, made this catastrophe with his hotheaded boasting."[38]

A dream, then, is a public responsibility; White Man's Dog "should have" told his dream. But his proximity to danger, and the excited state of mind this prompted, blinded him. His altered subjective state changes his perceptions, but more, it changes everything: "Already the *world* was out of balance." Rides-at-the-Door suggests here the close relationship of inner and outer in Pikuni culture: a dream is also "reason." The truth it speaks may not be clear, but it does not lie. The distinctions Western culture makes between the real and the imaginary, dream and waking experience, story and history, do not obtain. This intimacy of dream and reason mirrors that of human and nature and places grave responsibility on humans to keep the world in balance. Thus, the narrative in *Fools Crow* takes dreams seriously. They acquire a social and ethical reality when they are presented publicly. The dream places the subjectivity of the dreamer on view, linking it to the common imagination. This makes a person responsible not only for his actions but also for what he channels from the unconscious.

In addition to dreams, *Fools Crow* features the trickster Raven as a character who leads White Man's Dog to Skunk Bear, a wolverine who becomes his power animal. Raven speaks to White Man's Dog, and the narrative asks the reader to accept this; however the reader understands it, Welch offers the bird's speech not as metaphor but as simple fact. White Man's Dog's subsequent rescue of the wolverine represents a development in his consciousness and his capacity. His first vision quest had not yielded him a power animal, and now he has found one.

Later, after his sacrifice at the medicine pole, he has a dream in which he again frees the wolverine from a trap, and the wolverine teaches him a song. He also instructs White Man's Dog thus: "When you kill the blackhorns, or any of the four-leggeds, you must leave a chunk of liver for Raven, for it was he who guided you to me. He watches out for all his brothers, and that is why we leave part of our kills for him."[39] This powerful dream asserts a deeper kinship between the man and the animal: each hunts, and each honors the hunted. To live, each must take life, so each honors both those powers that guide the hunt and those that give their lives for the survival of the hunter. Because in Blackfeet culture, as in other traditional societies, no ethical distinction was made between humans and animals, hunting entailed considerable emotional stress. The people must eat, but this requires that animals sacrifice their lives. Hunting rituals mediate this anxiety and honor the sacrifice by ensuring that the hunt is undertaken in the spirit of the sacred. In leaving some of the liver for Raven, White Man's Dog sacrifices some of his bounty to acknowledge his gratitude, dependence, and complicity. The origin of the hunting ritual in the dream amplifies its personal emotional force. Skunk Bear reciprocates White Man's Dog's acts of kindness by conferring power on him, specifically the power of song.

The power song is a very special kind of utterance, akin to prayer. In *American Indian Literatures*, A. LaVonne Brown Ruoff writes of the emphasis American Indian people place on "living in harmony with the physical and spiritual universe, the power of thought and word to maintain this balance, a deep reverence for the land, and a strong sense of community."[40] In song people vocalize the thoughts that maintain balance; song invokes the presence of the spiritual in the physical; it speaks to the singer; it promises; it celebrates. Song maintains a relationship between humans and their fellow beings. David Abram, in *The Spell of the Sensuous*, argues that for traditional people language is not exclusive to humans. Trees, animals, even rocks speak. Wind and rain speak, and human speech involves a dialogue with other beings. Songs use repetition, both within the song and in singing it over and over, which can alter states of mind. Like prayer, song is not intended to communicate information; like prayer, song has the function of "establishing or consolidating relationship through intensifying the 'presence' of one being to another."[41]

Song also brings deep parts of the self into relationship with the living physical world. The power song expresses and engenders a relationship with a specific creature, in Fools Crow's case the wolverine. Later in the narrative White Man's Dog, now named Fools Crow, and Red Paint, his wife, visit the mountains. There, Raven instructs him to kill a white man who has been killing animals and leaving them. At first he resists, because he knows that to kill a white man at this point is to expose his people to danger, but Raven persuades him that his allegiance to "his brothers, the four-leggeds and the flyers," demands that he rid the mountain of this menace.[42] We see how song works when Fools Crow is stalking the Napikwan who leaves his kill:

[He] breathed deeply and saw a red wall come up behind his eyes. He felt sick and weak. He closed his eyes and called out to Sun Chief, to Wolverine, his power, to give him strength, to let him die with honor. Slowly, almost silently, a sound entered his ears. As the sound increased in volume, the red wall behind his eyes receded. Now he saw the slope clearly, the red bushes, the slender yellow grasses—and his gun. The sound was in his head and in the small meadow surrounded by the great mountains of the Backbone. The sound flowed through his body and he felt the strength of its music in his limbs, in his hands, in his guts, in his chest. He sprang to a crouch, then made a dive for his weapon. A *boom!* kicked up a patch of duff inches from his head. But the music had reached his heart. The weapon was in his hands, against his cheek, and he watched the greased shooter leave his rifle and he watched it travel through the air, between the trees, and he saw it enter the Napikwan's forehead above the startled eyes, below the wolfskin head-dress, and he squatted and watched the head jerk back, then the body, until it landed with a quivering shudder in the bear grass, the lupine, the windflowers. Then the sound was no more. Fools Crow's death song had ended.[43]

The song seems almost involuntary, an agency that enters his ears, clears his sight, inflames his courage, strengthens his body, guides his hand. It comes when he is nearly hobbled by fear, giving him the power of Wolverine to keep him mindful of his responsibility to all the animals. It is his death song, the reminder of his mortality, that inspires courage to do what's right. At the same time it is the song that enables him to take life, not rashly but in accord with moral principles. It contains and channels energy from the shadow into an appropriate act.

One more example underlines the power of dreams and their ethical quality in the Pikuni world. In the same dream in which he receives the power song from the wolverine, White Man's Dog dreams of making love to Kills-close-to-the-lake, his father's young wife, whom he has desired without fully acknowledging it ever since she joined their family. In the dream she tells him: "This is the place of dreams. Here, we may desire each other. But not in that other world, for there you are my husband's son." As the people pack up to leave the site of the Sun Dance, White Man's Dog meets Kills-close-to-the-lake, who tells him that on the same night she had a parallel dream. She too dreamed of him, but in the dream he vanished, and instead a wolverine appeared and ravished her. When the wolverine finished, he bit off her little finger, and it turned into a white stone. "Let this always remind you of your wickedness, sister," he told her. She says, "I threw myself into the white grass and wept, for he had revealed what I had kept hidden even from myself."[44] When she woke up, she found the white stone and left it with the sleeping White Man's Dog. Later, she sacrificed the finger at the Sun Dance, a powerful suggestion of the embodiedness of psychic life, an enactment of shadow knowledge.

White Man's Dog remembers his dream, but he does not remember that in it he made love with Kills-close-to-the-lake. Even so, the dreams have power: "White Man's Dog didn't know how or why, but Wolverine had cleansed both him and Kills-close-to-the-lake. He had also given White Man's Dog his power, in the white stone and the song."[45] In this respect the narrative expresses vividly the quality of dream, "the seemingly self-generative and autonomous power of the dream image to appear without apparent volition on the part of the dreamer, the astonishing power of the simplest image to provoke an extreme emotional charge, and the helplessness of the dreamer in the face of his own creation."[46] While White Man's Dog feels cleansed, Kills-close-to-the-lake suffers a reminder in her maimed hand of the "wickedness" she had kept in her shadow. She seems to have been cured of her desire for White Man's Dog, but even this cannot save her, later in the narrative, from falling into a shameful liaison with his brother, Running Fisher. Here the narrative comes close to acknowledging the shadow side of Pikuni culture in the dependency and powerlessness thrust on some women.[47]

Still, from White Man's Dog's perspective, Wolverine has cleansed them. Again the public dream—even a dream only so public as to be shared by two people—has ethical force. The paired dreams free desire from shadow without requiring White Man's Dog to act on what he feels. He can now live wholeheartedly with his new bride, Red Paint. A Western interpretation might focus on the animal figure in the dreams as a representation of instinctual energy. Honoring such instincts in consciousness disarms their power to manipulate, so the two young people no longer need to suffer the guilt of their illicit desire. But the narrative says something different: "Wolverine had cleansed both him and Kills-close-to-the-lake." White Man's Dog does not even have to remember his dream accurately for its power to work.

Ritual and Psyche

After the raid on the Crow horses, White Man's Dog dances the Sun Dance to thank the sun god for his success. In the Sun Dance a dancer's flesh is pierced with a bear claw and serviceberry sticks inserted beneath the flesh. These are attached to rawhide lines tied at the other end to the Medicine Pole. The dancer circles the pole, praying and dancing in the four directions, until he pulls the sticks out, tearing the flesh again. This ritual ordeal serves as a transition for White Man's Dog, moving him toward his role as a warrior.

Hunters and warriors kill, after all, and both risk death in the process. The Sun Dance allows White Man's Dog symbolically to take some of the violence he has performed and embody it, to contain the tension between his love of life, with whatever shadow elements of cowardice that may imply, and his desire for glory, with whatever shadow elements of hubris that may imply. Because it is symbolic, the ritual allows him to accommodate extreme desires and hold them simultaneously in his body, increasing the likelihood that he will grow in consciousness as a consequence. It helps to transform White Man's Dog from a young horse raider into a warrior and a man.

Richard Schechner describes the "quintessential . . . task" of a ritual as "to keep open a road" between ordinary and nonordinary realities.[48] The Sun Dance sacrifice performed by White Man's Dog is a way of keeping such a road open, recognizing publicly White Man's Dog's dependence on larger forces and sacrificing some measure of ego—or flesh—in humility before these forces. After he sacrifices, White Man's Dog has the cleansing dream of Wolverine and Kills-close-to-the-lake. While he dances in honor of Sun Chief, not Wolverine, the boon he receives for his sacrifice comes from the animal. The narrative thus conflates the powers of animals, divinities, and dreams. Animals, even animal helpers, have a frightening otherness that remains in tension with their helpful, familiar qualities. Wolverine has power in part precisely because he is a wild animal. Divinities, likewise, have vast powers that awe and humble humans. And dreams channel power that comes from both these sources, or from some intrapsychic force experienced as Other. The ritual allows White Man's Dog to confront the dangers of all three safely and to release their energies into his experience without being overwhelmed. It enacts the relatedness, dependency, and humility that are imposed on the ego when it encounters the reality of the psyche. The sacrificial recognition of his relationship to greater powers allows White Man's Dog to receive power, keeping the ego in an appropriate relation to divine forces and, in so doing, also channeling the energies of transcendent powers to consciousness. In the dream Wolverine teaches White Man's Dog his power song, which he must know consciously in order to use. However, he never believes that his knowledge of the song constitutes his power. He must use it wisely; through it the power of Wolverine enters him. Trusting Wolverine, he gains confidence.

Both dream and ritual, then, represent extrarational experiences in symbolic form. Today, most people dismiss dream, and both religious and social rituals tend to be perfunctory. Dream and ritual states of mind and energy mostly occupy shadow. If they're not shameful, they are at least undeveloped. For the Pikunis, however, dream and ritual contained power, both personal and social. Animal power, the power of being an animal and the power of being among other animals, came to people through their receptivity to interior realities, as well as through their connections with real animals. Whereas Westerners have fairly rigid boundaries of self and not-self, the Pikunis seem to have had greater conscious access to psyche. The narrative of *Fools Crow* expresses this notion in its movement, without barrier, from what we could call "realistic" to "symbolic" landscapes.

Shadow in Fools Crow

There are two different experiences of shadow in *Fools Crow*. One occurs at the narrative level, the other at the mythic. On the narrative level Welch balances Fools Crow with his boyhood friend, Fast Horse. Early in the novel the Lone Eaters banish Fast Horse for the foolish self-indulgence of boasting loudly of his prowess during the horse raid on the Crows. Fast Horse then joins Owl Child and his band of marauders, who take revenge on individual whites for acts of aggression or simply for their occupation of the Blackfeet land. In 1869 a group like this one murdered a settler named Malcolm Clark. Moreover, the novel's account of the white authorities who demand the surrender or death of Owl Child is also based on real events. As Fast Horse and Owl Child advocate all-out war against the whites, they also become more and more involved with frontier habits—drinking, whoring, adventuring, and rejecting traditional ways. Thus, Fast Horse represents a shadow figure for Fools Crow; the entwining stories of the two contemporaries help Welch explore both the consciousness of Fools Crow and the values of the Pikunis.

Part of the shadow embodied in Fast Horse is individualism, and Fools Crow becomes conscious of its appeal when he rides out in search of Fast Horse:

> He chewed on the cold belly fat that Red Paint had thrown in as a treat and suddenly, unexpectedly, felt excited. He was enjoying himself. He had not been without another person for some time. . . . The thought came into his mind without warning, the sudden understanding of what Fast Horse found so attractive in running with Owl Child. It was this freedom from responsibility, from accountability to the group, that was so alluring. As long as one thought of himself as part of the group, he would be responsible to and for that group. If one cut the ties, he had the freedom to roam, to think only of himself and not worry about the consequences of his actions. So it was for Owl Child and Fast Horse to roam. And so it was for the Pikunis to suffer.[49]

This passage suggests the appeal of our cherished American freedom to pursue our happiness. At first Fast Horse seems free of the constraints of Pikuni caution, but Fools Crow knows that Fast Horse and Owl Child murder recklessly and endanger their people. Throughout the narrative Fast Horse refuses to acknowledge his responsibility for the Crows' mutilation of Yellow Kidney, just as Owl Child denies culpability in his killing of Bear Head. The destruction of Heavy Runner's village at the end of the novel seems to come in direct retaliation against the self-indulgent violence of Owl Child. We come to see his individualism as a terrible hubris, not romantic and free but reckless and cold. At the same time Owl Child and his band scorn the Pikunis for their refusal to fight the invading white settlers. While the narrative (and history) makes clear the violence of the white conquest, the story also exposes the danger caused by those who fail to honor community. It also, however, raises questions about the vulnerability of a culture that excludes the energy of these wild young men.

In both *Fools Crow* and *Things Fall Apart*, shadow at the level of character has very Western qualities: shadow appears in individualistic, impulsive, and self-indulgent behavior. Okonkwo's arrogant and selfish actions carry shadow for Igbo society. His failures of self-restraint and his pride perform parts of Igbo culture at odds with the peaceful rounds of ritual life. Okonkwo angers the god. He projects his shadow on his father, Unoka, which cuts him off from sources of nourishment that would have allowed him to adapt to new conditions. Fast Horse's individualistic militancy and his refusal to acknowledge his own complicity in the mutilation of Yellow Kidney constitute shadow potentials of the Pikuni culture. While Achebe shows his Igbo characters projecting shadow onto the few whites they encounter, this is less so in Welch's narrative.

Myth and Shadow

When Fools Crow rides off into Feather Woman's land, Welch moves beyond the narrative level, evoking shadow at the mythic and cultural level. This story compresses the pain of a century's experience of colonization into a few pages, forcing the reader to confront history that has been stored in shadow. Fools Crow's visit to Feather Woman is a kind of descent into dread and grief. While the victims of violence often blame and hate themselves and each other, the conquerors and their heirs have ignored or romanticized this violent past. Thus, every reader is granted the opportunity to stare into shadow. Welch confronts the Indian reader with at least the possibility that some flaw in the culture itself, represented by Feather Woman's original sin, brought about its ruin. This device allows the Indian reader to encounter shadow rather than self-pity, which cannot lead to change. Out of the painful, shameful experience of shadow, however, can come renewed energy. The non-Indian reader, too, encounters shadow as the bloody past refuses to be forgotten. This new capacity to see Indian persons and practices in context may dispel the reader's romanticized view of Indians and lead to a withdrawal of shadow projections, whether of noble or savage.

Feather Woman recounts her story, telling of how an act of disobedience cast her out of her home in the sky. Feather Woman broke the one rule she was given, and her curiosity set her at odds with the divine powers. Her downfall, however, came not from a desire to be godlike but rather from her homesickness, and the Pikunis who follow her also feel that bond of community at the center of their experience. But once she was banished back to earth, she could no longer return to her husband, Morning Star. Her son, Poia, however, made his way back, and after earning the gratitude of Sun Chief, he brought the Sun Dance ceremony and the elkskin robe back to his mother and her people, before returning to his father in the sky.

From her point of view, Feather Woman is responsible for the people's current misery. That is to say, her story plunges Fools Crow into shadow. The narrative here effectively captures the tone of the encounter with shadow: energy leaves, hope departs, and shame and hopelessness weigh one down. Fools Crow's depression is palpable. But Feather Woman breaks the spell by her proclamation of faith that one day she will return to her husband and son, "and your people will suffer no more."[50] Fools Crow is filled with compassion for her loneliness and shame. He embraces her shadow, which allows him to see the designs Feather Woman has been making on a yellow skin: four visions—of smallpox; massacre; the extinction of the blackhorns; and finally, Pikuni children watching happy white children playing in the white school yard. "He had been brought here," Welch writes, "to the strange woman's lodge in this strange world, to see the fate of his people. And he was powerless to change it, for he knew the yellow skin spoke a truth far greater than his meager powers, than the power of all his people."[51] This vision endows Fools Crow with a consciousness hidden from his people, prophetic and tragic.

Alan Velie argues that *Fools Crow* follows the form of a traditional historical novel, much like Sir Walter Scott's novels of the wild Scottish clans. Velie claims that "the Blackfeet, like the Scots, are a warlike people who love nature, have little use for material possessions, live in the wilds, and are crushed and civilized by the less courageous but more numerous Anglo Saxons.... The appeal of the traditional historical novel is that it makes the reader long nostalgically for a way of life that has been destroyed."[52] I believe Welch chose to end *Fools Crow* with a focus on Blackfeet culture in order to foreground the role of story itself. The tragic vision concludes with Feather Woman's reassurance to Fools Crow: "Much will be lost to them. . . . But they will know the way it was. The stories will be handed down, and they will see that their people were proud and lived in accordance with the Below Ones, the Underwater People—and the Above Ones."[53] Story, particularly for an oral culture, knits time and space, ancestors and the living, humans and the more-than-human world. Story restores order. It draws listeners in to a meaningful sequence that reframes experiences so that they reach a new perspective, individual experience placed in the context of a larger narrative. As Karen Armstrong explains: "A myth . . . is true because it is effective. . . . It forces us to change our minds and our hearts, gives us new hope, and compels us to live more fully."[54] Myth ensures that culture will persist; story, thus, is a shadow for the missionary-school consciousness, a trickster. Story is power.

RITUAL, MYTH, AND DEPTH PSYCHOLOGY

Many people today feel a lack of meaningful communal rituals that can serve as containers for the numinous or frightening energies of Self and shadow. Psychoanalysts speak of the analytic hour as a *temenos*, a safe container, and the analytic session itself has ritualistic qualities, but there is little in public life that satisfies what Paul Shepard calls a "nostalgia in the bone" for connection with the extrahuman world around us and the psyche within us. Shepard argues: "As born anti-historians, our secret desire is to explicate the inexplicable, to recover that which is said to be denied. It is a yearning, a nostalgia in the bone, an intuition of the self as other selves, perhaps other animals, a shadow of something significant that haunts us, a need for exemplary events as they occur in myth rather than History."[55] Shepard's fascination with the primitive, his desire "to explicate the inexplicable, to recover that which is said to be denied," sounds like the urge to recover shadow, to retrieve into consciousness some of the energy and connection lost to an acculturated historical mind. For Shepard, as for Conrad, going in offers the risk that we will lose our carefully constructed identities; face darkness; discover a second nature, instinctual, sensual, and wild. The longing is not for immersion in one or the other way of knowing, but rather for a consciousness that can contain both. In the cultures of *Things Fall Apart* and *Fools Crow*, ritual permits characters access to this "second nature." In *Fools Crow* ritual and story suggest ways to move between—or even to contain—the outer and inner, human and animal, ego and psyche, historical and traditional.

Fiction cannot do what ritual can, but novels like *Fools Crow* approximate this containment of contradictions. In doing so, Welch's work achieves what Joseph Meeker, a leading ecocritic, calls a comic worldview, an ethos of regeneration. Meeker argues that comedy is the literary form for ecologically based literatures. "Tragedy," he says, undertakes to "demonstrate that man is equal or superior to his conflict . . . [while] comedy grows from the biological circumstances of life."[56] Welch resurrects the culture and thereby subverts history. If he succeeds, it's partly because of the land itself, its annual regeneration, the inspiration it offers. Like Raven, Feather Woman is a kind of trickster figure, one of the "holotropes of imagination," in Vizenor's words.[57] She recenters history in a Pikuni worldview. This reestablishes a frontier that Owens calls "always unstable, multidirectional, hybridized, characterized by heteroglossia, and indeterminate."[58] In such a liminal space, change is possible.

I want to suggest here that the recovery of connection with nature may be tied to a rediscovery of the numinous. Together, these two may both spring from and nourish new attempts to restore wildness to the land and to psyche. In the next chapter I explore cultural resources and political strategies for returning humans to a more meaningful relationship with the land. Three such strategies—wilderness protection, reinhabitation, and restoration—serve as the organizing ideas for the three chapters that follow the next. Each considers novels whose action offers hope for new connections with nature, without and within the human.

Toward Recovery

Seeking a Psychology of Renewal

> Cartesian dualism has insisted on separating subject from object, us
> from them. It has, indeed, made voyeurs of Western man, exaggerat-
> ing sight by macro- and micro-instrumentation, the better to learn
> the structures of the world with an "eye" to its exploitation. The deep
> bonds between body and mentality, unconscious and conscious think-
> ing, species and self have been treated without respect, as though irrel-
> evant for analytical purposes.
> —Victor Turner, *From Ritual to Theater*

ALDO LEOPOLD argues in *A Sand County Almanac* that we need a relationship with the land before we will care enough to defend it against
the economic imperatives structuring our culture: "An ethic to supplement
and guide the economic relation to land presupposes the existence of some
mental image of land as a biotic mechanism. *We can be ethical only in relation
to something we can see, feel, understand, love, or otherwise have faith in.*"[1]

The preceding two chapters might suggest that Western culture is hope-
lessly alienated from nature or that I am romanticizing the virtues of traditional knowledge of self and habitat while demonizing the industrial world.
While I hope not to submit to such a simplistic dualism, I do believe that the
dominant ideas driving global capitalism are divorced from intimacy with
the land and that one consequence is that the identity experienced by most
people under capitalism allows them access to only a small portion of their
own "natural" possibilities. Not many people today have an opportunity to
"see, feel, understand, love, or . . . have faith in" the land.

At the same time there are rich seams in Western culture that celebrate the continuity of humans and the rest of nature, found in myths, folktales, and traditions. This chapter explores both ecopsychology and some of these traditional Western stories of connection. It also examines the worldview, values, and ecological practices that have long anchored American Indian cultures to the land. Finally, it investigates contemporary ideas of wilderness and bioregionalism as practices of the land ethic and as paths toward psychological reconnection with nature, without and within.

STORY, MYTH, AND ECOPSYCHOLOGY

One way toward a feeling connection with the land is through myth. Like Freud, Jung looked to myths and symbols to provide metaphors for psychological processes and conditions:

> Myths and fairy-tales of world literature contain definite motifs which crop up everywhere. We meet these same motifs in the fantasies, dreams, deliriums, and delusions of individuals living today. . . . The more vivid they are, the more they will be coloured by particularly strong feeling-tones. . . . They have their origin in the archetype, which in itself is an irrepresentable, unconscious, pre-existent form that seems to be part of the inherited structure of the psyche and can therefore manifest itself spontaneously anywhere, at any time. Because of its instinctual nature, the archetype underlies the feeling-toned complexes and shares their autonomy.[2]

In Jung's theory myths and folktales arise out of the same instinctual forms across cultures—issuing, that is, from our inherited nature, finding symbols in human habitat that yield knowledge of psyche and of human kinship with the rest of life.

The "strong feeling-tones" associated with myths lend them the power to reframe experience because they speak to a liminal part of the mind. Linda Hogan proposes that myth represents an originary way of knowing, with roots in both Western and traditional cultures. She points to the mythical Orpheus as an instance of a human who could communicate with animals, plants, and minerals, and to Psyche, whose misery the ants and reeds alleviated by sharing her labor and passing on their secrets.[3] Paula Gunn Allen says that myth "shows us our own ability to accept and allow the eternal to be part of our selves. [Myth] allows us to image a marriage between our conscious and unconscious, fusing the twin dimensions of mind and society into a coherent, meaningful whole. . . . It makes us aware of other orders of reality and experience and in that awareness makes the universe our home. It is a magic: it is the area of relationship between all those parts of experience that commonly divide us from ourselves, our universe, and our fellows."[4]

Karen Armstrong's *A Short History of Myth* traces the evolution of myths from the Paleolithic, or hunter-gatherer, cultures, through the Neolithic, or agricultural, cultures and the rise of cities, to what she calls the Axial Age. Because mortality is the most difficult experience to comprehend, Armstrong maintains, myths have placed death, catastrophe, dismemberment, and bloodshed at the center of consciousness. In this way they offer a narrative structure that makes it possible for people to face their fear of death and confront shadow elements of their own experience. Seeing that everything in nature dies, and that each entity in nature has its own power, myths link the fertility and the destructiveness of the natural world. Hunting and planting myths make human responsibility for the natural world a matter of sacred duty.

Moreover, Armstrong says, mythic thinking requires ritual participation for its truth-value to be effective. Ritual aligns mythic thinking with the longing for larger meanings and allows participants to construct order. Armstrong is particularly interested in the inner states that myth and ritual address: imagination and ecstasy, as well as dread and anxiety. Myth "is a game that transfigures our fragmented, tragic world, and helps us to glimpse new possibilities," she writes. Myth is true to an inner, not an outer, logic. Armstrong argues that since Bacon the West has lost access to *mythos*, which she sees as complementary to *logos*. Both, she maintains, are necessary: "A myth could not tell a hunter how to kill his prey or how to organize an expedition efficiently, but it helped him to deal with his complicated emotions about the killing of animals."[5] Armstrong follows the story of humans' estrangement from nature in the narrative of the movement away from myth, finding in the absence of mythical thinking and practice a source of contemporary alienation and despair.

Simon Schama, in his 1995 book, *Landscape and Memory*, explores the persistence in Western culture of myths and traditions that link us with nature. Schama provides a richly detailed and entertaining excavation of the gold in dark places, often obscured from view by the neon and glitter of the international commercial enterprise. He organizes his book around three features of the land: forests, rivers, and mountains. While the vastness of oceans and the heady pinnacles of mountains have long invited experiences of transcendence, forests seem particularly apt homes for folktales and myths. After all, the folk lived near or in forests, which provided livelihood and protection from authority but also exposed people to the dangers of wild animals and sometimes wild men. While the clearing represents space humans have domesticated and the deep forest the frightening wild, the edge of the forest stands as a liminal space psychologically as well as ecologically. The myths and folktales that have grown up around forests provide metaphors for states of consciousness that depth psychology has been quick to explore, often providing models for confrontations with shadow.

These stories connect deep fears and longings with nature and provide images that contain complex feelings. Red Riding Hood may be frightened of the wolf, but she certainly lets herself be tricked; Hansel and Gretel seem to need the deep and pathless wood to confront the witch in their stepmother and to rescue their father from her enchantment. Frogs and bears turn into princes, but only if you befriend them. Wild nature resonates with the human unconscious. Nature's justice, as Schama points out, differs from the city's: unconcerned with preserving power and property, natural justice rewards virtue or, in the case of such forest figures as Robin Hood, redresses injustice. The outlaw, robber, or avenger finds refuge in the forest.

Like Schama, Robert Pogue Harrison, in his 1992 *Forests: The Shadow of Civilization*, traces schisms and fault lines in Western thinking, noting that Western culture is not the same as Western Enlightenment modernism. Harrison locates the origins of the Western estrangement from nature in the ancient myths and stories of the Greeks, of Gilgamesh, and of the Romans. Drawing on Vico, Harrison evokes a race of giants who slash a clearing in the forest and, seeing the light of the sun, imagine a god that blesses their civilization. The light (of reason?) that streams through a cleared canopy engenders laws, institutions, and history. Civilization, then, can only exist where the forest has been destroyed; it is the "shadow of civilization." To illustrate his theory, Harrison examines Greek myths and divinities associated with the forest. He documents in myths the terror associated with nature's metamorphoses, which remind humans of mortality, our common lot with animals and plants. Artemis, the Greek goddess of the earth and the forest, is a figure for the inevitable changes of form enacted in processes of death, decay, and reconfiguration. She images the material nature shared by all organisms. The "truth" of Artemis, which Actaeon died for seeing, is "the preformal kinship of all creation."[6] Although Harrison doesn't use the concept of "shadow" in the Jungian sense, its connotations in his work are very similar: the gods represent what humans try to deny about life, and the human heroes act out the ego's desire to avoid facing its mortality. Thus, myths take the problem of shadow as a central reality. In service of the god, Dionysian maenads enter a frenzy of dissolution or descend into the unconscious, as we see in Pentheus's mother, who does not recognize the son whose head she impales. Like the forest, the god is the antagonist of the human constructions that allow people to pretend that they are not-nature.

Death is in the forest, in shadow, vigorously self-denied. Likewise, states of mind that are not focused and rational belong in the forest: intuition, visionary experience, dream, imagination, nostalgia, wisdom, epiphany, as well as bewilderment, confusion, and dread. In an analysis of Rousseau's *Confessions*, Harrison calls the forest of Saint-Germain, where Rousseau had his inspiration, "the preserve of imagination's storehouse of images of remote antiquity. Intuition conspires with the forest's presence to produce in the mind an image of origins." Whether the forest inspires intuition or fosters it, Rousseau, walking there, experiences "the difference between finding oneself inside or outside of the forest."[7] Outside it he could be as practical as the next French Enlightenment intellectual; in it he opened himself to the workings of imagination. (He is freed to do this because his wife and two servants are taking care of the meals and the house.) Like the Edward Abbeys of our time, Rousseau enjoyed a privilege that made possible his wilderness (or at least exurban) intuition, but this does not invalidate the power of wilderness to inspire. If, as Harrison argues, Rousseau simply inverted the nature-culture hierarchy in order to have the pleasure of criticizing his peers (a shadow pleasure), he nonetheless inspired other Western thinkers who have kept alive the aboriginal Western attraction to the forest as a place to experience something other than instrumental reason.

Harrison provides a fascinating history of European cultural ambivalence and practical conquest of the forest, but he doesn't consider the cultures of the people who live there. Does it not make sense that people who live intimately with the forest—or the plains or the desert—should have different assumptions about nature, different approaches to knowing it, and different shadows too? If, as Harrison says, "soul and habitat . . . are correlates of one another," then people whose relationship to habitat is radically different from the Western one will have different experiences of soul—different psychologies and different cultures.[8]

Harrison comments, "*Where divinity has been identified with the sky, or with the eternal geometry of the stars, or with cosmic infinity, or with 'heaven,' the forests become monstrous, for they hide the prospect of god.*" He calls religion, matrimonial monogamy, and burial of the dead the "universal institutions of humanity."[9] But he is wrong: not all cultures bury their dead, and not all are monogamous. Many American Indian cultures placed their dead in trees; some Northwestern Indians committed their dead to the rivers; in the Southwest some people entombed their dead in the walls of their homes. Many traditional cultures observe a close communion between the living and the ancestors. Because of their conviction that humans are of the earth, these cultures have a different relationship with death than does the West. Harrison comments that for Vico, whom he admires, "humanity in its very essence is a historical, that is, extraforestial, phenomenon."[10] But for traditional, cyclical cultures, this is not true either. Western culture has located mortality as the central problem of humans, its emphasis on linear time driving Western culture to establish monuments to distinguish the human from nature, where death is the common lot. Harrison's mood in concluding his study is pessimistic. Perhaps because he confines his study to Western culture, he seems to feel that the city is on an irreversible path to the desertification of the forest. In the Western preference for self-deception, encoded in rhetoric, he locates a failure to acknowledge, restrain, and incorporate the shadow. In this respect he has a postmodern bent, concluding as he does that "because we alone inhabit the *logos*, we alone must learn the lesson of dying time and time again. . . . When we do not speak our death to the world we speak death to the world."[11]

This imprisonment in *logos*, Harrison points out, springs specifically from the contemporary domination of an ethic of utility that shapes a political discourse in which nature must be spoken of in resource terms. He comments, "It remains to be seen whether one day a less compromised, less ironic language will become possible—a language of other rights and other interests, a language, in short, of other worlds."[12] This is a crucial issue for today's ecopoets and novelists, many of whom acknowledge this need for a new language and even take a go at it, often inspired by the traditional values of cultures Harrison overlooks. Such a new language might be the idiom of the mountain, the cry of the wolf, the arc of the dolphin. It might be the language of symbols—not in the postmodern sense, in which discursive language is seen as a symbolic realm from which there is no escape, but rather in the Jungian sense, in which the unconscious may generate a symbol capable of transcending what appears to be an irresolvable dilemma.

An antidote to the narrow rationalism of the modern period, myth supplies symbols for psychic experiences that elude discursive analysis; at the same time it connects people today with the emotional experiences of humans who have inhabited the planet for millennia. Myths offer metaphors that make suffering comprehensible and even noble. For example, the image of dismembering, found in the stories of Osiris, Dionysus, Orpheus, and many others, focuses the experience of loss and figures it as essential to the transformative work of re-membering. Myth suggests a way to live beneath the trivia; it sends rhizomes into other worlds. Myth speaks to the experience of the sacred in nature, the power that humans encounter in relationships with other forms of life. It offers relief from the ego's constant counting. Vegetative cycles of nature provide metaphors for renewals of the human spirit that may seem as miraculous as spring, connecting human well-being with the health of plants and planet. Science provides a way to talk about nature, and psychology a *logos* of mind, but myth offers a language in which to engage the unconscious.[13]

TRADITIONAL CULTURES AND ECOPSYCHOLOGY

Louis Owens remarks that the "displacement of humanity from nature points to perhaps the most profound cause of humankind's destructive relationship with our environment." He goes on to say, "Unlike the Western European, in a traditional world view the Indian is not removed from and superior to nature but rather an essential part of that complex of relationships we call environment."[14] Many non-Indian people in the environmental and conservation movements have argued the necessity of learning from the practices of American Indians how to reorient contemporary culture toward sustainable living based in a land ethic. Indeed, many elements of traditional American Indian cultures can contribute to an understanding of what ecopsychology might mean in daily life.

Traditional cultures hold the land to be sacred. Barre Toelken observes that "in many . . . native religions, religion is viewed as embodying the reciprocal relationships between people and the sacred *processes* going on in the world. It may not involve a 'god.'"[15] Writing about Apache people, David Abram notes that the "ancestral wisdom of the community resides, as it were, in the stories, but the stories—and even the ancestors themselves—reside in the land."[16] Place, he says, is an active participant in human events, and sacred, or even communally significant, events are meaningless without reference to place.

Fundamental beliefs, encoded in creation stories, suggest ways to view the sacred land as a complex of relationships. In Laguna Culture Spider Woman is the "spirit that pervades everything," the creator and matrix who has being in the land and in her many names, according to Paula Gunn Allen.[17] Thus, the traditional culture of the Pueblos holds "a mental image of land" as a set of relationships, a web, not a chain. This image embodies the traditional worldview, grounded in what has in Western thought become the science of ecology. While ecologists speak of food webs, traditional people created rituals to acknowledge their dependence on other species for survival.

For many people of North America, the creation story involved the emergence of people and other animals from the earth, from under ice, or from a flood. Life, including human life, rose from the land and owes its survival to continuing reverence for the land. Traditional religions and languages express the people's reverence for a *particular* place. Religion rooted people, so they had no incentive to impose their religious views on others who inhabited a different place. Joseph Epes Brown remarks: "Across this diversity [of American Indian cultures] . . . we are in fact dealing with what may be called dialects of a common language of the sacred." "Each being of nature," Brown says, "every particular form of the land, is experienced as the locus of qualitatively differentiated spirit-beings, whose individual and collective presence sanctifies and gives meaning to the land in all its details and contours. Thus, it also gives meaning to the life of man who cannot conceive of himself apart from the land."[18] The sacred site for each group helps to define a person's identity—literally, the individual's standing in relation to a ritually defined center of the universe.

The ancient Greeks also connected their worship, healing, and divination with particular places, often associated with a chthonic animal or deity. "Marvelous cures have a tendency to occur in particular places, for sanctity is bound up with locality," writes C. A. Meier. "Thus in antiquity countless healing shrines were firmly bound to one geographical spot, just as they are today. Looked at psychologically, this means nothing less than a geography of the human psyche."[19] According to Vine Deloria Jr.: "The vast majority of Indian tribal religions have a center at a particular place, be it river, mountain, plateau, valley or other natural feature. . . . In part the affirmation of the existence of holy places confirms tribal peoples' rootedness."[20] In *Things Fall Apart* villages must remain where the ancestors' spirits convened, and the oracle is closely associated with a cave. Thus, these cultures give rise to a psyche that is closely linked with the land, which is seen as sacred.

The sense of connection between the people and the land mirrors the connections people feel with one another. Leslie Marmon Silko recounts how the Pueblo people tell stories with everyone, even the smallest child, expected to remember a portion, so that "the remembering and retelling [are] a communal process." A story might have several versions, depending on the storyteller, but the Pueblo people do not demand that one version be correct, since they "[seek] a communal truth, not an absolute."[21] Prominent features of the land make their way into stories, thereby passing on information people need for survival—the need to watch your rear on a particular butte, for example, or the virtues of an uncommon plant.

Vine Deloria Jr. elaborates on this idea of a communal history, arguing that in the recitation of stories at tribal gatherings, different versions of events were respected, since no one was trying to gain power over others. Even in large confederacies, such as those the Iroquois and Creek maintained, while weaker members knew who had power, no one attempted to convert them to an Iroquois or a Creek version of history.[22]

The regularity of ceremony in traditional life connects individuals to tradition and culture and acts as a container for shadow, with its urges to selfishness and individualism. Psychological health is thus connected to the health of the land: "A Navajo goes to the equivalent of a priest to get well because one needs not only medicine, the Navajo would say, but one needs to reestablish his relationship with the rhythms of nature. It is the ritual as well as the medicine which gets one back 'in shape.'" The "singer" reconciles the ailing person with natural cycles by performing what Barre Toelken calls a "sacred reciprocation."[23]

One function of rituals is to promote mindfulness: Toelken reports that Navajo people carry strings of beads in their pockets, made from juniper seeds collected carefully from supplies of seeds stored by small animals and chosen so as not to deprive the animals of food. The beads "represent the partnership between the tree that gives its berries, the animals which gather them, and humans who pick them up. . . . If you keep these beads on you and think about them, your mind, in its balance with nature, will tend to lead a healthy existence."[24] Like a rosary, these seed beads promote consciousness; reaching into the pocket, a person can finger them and return to balance, holding in mind the dependencies and reciprocities that make life possible.

Ceremony also regulates the ecology of an area, according to Roy Rappaport. His research among the Maring people of New Guinea showed him that relationships both with other local groups of Maring speakers and with the non-human species with which they shared their territory are regulated by protracted ritual cycles. Although the rituals which constitute these cycles are undertaken to maintain or transform the relations of the living with super-naturals . . . their operation helps to maintain an undegraded biotic environment, limits fighting to frequencies which do not endanger the survival of the Maring population as a whole, adjusts man-land ratios, facilitates trade and marriage, distributes local surpluses of pig throughout a wide region in the form of pork and assures to members of the local group rations of high quality protein when they are most in need of it.[25]

Ritual, in the traditional world, puts people in relation to the land, to one another, to other tribes, to the spirit world, and to their own inner world.

The openness to states of mind beyond that of the rational ego characterizes traditional ecopsychology. Native people observe transformations in nature and experience these transformations subjectively in varied states of consciousness, none of which is privileged as the only one that is "real." This applies, of course, to dreams, which are often the source of visions and great power. Leslie Marmon Silko remarks that landscape and dream are similar: "Both have the power to seize terrifying feelings and deep instincts and translate them into images—visual, aural, tactile—into the concrete where human beings may more readily confront and channel the terrifying instincts or powerful emotions into rituals and narratives which reassure the individual while reaffirming cherished values of the group. The identity of the individual as a part of the group and the greater Whole is strengthened, and the terror of facing the world alone is extinguished."[26] In this way the individual does not live alone in the world, as Western people so often do, but is surrounded by family, clan, and tribe; by animal powers, plants, and rocks; by ancestors, spirits, and subjective realities, all of which working together are responsible for maintaining the harmony that allows each element to thrive. Subjective, social, and ecological balance is the goal, and story and ritual the means.

In *Changes in the Land*, William Cronon examines the economic and ecological practices of the Indians of the Northeast that kept human populations in balance with the land. He notes how the different legal and psychological assumptions of the English settlers disrupted these balances. English fences, deforestation, and property laws interfered with traditional economies and disrupted ceremonial life. English use of the plow and the practice of agricultural monoculture depleted the soil, driving settlements out from the center. Domestic livestock altered plant communities, brought invasive plants, and resulted in the fencing of the land and the settlers' eradication of the natural predators of their livestock. New Englanders' and Europeans' demands for wood, for burning and for ship- and home-building, began to deforest the area. Inland, fur traders altered the traditional relationship to such animals as beaver and fox and introduced firearms and firewater. Whereas tribal people had mined copper for sacred purposes, taking only small amounts, the capitalists who followed the traders had different ideas. As Gerald Vizenor explains the process, "The woodland tribes in the middle of the nineteenth century were separated from their sacred places on the earth. White people were determined to exploit animals, human beings, minerals, the sacred, in their pursuit of wealth and domination, their manifest destinies perceived in the woodland."[27]

Cronon makes it clear that not only did the ecological assumptions of the two cultures clash, but the English also projected their judgments onto the Indians, justifying their taking of the Indians' land. For example, the English saw the Indian men's pursuit of hunting as a "leisure" activity and criticized them for "abusing" the women, who did all the agricultural work. At the same time the English called the Indians lazy for not "improving" the land and believed they were crazy for enduring hunger rather than accumulating enough surplus to feed themselves over the winter. English Puritan values about work and property determined their (in)ability to perceive Indian culture.

One consequence is the ignorance of most Americans today of Indian values and ecological practices. Because so many were wiped out by disease, and yet more by greed, expansion, racism, battle, starvation, and dislocation, and because an ideology of the "vanishing Indian" served the needs of government and settlers alike, the wisdom of traditional ecological practices is all but lost from public consciousness. It has been replaced by an image of the noble savage who can perform magic through rituals: a "quick fix" to substitute for the lifeways that preserved relations between humans and the land before conquest. For the conquered people this loss amounts to what the psychologists Eduardo Duran and Bonnie Duran call a "soul wound," a tear in the fabric of relations that tied humans with animals, plants, and minerals, disturbing the "centered awareness that . . . allowed for a harmonious attitude toward the world . . . the acceptance and being part of the mystery of existence."[28]

ECOPSYCHOLOGY, WILDERNESS PROTECTION,
AND BIOREGIONALISM

Individuals and organizations within the conservation community have proposed a variety of strategies for implementing a land ethic, including wilderness protection, green cities, bioregional or watershed-wide protected zones, green belts to allow for migration of species and continued evolution, moratoria on development, and many others. Three of these—wilderness protection; bioregionalism, or reinhabitation; and natural areas restoration—inform my examination of ecopsychology. Together, these strategies combine to constellate a land ethic and a way to think about the psychological dimensions of political change.

Wilderness Protection
The most influential division in U.S. thought about wilderness protection owes its historical origin to the rivalry between Gifford Pinchot and John Muir in the early part of the twentieth century. Pinchot, who founded the U.S. Forest Service, advocated the judicious use of wilderness for human purposes. This utilitarian, or resource-centered, approach continues to characterize the U.S. Forest Service. Critical of this anthropocentric ethic, the intellectual descendents of Muir propose an ecocentric, or "deep ecology," approach. In this view wilderness has intrinsic value. Wildness alone permits evolution to proceed without hindrance because it offers habitat in which species can survive and change. Arguing for wilderness protection, George Sessions cites Arne Naess's concept of the "ecological self," "which expands with increasing maturity through an identification with other people, to an identification with other species and nature, to the cosmos itself."[29] In the United States the Wilderness Act and the Endangered Species Act offer some protection for wild areas; these are essential legal constructs, constantly under assault from resource extractors and a critical locus of political struggle, as conservation organizations compete with the barons of resource extraction to define terms and frame public discourse.

Deep ecologists also frequently maintain that people need to have a personal experience of wild nature. According to Bill Devall, the first theme of deep ecology is "a new cosmic/ecological metaphysics which stresses the identity (I/thou) of humans with nonhuman nature." This entails a new psychology that "requires rejection of subject/object, man/nature dualisms."[30] The philosopher Joanna Macy speaks of the development of an "ecological self," attributing this in part to the threats of global annihilation that we live with: "As their grief and fear for the world is allowed to be expressed without apology or argument . . . people break through their avoidance mechanisms . . . into a larger sense of identity."[31] This dynamic is strikingly similar to the process of absorbing shadow, which can lead a person to a sense of self that transcends the ego. Charlene Spretnak argues that hope can be found in the stewardship programs of Jewish and Christian congregations. Theodore Roszak, who coined the term *ecopsychology*, emphasizes the continuum of mind and cosmos: "Mind, far from being a belated and aberrant development in a universe of dead matter, *connects* with that universe as the latest emergent stage on its unfolding frontier."[32]

Roszak is particularly strong in arguing that guilt does not motivate people to a green perspective nearly as effectively as the joy inherent in discovering connection with the rest of nature. Activism that focuses primarily on the damage humans do to the land can lead people to feel guilt simply for being human. Such feelings of shame are implicated in shadow, and they need to be addressed and contained. For environmentalists they can lead to destructive and self-destructive behavior.

Bioregionalism and Reinhabitation

William Cronon argues that environmentalists in the United States "mistake ourselves when we suppose that wilderness can be the solution to our culture's problematic relationships with the nonhuman world." Cronon suggests "an environmental ethic that will tell us as much about *using* nature as about *not* using it."[33] This sentiment, echoed by many people in the green movements of the developing world, is often at the heart of drives for reinhabitation and restoration.

Reinhabitation takes off from the drive to find or make a home; to become part of a place; to live locally, familiar with the flora and fauna, landforms, food, climate, vernacular, and rhythms of a place. Peter Berg defines a bioregion not in geopolitical terms but rather according to natural characteristics such as watersheds or natural barriers like mountain ranges or desert. Other bioregional features include climate, landforms, soils, native plants and animals, and local human cultures. Berg, defining *bioregion* as "a geographic terrain and a terrain of consciousness," cites the following as goals of bioregionalism: "to restore and maintain local natural systems; practice sustainable ways to satisfy basic human needs such as food, water, energy, housing, and materials; and support the work of reinhabitation," which might include education and employment, as well as political action to preserve the land.[34] Thomas Berry argues that bioregions are the natural context for reinhabitation and that the form of bioregions is community. A bioregion, he says, is a "self-propagating, self-nourishing, self-educating, self-governing, self-healing, and self-fulfilling community."[35]

Bioregionalism engages people in community both with other people and with the land. "The primary values, from a bioregional perspective," writes Ralph Metzner, "are not 'property rights' and 'development,' but the preservation of the integrity of the regional ecosystem, the viability of the biotic community, and maximizing economic self-sufficiency within the region. Political control should rest with the community of people actually living in the region: This is the concept of 'reinhabitation.'"[36] Bioregionalism, that is, engages humans as part of a larger biotic and abiotic system—or, using Aldo Leopold's language, "the land."

"Reinhabitation," according to Stephanie Mills, "means learning the whole history of one's bioregion or watershed, and developing a vision of sustainable ecological community from that knowledge, and from what we have been learning, in the last half-century, about elegant techniques of construction, gardening, recycling, energy conservation and waste treatment; ways of sophisticating old-style household and neighborhood frugality."[37] Although it is most often consciously practiced in rural areas, reinhabitation is not exclusively exurban. In cities and suburbs reinhabitation also entails investigating history, natural processes, the local flora and fauna, energy circuits, and climate, then adapting one's style of living as much as possible to the contours of the local: engaging in community gardening in abandoned lots; working with local school and church councils to restore schoolyards and parish areas to native diversity; landscaping homes with native plants and avoiding fertilizers, herbicides, and pesticides; convincing corporate employers to restore their corporate lands with native flora; using local construction materials; buying at farmers' markets; carpooling; and joining with neighbors for homemade entertainment.[38]

Restoration

The complement to reinhabitation in bioregional thinking is natural areas restoration. The goal of restoration is to return land to a condition of biodiversity. The practice of restoration arose from the observation that little wild land is left to preserve but that we may be able to return biodiversity to degraded remnants. While not everyone can or wishes to leave cities, many urban and suburban areas contain such remnants that have not succumbed to development. In many cases land has been conserved through local and state ordinance, as park or preserve. Cemeteries and railroad rights-of-way often boast significant varieties of native flora and fauna. However, such land has, in most cases, not been maintained, and as a result it has degraded through alterations of neighboring hydrology, agricultural and industrial processes, fire suppression, and the invasion of nonnative species. Practicing restoration most typically involves groups of volunteers under the direction of volunteer or professional stewards who donate labor to control invasive species; repair damaged areas such as stream banks; remove human structures and trash; collect and sow seeds of native species; and return natural processes, such as fire or fish runs, to the land. Local residents, including schoolchildren, may also train as citizen-scientists who participate in monitoring projects: one person may quarterly inventory the benthic macroinvertebrates in a stream to determine water quality, while another keeps track of butterflies in a section of prairie. In the process, restoration advocates maintain, human participants may also repair the alienation they feel from nature, restoring themselves to a sense of community; to a perspective on the human role in natural systems that has been corrected for hubris; and to a fuller, more integrated psychological life.

For American Indian nations restoration has a cultural urgency. Winona LaDuke writes about her fellow Anishinaabeg, many living below the poverty level, who continue to hunt deer and harvest maple syrup, berries, medicinal plants, fish, and material for baskets. However, much of their land has been lost, so many must collect their harvest on traditional land off-reservation. For them restoration means rebuilding a land-based community, recovering land through negotiation and acquisition, and political activism to return land seized by the federal government. All this is necessary to restore their economic capacity to live sustainably on traditional land.[39] On the Plains fifty-two tribes in eighteen states are raising buffalo, trying to build herds into viable economic enterprises and renewing bonds with traditions. Vine Deloria Jr. connects these efforts with those of Indians in the Pacific Northwest to preserve salmon or hunt whales: "What you're seeing are growing attempts of all kinds by Native Americans to return to a more traditional relationship with nature, a restoration, really, of their cultures. The elders have wanted to do this for a long time. Finally, tribes are in a position where they can devote resources to this effort."[40]

The remainder of this book looks at recent fictions that explore the intersection of wilderness, reinhabitation, and restoration with ecopsychology. In some cases the narrative action is mythic, in others realistic. In all cases, however, those characters who reconnect with the land also move in the direction of individuation; in most cases this individuation occurs primarily in community. My experience teaching most of these novels suggests that having images to associate with what, in life, are complex and lengthy processes helps readers imagine the potential for their own reconnection with nature and psyche.

Wilderness and Vision

Shadow and the Quest for Identity

We are small in this large, cold land. It feels like something else is here,
the way it does in solitude when a person faces their own life in the
night and turns in, toward their own dark wilderness.
—Linda Hogan, *Dwellings*

No matter how high the tech, *homo sapiens sapiens* remains at heart
what he's been for tens of thousands of years—the same emotions, the
same preoccupations.
—Margaret Atwood, from the notes to *Oryx and Crake*

J OURNEYING TO THE WILDERNESS in search of revelation is a feature of
many cultures, where wilderness ushers a person to whatever lies outside
culture or beyond understanding. Therefore, wilderness has been a location
both literal and metaphorical for rites of passage and retreats. In this chapter
I look at *Surfacing*, by Margaret Atwood, and *Housekeeping*, by Marilynne
Robinson. In both these novels the young protagonists' experiences in wilderness are central to their coming of age. Each finds that being in wild nature
fosters a reconnection with the undomesticated part of herself that has been
excised from consciousness and now occupies shadow. The Jungian concepts
of the symbol and the transcendent function help to illuminate the strategies
Atwood and Robinson use in resolving conflicts between the identity constructed for the protagonists by a sexist society and their experiences of the
wildness within themselves.

Historically, wilderness has held danger. It is land inhospitable to human
habitation—desert, mountain, deep forest, jungle, or swamp. In the Bible

"wilderness" is often a site for "moral confusion and despair."[1] Pilgrim settlers came to a new world they imagined as a hostile wilderness, hoping to found a New Jerusalem free from corruption. In wilderness one is exposed to thirst, disorientation, and threat from wild animals. A person risks comfort and safety there in order to seek visions, to converse with God, and to find him- or herself. While many writers on the history of the Americas point out that "wilderness" is a construct unknown to the people indigenous to the hemisphere, the Indians of North America had sacred places in unsettled areas, as well as sites of danger. These functioned as "wilderness" for the people. They were places where one could test endurance, live without shelter, and encounter the Other. Traditionally, then, wilderness has harbored both danger and power. It has offered humans the possibility of surprise, a humbling encounter with a world we did not create, a chance at a conversation with spirits and with the Self. Charlene Spretnak calls these "moments of awakening" that connect people both to nature and to themselves.[2]

The wilderness experience, generally, is not a wilderness life. To encounter the unconscious and then to stay there is to walk a trail to madness. But without wilderness, as without some access to extrarational psyche, both ego and culture become rigid, mechanical, and dry. The challenge is to find ways to connect humans with nature's autonomous life in order to promote a commitment to preserve, protect, and restore natural areas, habitat, and biological diversity. In psychological terms this means the development of what the Jungian writer Edward Edinger calls an ego-Self axis: a capacity to contain in the ego a connection with the unconscious; to cling to the apprehension that ego is not all there is, while avoiding the twin dangers of inflation and madness. The wilderness experience provides an image for this psychological capacity: when I stand at the base of a waterfall in the wilderness, I am moved by its power and size, and I feel how small I am and how vast the planet is. But I am also comforted to know that the waterfall will still be there when I return to my office, that it plunges and roars without human direction or control. The waterfall is an image of nature's self-regulating processes, including the processes of the unconscious. In a world full of stresses and demands, it's as good to know the waterfall is there as it is to know that I don't have to keep telling my kidneys to function or that my brain will produce startling dreams without my willing them. In the same way a powerful dream humbles me with its wit, vividness, and emotional charge, and I am glad that even when I'm balancing my checkbook or washing floors, psyche churns on beyond my conscious control. When I read that rivers have been reduced to dribbles by dams and the diversion of water upstream to keep golf courses green, I feel a personal loss, as well as a political challenge.

Surfacing and *Housekeeping* focus on young women constructing an ego. They are alone, lacking parents and community, and they find the options offered by the culture around them oppressive, mostly because of sexism. They struggle to find a voice, a place, and a way to live wholeheartedly. In both novels the wilderness signifies a site outside the social identity constructed for these young women by their elders and their culture. Wilderness provides energy and images that help them to resist or at least escape temporarily the constraints of society, while also assuming its traditional role as a place of danger, where one might starve, freeze, or even go mad. Both protagonists encounter shadow in the wilderness, the Other in themselves and in their personal histories, and these encounters endanger their fragile egos. These are not escape stories or romantic celebrations of wilderness: if the wild land is a "landscape of authenticity," it is not a place where the protagonists can escape from history.[3] These novels share an anxiety about whether their young protagonists will be able to find a community that will embrace and nurture the selves they discover in the wilderness.

SURFACE AND SHADOW

Margaret Atwood's *Surfacing*, published in 1972, follows the journey home and descent into a kind of feral madness of a nameless narrator so isolated from others that she never hears her own name spoken. It posits the Canadian wilderness as an alternative to a repressive and often brutal civilization in which the narrator seems paralyzed by claustrophobic social norms. However, the novel asserts not that she is escaping but rather that she is being drawn into the wilderness, which is ultimately both safer and saner than the predatory social world. When at the end she considers whether to reenter society, her encounter with wild nature has, at least, given her a voice.

We see the narrator's city life only through flashbacks and memories. As the novel opens, the narrator and her three friends are traveling north to the remote cabin from which her father has gone missing. The journey serves as a transition, making the city seem less real than the series of bizarre and anomalous sights they encounter, including a house made out of bottles and a gas station featuring a family of stuffed moose dressed in sex-stereotyped clothing. The trip itself seems like a passage through a dream.

The farther the narrator travels from the city, the more her conventional ways of understanding the world become problematic. First, nationality and language begin to crack: the action takes place in Francophone Canada, where the narrator's English is foreign. Her difficulty speaking extends to her traveling companions, her lover and another couple: conversations are aborted, superficial, overheard, dissimulated. She cannot even trust the language in her mind. Her challenge in finding a voice is amplified by the sexism she encounters everywhere. The women wait on the men, cook, clean, and serve. In spite of her superior wilderness skills, the narrator still jumps to bring the men a beer.

Nothing is what it seems. Even the land, which appears pristine and wild, disguises the predatory activities especially associated with Americans. On the way to the cabin, the narrator notices a "pit the Americans hollowed out. From here it looks like an innocent hill, spruce-covered, but the thick power lines running into the forest gave it away. I heard they'd left, maybe that was a ruse, they could easily still be living in there, the generals in concrete bunkers. . . . There's no way of checking because we aren't allowed in." Surveyors from the power company are planning a project that will raise the level of the lake and flood much of the land. They are cutting trees. Someone—one of the surveyors?—has killed a heron and strung it up from a tree, the image of lynched nature. Why? "To prove they could do it, they had the power to kill." Most of all, the Americans are identified as sport fishermen, greedy, brutal, and casual: "Raygun fishing rods, faces impermeable as spacesuit helmets, sniper eyes, they did it; guilt glittered on them like tinfoil."[4]

Retrieving Shadow in the Wilderness

The Americans carry shadow for the narrator, their pride and power lust the photographic negative of her own self-abasement and victimization. The Americans are strongly linked with the dead heron, not simply killed but displayed, a useless trophy. When she discovers that the "Americans" are really Canadian, the narrator retrieves a piece of her own shadow, recalling a childhood game in which she and her brother played at being animals: "our parents were the humans, the enemies who might shoot us or catch us, we would hide from them. But sometimes the animals had power too: one time we were a swarm of bees, we gnawed the fingers, feet and nose off our least favorite doll."[5] Even as a child she felt comfortable as the victim, but in this memory she has an insight about the ease with which victims can turn into victimizers. The power and viciousness she enacted as a child caused her shame, so her desire for power was cast into shadow, along with her capacity to destroy. The story she has been living is all about self-effacement.

Piecing together her memories is central to the narrator's journey. Her father's cabin houses scrapbooks that help her recall scattered bits of her early life, and her encounters with the natural world seem to help her reclaim even more of the memories she's distorted: "I have to be sure they're my own and not the memories of other people telling me what I felt, how I acted." To survive in her family and in her culture, she has resigned key experiences to shadow, losing their memory and being left instead with an ego composed of acceptable versions of history and other people's stories. Atwood provides an image of this psychic experience when the narrator reads the family book of photos: "I must have been all right then; but after that I'd allowed myself to be cut in two. Woman sawn apart in a wooden crate, wearing a bathing suit, smiling, a trick done with mirrors ... with me there had been an accident and I came apart. The other half, the one locked away, was the only one that could live."[6] She recognizes that she's excised vital parts of herself—"the only one that could live"—but because they are unconscious, she can't confront them. The scrapbook photographs and her father's pictographs become Rorschachs, receptacles for her projections. As she tracks down the originals of the pictographs, she becomes able to absorb some of the truth that she's repressed.

On her first trip to find these rock paintings, she encounters the dead heron and begins to withdraw her projection from the "Americans": "I felt a sickening complicity, sticky as glue, blood on my hands, as though I had been there and watched without saying No or doing anything to stop it: one of the silent guarded faces in the crowd."[7] This experience of shadow disturbs her deeply, precipitating her memories of her brother's animal laboratory, her sugarcoated pictures, the leeches they killed, the barbarisms of childhood. The shadow she confronts moves her further along a path to self-loathing, along which she must pass before she can move toward self-acceptance.

On her second excursion to locate the original rock paintings, the narrator has a fully developed encounter with shadow. Rising waters have submerged the images, so she has to dive to see them. This passage has a ritual quality. Three times she dives unsuccessfully, but on her fourth dive she encounters her shadow as a shape "drifting towards me from the furthest level where there was no life, a dark oval trailing limbs. It was blurred but it had eyes, they were open, it was something I knew about, a dead thing, it was dead." This may, of course, be her father's drowned body, but the narrator interprets it as an image of the fetus she aborted. At this point she is caught in a flood of memory: she has never married, never borne a child. The abortion is the shadow truth of the stories of marriage and a child that she's constructed for herself to protect her from her complicity in the abortion: "Whatever it is, part of myself or a separate creature, I killed it. It wasn't a child but it could have been one, I didn't allow it." In this case the abortion offers an image for the experience of denial, of casting part of oneself into shadow. She has become "a faked album, the memories fraudulent as passports; but a paper house was better than none and I could almost live in it." Because the memory was erased, the grief could not come out; it feels like "a cyst, a tumor, black pearl."[8] She is filled with self-loathing, prompting her to seek to shed her human form.

Wilderness and Transformation

To reach this point, the narrator has had to dive deep into the lake, the image rising from its depths. Increasingly, her insights come directly from experiences in the wilderness, which grants her escape from the faked images of human culture, including her own conscious mind. Nature offers her a retreat from the unacceptable alternatives presented by her culture, where she can either conform to gender roles or suffer isolation, but nature also leads her to confront a more personal conundrum. In constructing for herself an ego that is innocent, she has cast into shadow all her guilt, aggression, and desire for power; as a consequence she believes that one is either innocent and good or guilty and evil. This experience of a set of extreme alternatives is what Jung called an *enantiodromia*: an intolerable situation characterized by an exclusive dichotomy. In *Memories, Dreams, Reflections* Jung writes: "Insofar as analytical treatment makes the 'shadow' conscious, it causes a cleavage and a tension of opposites which in their turn seek compensation in unity. . . . The conflict between the opposites can strain our psyche to the breaking point."[9] For the narrator to believe herself "good," she must deny responsibility for her choice to have an abortion. She has projected her own destructive impulses onto Americans so she can retain an innocent self-image. In confronting shadow, then, she experiences deep shame and self-loathing. For her the question is whether she's worthy of living if she has aggressive or selfish drives.

The Transcendent Function

Jung believed that you can't *reason* your way out of such a dilemma, but if you suffer it, if you can contain both possibilities in consciousness (and not split one off), something beyond the ego may offer a third alternative, in the form of a symbol. Jung called this capacity of the psyche to resolve the insoluble the "transcendent function": "If all goes well, the solution, seemingly of its own accord, appears out of nature. Then and only then is it convincing. It is felt as 'grace.'"[10] A symbol generated by psyche, in dream, imagination, or trance, is "a living, organic entity"; it "points to something essentially unknown, a mystery."[11] Its purpose is to *transform libido from one level to another, pointing the way toward future development.*"[12] For the transformation to occur, symbols must be attended to, integrated in some way, often in art. This is what Jung meant by living a symbolic life.

Usually, however, before this can happen, the individual must enter a liminal state where there is real danger of psychological collapse. In deconstructing the old matrix of meaning, the narrator of *Surfacing* renders herself vulnerable, because her ego is so frail that she may not be able to contain what she discovers about herself. The wilderness provokes this liminal state where the constructions of her earlier life break down. Before she can receive a symbol that may enable her to reconstruct her identity, she has to experience a frightening immersion in nature. Andrew Samuels calls this "a transformation downward: Down into the lake, down into the animal world, down (if you will) into the unconscious. This journey downward involves the narrator in nothing less than a transcendence of her human body."[13] As the narrator comes closer and closer to wild nature and to psychologically liminal space, she becomes more and more paranoid. She has some reason to distrust her companions, but as her apprehensions become general, she becomes more feral. She sheds language like a flimsy garment. Although she has long known the names and uses of the plants, she now wants to apprehend them directly, "the names of things fading but their forms and uses remaining, the animals learned what to eat without nouns. Six leaves, three leaves, the root of this is crisp."[14] Jung considered sensation and intuition nonrational functions, and these capacities of the psyche emerge in the narrator's search for something authentic. The process accelerates when she finds what she believes is a gift from her mother, as the pictogram that led her to the encounter in the lake was a gift from her father. In a scrapbook she finds a picture she made as a child, when her imagination was less corrupted, of a pregnant woman whose baby could be seen looking out and a man with horns and a tail. She identifies herself as the baby and the man as God. To even the advantage, she had given God horns and a tail, just like the devil's. Thus, the male figure unites opposites and provokes a high level of response in the narrator, who determines that she must absorb her human form into the natural world. As she leads Joe outside to impregnate her, she thinks, "My tentacled feet and free hand scent out the way, shoes are a barrier between touch and the earth." She vows that when the baby is born she will "lick it off and bite the cord. . . . I will never teach it any words."[15]

The more she moves toward an animal existence, the more she speaks a language of dream: "Through the trees the sun glances; the swamp around me smolders, energy of decay turning to growth, green fire. I remember the heron; by now it will be insects, frogs, fish, other herons. My body also changes, the creature in me, plant-animal, sends out filaments in me; I ferry it secure between death and life, I multiply."[16] She is becoming wild, but she is also moving the center of consciousness from ego to Self; identifying with the transformative power of nature; shedding old skins of language, subservience, and old constructed identities. The transcendent function, activated by the image she drew as a child, facilitates this transformation of libido.

After the others leave the island, the narrator can no longer live in the house. Moving out of doors, she returns to the matrix, or the symbolic mother, where sensation and intuition keep boundaries fluid. Believing herself pregnant, like the woman in her childhood drawing, she is both mother and god-father, container of good and evil, creative and destructive power. Parts of her own being that were cast off in childhood return, even as she becomes more and more part of a regenerated place: "The forest leaps upward, enormous, the way it was before they cut it, columns of sunlight frozen; the boulders float, melt, everything is made of water, even the rocks. In one of the languages there are no nouns, only verbs held for a longer moment. . . . I lean against a tree, I am a tree leaning. . . . I am not an animal or a tree, I am the thing in which the trees and animals move and grow, I am a place." If hers is a kind of vision quest, it would seem that what the narrator seeks is something real that transcends, or precedes, language, knowing, and judgment: the land, God, the Other, the Self. These are the presences that she intuits but that language and ego cannot contain nor define. In her hallucination she expands her imaginative power. Seeing a fish jumping in the lake, she perceives "a fish . . . an idea of a fish . . . carved wooden fish . . . antlered fish thing drawn in red on cliffstone . . . flesh turned to icon. . . . How many shapes can he take."[17] The fish becomes an authentic symbol, offered by nature and her unconscious working in consort; it unites possibilities of life, art, philosophy, and religion. As a symbol it allows her to understand her life as part of the natural continuum of life, death, and transformation.

Return

The narrator's recovery is swift if incomplete. She has summoned her dead parents; they came, and they left. Her experience, this regression in search of renewal, has allowed her to acknowledge her shadow; in doing so, it may have given her a way out of her dilemma: "I have to recant, give up the old belief that I am powerless and because of it nothing I can do will ever hurt anyone."[18] This in turn positions her to reconstruct an ego that can survive in the city, with her lover, Joe, using words. She appears poised to enter a genuine adulthood in a reality neither demonic nor benevolent. Atwood thus reasserts the issue of language as the medium of relationships, acknowledging its potential for misunderstanding and the risks of its use. She seems to imply, however, that the narrator's new symbolic consciousness may equip her to face even a painful failure. The text encourages the reader to believe she will reenter the social world despite her misgivings. Joe, after all, "isn't an American. . . . I can trust him." Atwood leaves her narrator undecided, and in the end "the lake is quiet, the trees surround me, asking and giving nothing."[19]

Atwood, however, undermines this resolution in her 1972 critical work *Survival*, in which she makes fun of the "magic baby" that appears at the end of Canadian narratives, the sign of a hopeful future imported into the story, which indicates "evading rather than confronting failure and responsibility."[20] This suggests that perhaps it is not the narrator but the reader who must carry out the work of integration. The end of the novel challenges readers to imagine a future and, in doing so, to turn themselves into people capable of hope. In this Atwood's novel resembles *Housekeeping*, which also ejects its tender protagonist into the unknown.

In *Surfacing* the encounter with nature/the unconscious generates not so much new knowledge as a capacity to know in new ways. Before her descent the domination of reason in the narrator's consciousness represents the internalized presence of her father and hence of the patriarchal world. In her new condition she is aware of the power of nature and instinct and of her own complicity in life; she now has a symbol that joins together life and art. Her language has begun to approximate that of a poet, and her way of knowing has expanded to include intuition, sensation, and the apprehension of elements of herself that transcend ego. Perhaps the narrator's pregnancy may then be seen not as a magic baby but rather as the potential for the symbolic capacity. The return of ego-consciousness allows the narrator to incorporate slowly the emotional experiences of her union with the land/mother/unconscious and to withdraw her projections, recognizing in herself what she had looked for in a partner. This is a beginning, but not a fully realized new identity. The narrator entertains inflated fantasies about the fetus she may or may not be carrying; she is only at the beginning of a difficult new path. Now she knows that there's more to herself than the faux-innocent delusional ego she has rejected. She has encountered shadow and something like the Self. But she is young, and this is a novel about the generation of an ego that can handle daily life.

Shadow, Guilt, and Transformation

Critics disagree about the extent to which the narrator of *Surfacing* undergoes a transformation or achieves self-knowledge. Those who emphasize her immersion in wilderness, especially those who read through a feminist lens, seem to concur with the notion that she makes significant changes. The issue of voice is often central to their readings, the narrator's struggle with language standing in for the problem of her identity in the social order. Hilde Staels highlights the power of language (the patriarchal realm) to undermine any changes in ethics or identity.[21] David Ward focuses on the paradoxical quality of language: it is both the social order—the context and material for the construction of a persona that supports the maintenance of the patriarchy—and the means of affirmation of a subversive or more idiosyncratic ego. He argues that Atwood "maps a transition in which release from language becomes a condition for the discovery of self."[22] This claim could also easily work as a statement about the apprehension of Self: the persona and ego exist in a world of boundaries, but the Self does not. When the narrator moves outside her house, she falls into metaphor because discursive language is inadequate to the experience of Self, which is not silent but filled with words loaded with emotion.

Those who read from a postcolonial perspective focus instead on the narrator's failure to recognize that the comfort of white Canadians rests on the dispossession of First Nations people. For them the ethical weight of the novel relies on the reader's awareness of what has been erased. Janice Fiamengo quotes a 1972 interview in which Atwood said of the narrator of *Surfacing* that "she wishes to be not human, because being human inevitably involves being guilty." From this Fiamengo develops an argument that the narrator's guilt has its roots in her inability to acknowledge the appropriation of Native lands—the basis of the Canadian nation, as well as the locus of the narrator's transforming wilderness experience. Fiamengo argues that "recognizing Canada's heritage of violence is painful but necessary if English Canadians are to escape from their recurrent, paralyzing fantasy" of innocence. She points out that Americans (and "Americans") "function as the self-justifying other" that enables the narrator to sustain her innocent persona; when she discovers that the canoeists are Canadian, "she sees herself now as completely contaminated and guilty."[23] As the narrator becomes able to admit shadow into consciousness, she finds her "inner American," but she is caught in a national double bind, both victim of an alien power and beneficiary of the victimization of First Nations people. Particularly because there are some resemblances between the narrator's immersion in wilderness and the vision quest ritual, Fiamengo and others concentrate on her guilt over the appropriation of aboriginal land. Yet to me the narrator's excessive guilt and self-loathing seem more consonant with the experience of personal shadow, while it's left to the reader to confront the political realities of erasure.

However, it seems possible to extend this notion of guilt to embrace Atwood's contention that the narrator "wishes to be not human." Wilderness in Canadian literature is often used as a sign of Canadian identity, the "white myth" of an empty land that is both dangerous and free but also "indecipherable" to European explorers and settlers.[24] When wilderness signifies whatever is outside of culture, it provokes questioning of what it means to be human, a human animal. In the passages in which the narrator descends into the unconscious, she feels herself variously "amphibian," mammalian (using a blanket "until the fur grows"), and "a place." It is specifically her *human* condition that she seeks to escape: ego, rationality, and persona—the "sickening complicity, sticky as glue," that she feels in the death of the heron.[25] She now feels guilty for living, just as earlier she refused any responsibility. The guilt of being human has to do with the taking of life in order to live, extending to knowledge of the cost to the planet of each human being, particularly in developed countries. At the most obvious level, it has to do with the destruction humans cause with our "American" ways; at the most subtle level, it has to do with the knowledge that even subsistence living requires taking life.[26]

First Nations people living traditionally had rituals that mediated their impact on their habitat. Hunting required ritual, as did planting, harvesting, war, and daily social life. Whatever other power these rituals held, they kept people mindful of their responsibility, their destructive power, and their dependency on other species. The narrator of *Surfacing* explicitly associates Christ's death with the deaths of animals: "The animals die that we may live, they are substitute people, hunters in the fall killing the deer, that is Christ also. And we eat them, out of cans or otherwise; we are eaters of death, dead Christ-flesh resurrecting inside us, granting us life. Canned Spam, canned Jesus, even the plants must be Christ. But we refuse to worship; the body worships ... but ... the head is greedy, it consumes but does not give thanks."[27] The narrator understands that she lives on the deaths of others, but she cannot find in Christianity an appropriate sacramental response. Guilt and shame accompany the experience of shadow: the knowledge of one's rage, lust, self-serving meanness, and so on, induces powerful emotional responses.

To live with shadow, however, does not mean to spend every day consumed by guilt but rather to allow mindfulness of one's capacity for hurtfulness. Ritual is a means to this mindfulness. The narrator of *Surfacing* seems drawn to ritual. She thinks, "If I do everything in the right order, if I think of nothing else." At this point in the narrative, she is overwhelmed by the psychic energies she has engaged, and she seeks to placate or mitigate their power. As she surfaces from her temporary psychosis, she vows "to refuse to be a victim"—to own her shadow—but she also resolves to live in relationship, which is to say, to be mindful of her effect on others.[28]

Whether the narrator will also develop means for living less destructively on the planet, more mindfully in relation to history, Atwood leaves us to imagine. This is not an activist narrative, but what Andrew Samuels identifies as its trickster quality provokes a reader to political thoughts and, possibly, action.[29] The novel itself seems unresolved regarding the appropriate response to the knowledge of guilt. The ethical impact of the narrative depends on the reader's careful willingness to consider that present comfort rests on prior dispossession or other violence, for which the narrator's abortion can be read as a sign. This is not knowledge that can be "overcome," although it can be held in consciousness and potentially transformed into action. There is no cure for being human, or for being white, but there are more or less ethical ways to live with the condition.[30]

HOUSEKEEPING: *SHADOW, MEMORY, AND THE TRANSCENDENT FUNCTION*

While *Surfacing* holds out the possibility of a return to city life, in *Housekeeping* the action takes the female characters through the wilderness to a life as transients, in which they relinquish the hold of a civilization that comes to seem treacherous and restrictive. As normal processes of domestic life break down, the consciousness excluded from such persona-driven living emerges from the shadows. The out of doors appears safer and more nurturing, a place where Ruthie, the young central character, can begin to absorb shadow. Written a decade after *Surfacing*, this is also a narrative of youth, but Robinson appears less optimistic than Atwood about the possibility of constructing an authentic life within society. Although Ruthie achieves access to nonrational parts of psyche, there are losses attendant on forsaking civilization, of which loneliness is the most prominent.

A lake is also at the center of *Housekeeping*, the most important presence in the town of Fingerbone, traversed by a railroad bridge. The action begins with the death of Ruthie's grandfather years before. His train derailed and fell into the lake, which swallowed it and all traces of its passengers. Characteristically of this novel, the facts about the event are uncertain: the train "slid . . . into the water like a weasel sliding off a rock," leaving no witnesses. Since it plunged into the depths of the seemingly bottomless lake, no reliable evidence of its location was ever retrieved. All this gives the event a mythical quality and the lake an ominous personality: the lake had "sealed itself over" by nightfall, preventing recovery.[31]

In Fingerbone "one is always aware of" the "deeps of the lake, the lightless, airless waters below." The lake has many levels, including an ancient body of water, "smothered and nameless and altogether black," which lies beneath the present, mapped and charted lake. Above these levels are the groundwaters that rise in spring and flood the town; above these is "the water suspended in sunlight, sharp as the breath of an animal, which brims inside this circle of mountains."[32] This association of water vapor with breath, or spirit, encourages the reader to reflect that the human psyche, like the lake, has various levels of consciousness, from the very deepest unconscious to the ethereal light of spirit. These depths cannot be counted on to stay put either; they rise, and changes in consciousness are the normal order of things.

Like her grandfather, Ruthie's mother also died in the lake. Just as the train sank to the depths and could never be found, Ruthie's mother Helen's suicidal dive into the lake has dropped from polite public awareness. People will not talk to Ruthie and her sister, Lucille, about their mother, since the shame attendant on suicide makes the subject taboo. In consequence, loss and memory obsess Ruthie, and the lake becomes her image of the unconscious, guarding access to the pain she must work through, mostly alone. After her grandmother's death Ruthie dreams she's walking on the frozen lake, but the surface reveals itself to be made up of hands and arms and faces. She associates death with "the depths, . . . the undifferentiated past," and with "some other element upon which our lives floated."[33] Like a *memento mori* the lake holds the lost past and also tempts Ruthie with thoughts of a magical resurrection. But at this point in the story she has no access to it. It is frozen.

The death of the grandfather, the "silent Methodist Edmund," has liberated the women of his family from the male gaze, providing the necessary conditions for Ruthie's eventual choice to sidestep patriarchal culture altogether. *Housekeeping* has no significant living male characters and only brief mention of Edmund, who was a naturalist and a collector, a type with many antecedents both literary and living. He dug up wildflowers from the woods and brought them home to plant in his garden, but they always died. When spring called to him, he picked up souvenirs such as a bird's wing or a jawbone: "He would peer at them as if he could read them, and pocket them as if he could own them. This is death in my hand, this is ruin in my breast pocket." As a character Edmond establishes an equation of domestication and death; thus, his death frees his family of women from such constraint, "from the troublesome possibility of success, recognition, advancement. They had no reason to look forward, nothing to regret."[34] In the absence of an effective father, nothing draws these women into the world. His death, however, only appears to free them from the forward arrow of Western time into nature's cycles: the outside impinges, imposing its ambitions, its futurity, on children and grandchildren, as the promises of school and conviviality catch Lucille and the threat of the law finally propels Ruthie and her aunt Sylvie loose. Indeed, other than the grandfather, the only other significant male figure in the novel is the sheriff who comes to bring the judgment of the town—that Sylvie is not a fit mother and that Ruthie should be taken from her. Robinson does not complicate this identification of maleness and culture, but she does also represent the women of the town as arbiters of an oppressive, pinching, 1950s-style domesticity.

While she does not equate femaleness and nature, Robinson does link an unpossessive appreciation of wild nature with certain of the women. When she writes from the viewpoint of characters whom she associates with nature, Robinson often suggests a dimension just beyond the visible, not Platonic exactly, but a world that exists beyond language, on its own terms, independent of its value to humans. For example, she writes of the grandmother: "She felt the hair lifted from her neck by a swift, watery wind, and she saw the trees fill with wind and heard their trunks creak like masts. She . . . walked back to the house thinking, What have I seen, what have I seen. The earth and the sky and the garden, not as they always are . . . and she was quiet and aloof and watchful, not to startle the strangeness away."[35] She associates wind with spirit, which lifts the veil from her eyes, and she also sees wind mixed with water, in a preview of the novel's blurring of other boundaries. At the same time, however, Robinson refuses to romanticize nature, which, like the house, has dirty corners and boring repetitions. Moreover, nature includes decay and death, as well as beauty and mystery.

Housekeeping and Boundaries

The question of how to cope with mortality is at the heart of this novel, and housekeeping seems to be one response. Housekeeping as an activity is a ritual effort to forestall entropy, which is to say, to contain nature. The word *ecology* comes from the Greed *oikos*, or "house"; ecology, then, is the study of our home, while house*keeping* is the effort not to know but to domesticate nature. But time and nature conspire to undo what order domestic labor can achieve. Unlike work in the commercial world, housekeeping makes no progress. Clean clothes become dirty again, cooked food gets eaten, washed floors attract tracks, and the labor resumes. The human recipients of the labor, husbands and children, move through the household, swept on by growth and accident. Ruthie's grandmother, herself identified with the world behind the world, grieves at her children's defections to the outside and performs housekeeping tasks for her granddaughters as if they could right a world askew: "she whited shoes and braided hair and turned back bedclothes as if re-enacting the commonplace would make it merely commonplace again."[36] But her rituals cannot retrieve the past. In small and daily ways, the rituals of homemaking do foster intimacy and provide shelter. But housekeeping is powerless in relation to nature and mortality. The great cultural rituals celebrate and re-create order by reenacting the time of creation, but no ritual renewal halts change. Domestic rituals represent psychological attempts to recapture a family intimacy that is constantly under siege from both culture and nature: children grow and leave home; spouses stray; trains derail; precious objects get lost in a flood. The outside world and time interfere.

But *Housekeeping* offers an alternative image of keeping house. After their grandmother dies, Ruthie and Lucille's aunt Sylvie comes to care for them. Sylvie may not be the loving mother the girls long for, but she's better than foster care. Sylvie deals with change by herself becoming a drifter. She responds to nature and change not by attempting to deny or control them, but by opening the home to the outside, embracing cobwebs and windblown leaves. She brings night inside by turning off the lights. In this way she combines the comforts of a settled life with the wildness of transience. Under Sylvie the house becomes more and more immersed in the woods, and the boundaries between woods, lake, and house become less fixed: "Sylvie in a house was more or less like a mermaid in a ship's cabin. She preferred it sunk in the very element it was meant to exclude. We had crickets in the pantry, squirrels in the eaves, sparrows in the attic."[37]

Change becomes not the enemy but the way of life. Land and water merge: "The lawn was knee high, an oily, dank green, and the wind sent ripples across it.... And it seemed that if the house were not to founder, it must soon begin to float." Just as the house adapts to water, the lake, in its sheltered coves, appears domestic: "the surface [of the water] seemed almost viscous, membranous, and here things massed and accumulated, as they do in cobwebs or in the eaves and unswept corners of a house. It was a place of distinctly domestic disorder."[38] Allowing boundaries to blur in this way seems to permit Sylvie to merge with the processes of nature, with the woods for which she's named. The blurring acts as a kind of lifting of the veil, so that nature's continuities become more sensible than social distinctions. It also becomes the means for Ruthie to expand her senses so that she can explore and transgress other boundaries.

Darkness and Liminality

Like the narrator of *Surfacing*, Sylvie is a kind of female trickster. Under her tutelage and model, Ruthie slowly begins to see past the categories of the town. The town has one way of knowing and judging, which has to do with propriety and conformity to social norms, enforced by a set of "demure but absolute arbiters who continually sat in judgment of our lives." We learn of the town's judgments mostly through Lucille's eyes, as she squirms under the "gaze of the world" and urges Ruthie that they must "*improve* [themselves]" to win its approval.[39] Lucille regularly interrupts the communion Sylvie and Ruthie find with darkness, the lake, and the woods, by singing, turning on lights, or remarking bitterly on the shabbiness of the household. When she keeps a diary, it consists of lists and instruction. She exists in the novel to provide the contrast that sharpens our understanding of Ruthie's choices and heightens our awareness of how really odd Sylvie is; if they were characters in a dream, Lucille would be the light of persona and Sylvie the dark unconscious. Ruthie is our ego, our eyes. Through her we learn some new ways to apprehend the world.

One of these new ways of knowing involves an acquaintance with the night, with darkness and absence and pain.[40] The flood that follows Sylvie's arrival disorients the town and prompts Ruthie to wonder about the world's stability. In a very dark night, she reflects: "When we did not move or speak, there was no proof that we were there at all. The wind and the water brought sounds intact from any imaginable distance. Deprived of all perspective and horizon, I found myself reduced to an intuition, and my sister and my aunt to something less than that."[41] Here is the language of a mystic. Here is also the language of ego confronted with its smallness. Darkness changes Ruthie's way of assimilating the world, bringing intuition to bear where vision is lacking. Often associated with women, intuition offers an alternative to the instrumental reason that insists on demonstrability and usefulness.

Throughout *Housekeeping* darkness makes Ruthie conscious of loneliness and serves as a transition to liminal experience. Meditating on the condition of tramps and outsiders in train stations, Ruthie thinks: "When one looks from inside at a lighted window, or looks from above at the lake, one sees the image of oneself in a lighted room, the image of oneself among trees and sky—the deception is obvious, but flattering all the same. When one looks from the darkness into the light, however, one sees all the difference between here and there, this and that. Perhaps all unsheltered people are angry in their hearts, and would like to break the roof, spine, and ribs, and smash the windows and flood the floor and spindle the curtains and bloat the couch."[42] In the first scenario, looking from inside out, one sees as those at the centers of power see, blinded by their own image. In the second, looking from outside in, one sees as those at the margins see, hyperconscious of their powerlessness and dispossession, filled with anger. The problem exists because of the opposition of darkness and light; the habitual cultural preference for light stands in for the privileged half of many other dualistic contrasts, as between center and margin, reason and instinct, culture and nature. With the two posed in opposition—inside looking out or outside looking in—the result is self-deception or rage.

Robinson offers two images, however, that simply unlatch the opposition. The first is Sylvie's preference for eating dinner in the dark. As the family eats, they look from the unlighted kitchen out a window "luminous and cool as aquarium glass and warped as water"; they listen to the night sounds of crickets and nighthawks, which seem unusually loud, "perhaps because they were within the bounds that light would fix around us, or perhaps because one sense is a shield for the others and we had lost our sight." Ruthie's theory proposes that light, like ego, can obscure as well as illuminate, can prevent knowledge as well as promote it. Poised in darkness, Ruthie's receptiveness is contrasted with the posture of her light-named sister, Lucille, who looks longingly into the lighted town from the margins that shame and terrify her. Later, after spending the night out in the forest with Lucille, Ruthie remarks, "I simply let the darkness in the sky become coextensive with the darkness in my skull and bowels and bones."[43] This surrender to darkness—or openness to liminality—appears to offer an alternative to the contradictions involved in looking in or looking out. Darkness allows senses other than the visual to bring in information and in that way stills the probing ego to receive.

Imagination augments receptiveness as Ruthie moves toward new ways of knowing. As she comes to know darkness, her imagination grows. One day she and Lucille observe Sylvie walking way out on the railroad bridge, and Ruthie begins to fantasize frightful possibilities. If Sylvie were to be blown off, or a train were to overtake her, no one would believe it wasn't a suicide, like their mother's, and the girls would once again be abandoned, baffled, alone, ashamed, grieving. Ruthie entertains her imagination, does not shy away from the pictured horror: "And then imagine that same Sylvie trudging up from the lake bottom, foundered coat and drowned sleeves and marbled lips and marble fingers and eyes flooded with the deep water that gleamed down beneath the reach of light. She might very well have said, 'I've always wondered what that would be like.'" Confronting her fears in imagination, Ruthie begins to develop the capacity to face, name, and explore them, keeping them available to consciousness. Lucille, by contrast, characteristically moves to interrupt alternative possibilities: she turns lights on, speaks loudly, cleans vigorously, and consigns her fears to shadow. As Lucille becomes more and more estranged from Sylvie and Ruthie, she begins to see through the eyes of her "familiar" from school and finds herself "galled and wounded by her imagined disapprobation."[44]

Imagination is also Ruthie's ally in relation to loss and confusion. Finding a brochure for the missionary venture that claimed her aunt Molly, Ruthie fantasizes about the phrase, "I will make you fishers of men," picturing how "such a net, such a harvesting, would put an end to all anomaly." She imagines a resurrection and redemption of all those souls lost in the lake: "There would be a general reclaiming of fallen buttons and misplaced spectacles, of neighbors and kin, till time and error and accident were undone, and the world became comprehensible and whole." The redemption here is a "rescue" from fragmentation, loss, alienation; moreover, it is possible only outside the boundaries of town, of reason, of law—in and inspired by the natural world. Ruthie continues to play with fantasies of resurrection, all expressed as subjunctive, playful, and longing, existing in psychological reality: "Say that this resurrection was general enough to include my grandmother, and Helen, my mother. Say that Helen lifted our hair from our napes with her cold hands and gave us strawberries from her purse."[45] The "say that" construction locates the expressions in the semiotic realm of wish fulfillment, but like her fear fantasies, these imaginings allow Ruthie to keep her grief and pain alive to herself, so that they don't have to be buried in shadow.[46] Lucille, she remarks, "went to the woods . . . to escape observation. I myself felt the gaze of the world as a distorting mirror that squashed her plump and stretched me narrow. . . . But I went to the woods for the woods' own sake." Echoing the language of *Walden*, Ruthie can learn from nature's rhythms to turn her back on the world's scorn and live with her losses. The imaginary realm she develops offers her images of a redemptive wholeness. Like darkness, the woods seem to give her "proximity with our finer senses." Since she "made no impact on the world," she is "privileged to watch it unawares." Her inner darkness is filled with loss, with the ghosts of mother and grandmother, and it is her only truth: "everything that falls upon the eye is apparition, a sheet dropped over the world's true workings."[47] More and more the natural world to which she turns mirrors her own inwardness, the imaginary coexisting with shadow and offering her glimpses of safety.

Wilderness and Shadow

At the book's crisis Sylvie engineers for Ruthie a rite of passage that requires her to encounter shadow so that she can move past its hold on her. Sylvie takes her out at dawn in a stolen boat to visit an abandoned house in the mountains; they return to town the following morning in a boxcar. The journey is a pilgrimage to the heart of Ruthie's darkest fears and losses.

Sylvie abandons Ruthie for the day to face the ghost children who live alone in the woods.[48] This act appears heartless, but it works. Edward Whitmont, a Jungian analyst, comments: "There is . . . no access to the unconscious and to our own reality *but* through the shadow. . . . It is not until we have truly been shocked into seeing ourselves as we really are, instead of as we wish or hopefully assume we are, that we can take the first step toward individual reality."[49] In these ghost children Robinson captures the liminal quality of shadow, as it flickers just outside the range of consciousness. Ruthie muses: "I knew why Sylvie felt there were children in the woods. I felt so, too, though

I did not think so. . . . I knew that if I turned however quickly to look behind me the consciousness behind me would not still be there, and would only come closer when I turned away again. . . . It was persistent and teasing and ungentle, the way half-wild, lonely children are." The ghost children are the image of Ruthie's own abandonment and loss, the personal shadow of one who has been "turned out of house." Ruthie feels her mother's death as an abandonment and a cause of shame. Since no one will talk of it, there is no way for Ruthie to grieve through it, so the death is always there, along with the loneliness. She speaks of "the embarrassments of loneliness," which she calls "an absolute discovery."[50]

This entire passage has the quality of dream or of the liminal state in which a dream may recede. Ruthie pulls out planks from the cellar hole, imagining herself the rescuer of the children; she imagines herself in their place. Finally, she concludes: "It is better to have nothing, for at last even our bones will fall. . . . Let them come unhouse me of this flesh, and pry this house apart. It was no shelter now, it only kept me here alone." This meditation slides to thoughts of her lost mother, who "was a music I no longer heard, that rang in my mind, itself and nothing else, lost to all sense, but not perished, not perished."[51] Radical loneliness, abandonment, and mortality occupy Ruthie's shadow. Unlike Lucille, she cannot deny and pretend in order to live in town. But neither can she sink into the oblivion of psychosis: she knows that the children are not real, and she does not pretend that she can live in the wilderness, in the past, or in shadow. At the heart of her experience is a dilemma: How can she function in the world feeling all this? But how can she deny what she now comprehends? In other words, what do you do once you've seen your shadow?

Shadow and Self

Ruthie and Sylvie must cross the lake again in the night to return to Fingerbone, and on the water Ruthie engages a meditation that suggests a brush with the vast unknown Self, which has been evoked throughout the narrative in relation to the lake. In Jung's thought ego, shadow, indeed all of psyche is contained in the Self, which is the archetype of wholeness, the force moving a person toward individuation. The lake is linked with the unconscious earlier, but what was then frozen has now become fluid. In the boat Ruthie thinks, "It was the order of the world, after all, that water should pry through the seams of husks, which, pursed and tight as they might be, are only made for breaching." As she imagines being engulfed, she comes close to identifying with the Self; she "toyed with the thought" that the boat might capsize and that she, "the nub, the sleeping germ," might swell to bursting. Using again the "say that" construction, she imagines, "my skull would bulge preposterously and my back would hunch against the sky and my vastness would press my cheek hard." This is followed by a birthing, "a final one, which would free us from watery darkness."[52]

To live in this consciousness would be almost unbearable, and the passage reveals the danger of engaging with the unconscious. In her identification with water, Ruthie finds the darkest thought of all: "like reflections on water our thoughts will suffer no changing shock, no permanent displacement. ... They persist, outside the brisk and ruinous energies of the world." Anyone who has tried to stop thinking about a loss will understand the grief in this statement: the ego, despite its best efforts, cannot control psyche. For all our marathons and email and zippers, we are part of the lake, part of the woods, part of nature. The lake is full of people (literally and metaphorically): "below is always the accumulated past, which vanishes but does not vanish, which perishes and remains."[53]

Ruthie's emotions are frightening because she has never been allowed to express them in a way that will reassure her that she will not simply sink into endless grief. She needs a container for her grief, and in this climactic scene Sylvie is able to offer her a center of safety where she can allow the feelings to flow through her without being consumed by them. Without some containment grieving cannot occur because the power of the emotions would be overwhelming; as Ruthie images it, she would burst. But with Sylvie at the oars, she can embrace another image that provides a way to move past the dilemma of despair or denial. As she watches Sylvie row against the wind, Ruthie finds an image of "the mystery": "Watching Sylvie seemed very much like dreaming, because the motion was always the same, and was necessary, and arduous, and without issue, and repeated, not as one motion in a series, but as the same motion repeated because here was the mystery, if one could find it. We only seemed to be tethered to the old wreck on the lake floor. It was the wind that made us hover there. It was possible to pass out of the sight of my grandfather's empty eye, though the effort was dreadful."[54] Robinson's prose is full of images like this, rich and suggestive and dreamy. Here, the image seems to pull Ruthie from the whirlpool of despair; she *can* move beyond her past, beyond hopelessness, but only through the same motion repeated without the expectation of progress. The image contains its opposite—both movement and stasis—and that gives it power. When the shadow begins to be absorbed into consciousness, it does not disappear, but it loses some of its compulsive quality. This insight forms the beginning of Ruthie's capacity to live a symbolic life, guided and enriched by the language of the psyche, as revealed in dreams and imagination. Thus, ego tempers its isolation by its relation to a larger psyche that is the source of energy and comfort.

Transience

With this new consciousness Ruthie can accept the town's attempt to take her from Sylvie's care as a symbolic behavior. Fingerbone is not defending itself against the fear that harm might come to a child because of a negligent caretaker. It is protecting itself against the knowledge of mortality embodied in transients, who "wandered through Fingerbone like ghosts, terrifying as ghosts are because they were not very different from us." Sylvie represents the shadow of the town's belief that waste disappears when we throw it "away." When the ladies of the town come to visit and inspect, they find solid waste stacked to the ceiling. The dust, cans, newspapers, and cobwebs that they work so hard to get rid of, Sylvie keeps, "because she considered accumulation to be the essence of housekeeping."[55] As a shadow Sylvie herself must be controlled. So, threatened by the sheriff, Sylvie pulls a trickster move and burns down the house. Together she and Ruthie cross the bridge out of Fingerbone. They do not intend to live in the wilderness, and they do not *choose* to leave Fingerbone, but they cannot keep the family intact and stay in town.

In *Housekeeping* both nature and culture are complicated; as Karen Kaivola points out, "Ruth's decision to follow Sylvie seems both good and bad. The town's attempt to come between Ruth and Sylvie seems infuriating yet understandable. To read *Housekeeping* is to wrestle with such oppositions and experience contradictory responses."[56] The reader's challenge is to refuse splitting, to contain the complexity of both nature and culture. Thus, we have something that looks like an *enantiodromia*: The socially regulated, safe life of Fingerbone is intolerable, but the wilderness, the lake, loss, the flux and entropy of nature are unbearable. Ruthie can't live within the constructions of community, and she can't live up on the mountain: the cabin testifies to the fate of those who try. The town will not tolerate their presence in Sylvie's permeable house. So transience is a kind of third way, a condition of betweenness. And the bridge is the image that emerges as the symbol of this synthesis. As such, it evokes the transcendent function.

The bridge is the way out of Fingerbone. It leads not to the wilderness but to a life of transience, a life made possible by the train itself. Readers' responses to *Housekeeping* tend to depend on what they make of transience.[57]

The life of a drifter is certainly not comfortable, but Ruthie and Sylvie scrape by. Ruthie takes an occasional job, but finally "the imposture becomes burdensome," and she jettisons her imitation of a working person, free from its constricting expectations. She feels "so unlike other people."[58] Missing from the women's lives is any experience of romance or eroticism. Indeed, they are so marginal that Robinson spends only a few pages imagining their new life. It hardly seems the point. It's almost as though transience were an image for what Keats called negative capability, "that is, when a man is capable of being in uncertainties, Mysteries, doubts without any irritable reaching after fact and reason."[59] Only by living with the unknown can the new emerge, and Robinson can do little more at this point in history than leave her reader in this liminal place, although she does also leave the reader with some new capacity to respond to liminality.

Throughout *Housekeeping*, increasingly toward the end of the novel, a quality of imagination—a capacity to suspend disbelief, to entertain impossible or apparently exclusive possibilities—allows the bridging of the ordinary and the extraordinary. Meghan O'Rourke quotes Robinson as saying: "As a child, I couldn't see any bridge between where I was in my mind and the world around me. . . . If I couldn't write, I don't know what would happen, because that is the bridge, you know."[60] In *Housekeeping* the literal bridge is dangerous, the site of the original disaster, but also necessary, even thrilling. Without it the town would be isolated. In this the bridge is like writing, imagination, the liminal, the subjunctive voice that carries Ruth from the surface to the depths. But Robinson also weaves a visionary quality throughout the narrative. Watching Sylvie brush her hair, Ruthie sees her mother in her aunt, a kind of resurrection: "[Sylvie] would brush her hair all to one side, and put down the brush and look at herself. Then she would brush it straight back, and roll it and pin it at the nape, and look at herself." She remembers that the night before they came to Fingerbone, the night before she killed herself, her mother Helen had brushed her hair just this way. She asks: "Was this coincidence just another proof of the conspiracy of the senses with the world? Appearance paints itself on bright and sliding surfaces, for example, memory and dream." Absence and presence converge: Helen lives again in Sylvie—sort of. Her aunt and her mother resemble one another genetically, but the likeness is not perfect, the resurrection incomplete. The present shimmers and recedes, a palimpsest; the past is never sure. Full-bodied life cannot be counted on; it's rarely more than "bones, bones . . . in a fine sheath of flesh like Sunday gloves." What gives comfort also reminds one of loss, and vice versa: Ruthie's memory of what she has lost brings her beloved mother back into consciousness. Always behind the visible is the invisible, and only in the dark do they come together: "For need can blossom into all the compensations it requires. To crave and to have are as like as a thing and its shadow."[61] The passage sweeps the mundane and the transcendent into a meditation on time, memory, loss, and desire. The movement of attention neither polarizes nor denies. Thus, by confronting readers with complex images, Robinson stimulates the development of a symbolic capacity. Loss and redemption coexist, at least in the state of consciousness made possible by Ruthie's wilderness sojourn, which gives her and Sylvie the courage to cross the bridge and live as hoboes, rich in imagination, conscious of mortality, adrift on the land. If the image of the stolen boat seems a gesture in Wordsworth's direction, the preference for transience in this novel harkens more to the world of Samuel Beckett's tramps, who haunt the interstices of urban life.

In the end *Housekeeping* can also be read as a trickster narrative in the sense developed by Gerald Vizenor. "Trickster narratives," he says, "are suspensive, an ironic survivance; trickster metaphors are contradictions not representations of culture. The peripatetic trickster is a deverbative narrative in translation, a noun derived from a verb."[62] A transient is peripatetic, and "Ruthie" and "Sylvie" names derived respectively from the experiences of grief and forest. The novel itself makes shadow more real than culture, darkness more revealing than light. As a female-centered narrative, *Housekeeping* also represents a very female shadow. Its shadow issues are not violence and rage; rather, Sylvie's failure to keep house, her transgressions of property boundaries, and her nonchalance about the girls' whereabouts represent the shadow of female domesticity and the indifference that is a dark side of the mother. Sylvie is no harbor for the orphaned girls, and nature is not the romantic ideal of beauty and peace. Once Ruthie learns this, she understands that "if you do not resist the cold, but simply relax and accept it, you no longer feel the cold as discomfort."[63] The trickster suggests that if culture is a lie, so is the fantasy of a redeeming mother. Like *Surfacing*, *Housekeeping* entrusts the future to its readers, whose capacity for survivance it has expanded.

CONCLUSION

Wilderness is not a place to live. It needs protection so that animals other than humans will have habitat and safe migratory routes and so that biological diversity can continue on the planet. But humans also need to protect wilderness so that we can find, there, a site for confronting and transforming ourselves.

These two novels are stories of the first part of life. Neither one goes beyond the recognition that social forces construct psyche and impose burdensome limits on individuals to suggest how a person might find a way to live in the social world. That is, both leave the rupture of nature and culture unbridged. Both suggest the necessity of wilderness, but neither takes its characters past the wilderness encounter to live more wholesomely with nature or psyche.

In the next chapter I explore novels in which the central characters return to a place and a culture, offering richer images of a renewed relationship between humans and the natural world. In these works the land to which the characters return constitutes a home, the characters reinhabiting a place—and a culture—that offers an alternative to alienated life in mainstream America. This return prompts, or rewards, a painful transformative process in the protagonists that represents the beginnings of individuation. These are narratives of hope that present an antidote to the gloom that constitutes much of the environmental message.

Reinhabitation

Land, Myth, and Memory

Words used properly and in context . . . return us to ourselves and to
our place in the world. They unify the inner and outer.
—Linda Hogan, "Who Puts Together"

S URFACING AND *HOUSEKEEPING* reveal characters who find in wilderness a way out of the constraints of cultural expectations. Wilderness
offers them an encounter with something authentic and Other, a site where
they can strengthen the ego in order to begin to allow shadow material to
come to light. In addition, these characters gain access to nonrational ways
of knowing. Thus, wilderness has a vital function in psychological life, most
crucially in times of transition. Protecting the wilderness is essential to healing the disconnect that has resulted from the estrangement of humans from
the natural world. But the wilderness is not a place to live.

Here I look at N. Scott Momaday's *The Ancient Child*, Leslie Marmon
Silko's *Ceremony*, and Barbara Kingsolver's *Animal Dreams*, all novels of reinhabitation, representing characters who transform their lives through contact
with the land. Although wilderness is part of this process, location in a home
place provides the necessary conditions for psychological change. Further, because these novels immerse their characters in the matrix of land and community, the question of mothers occupies a central place. I use Jungian and
post-Jungian ideas about the mother archetype, in both its nurturing and its
destructive aspects, to discuss damage to land and psyche, as well as potentials
for healing.

Other ways of knowing also feature in these novels. Specifically, psychological "homing" requires that characters struggle with shadow material associ-

ated with their families of origin. Because maternal energies have been absent, these characters' emotional lives have been relegated to shadow. Confronting shadow thus releases them to engage what Jung called the feeling function, a way of knowing that complements the thinking function. "Knowing" also appears as a culturally constructed activity, as the protagonists struggle with competing narratives about how to make sense of themselves, the world, and life.

Moreover, "home" is problematic in all three novels, since the land has been compromised by centuries of abuse, the culture perforated by suppression and distortion. Yet "home" is a crucial construct, the locus where people must struggle to develop and practice a land ethic that allows them to live sustainably, honorably, and sanely. In this respect homing is an earth story, and together these novels constitute a new geography of home.

Reinhabitation, as we have seen, is an environmental strategy. While the novels here do not grow directly out of that movement, they do express its spirit. William Bevis argues that for American Indian writers "homing in" is "a primary mode of knowledge and a primary good."[1] This "homing in" may be a discovery of both a culture and a place that have been lost, as in *The Ancient Child*, or it may be a recovery of a place and community of origin, as in *Ceremony*.

Return and reconciliation in these two American Indian novels can take a mythic form because the protagonists are returning not only to place but also to culture. The intimacy of the people with the land lives on in myths that celebrate origins and spirit presences, as well as in cautionary tales that warn of the consequences of estrangement. Reanimating the myths is a way of resisting the stories of a consumer culture that projects shadow onto traditional ways. In *Animal Dreams* myth is less important. The hometown to which the protagonist returns has its own origin story, but there is not the same kind of cultural cohesion that is available in the other two novels. Perhaps in consequence, *Animal Dreams* is the most overtly political of the three.

THE ANCIENT CHILD

N. Scott Momaday's *The Ancient Child* traces the return to place and culture of Set, an accomplished artist who has only dim memories of his Kiowa father and stories about his mother, who died giving birth to him. His progress toward recovery of a traditional identity and life represents a kind of reinscription of the "vanished" Indian onto the land. From a totally assimilated life in San Francisco, where his Kiowa identity barely figures, he returns to the cultures and land of his parents through the action of an anima figure named Grey, herself a mixed Kiowa/Navajo medicine woman who is closely linked with the land. This process allows him to absorb maternal energies that open him to receptivity and align him with the land itself. The "homing" of Set appears as a culturally specific version of the process Jung called individuation, in which an anima figure acts as a guide to the unconscious.

Myth gives shape and meaning to *The Ancient Child*. The Kiowa story of Tsoai asserts the close relationship between the people and the land. In this story a boy becomes a bear. His seven sisters run from him. They encounter the stump of a great tree, which invites them to climb up to escape their pursuer. As they do so, the stump rises into the air, and the sisters become the stars of the Big Dipper. The brother, who has come to kill them, scores the bark of the great stump with his claws. This story has long preoccupied Momaday, who earlier retold it in both *The Way to Rainy Mountain* and *House Made of Dawn*. It celebrates a sacred place, a site of power, and in so doing creates a relationship to a force that exists beyond human reckoning. This creation story culminates in the appearance on the land of the monolith called Tsoai in Kiowa and Devil's Tower in English. In *House Made of Dawn*, Reverend John Tosomah says of Devil's Tower that it is "as if in the birth of time the core of the earth had broken through its crust and the motion of the world was begun. It stands in motion, like certain timeless trees that aspire too much into the sky, and imposes an illusion on the land. There are things in nature which engender an awful quiet in the heart of man; Devils Tower is one of them. Man must account for it. *He must never fail to explain such a thing to himself, or else he is estranged forever from the universe.* Two centuries ago, because they could not do otherwise, the Kiowas made a legend at the base of the rock."[2] In Tosomah's explanation the land initiated the exchange, and humans told a story about it as a way of keeping themselves in right relation to the universe. In *The Man Made of Words*, Momaday says, "When one . . . tells a story, he is dealing with forces that are supernatural and irresistible."[3] Story is an obligation; it links the land with the deepest personal mysteries of identity and transformation. In *The Ancient Child* Set must come to terms with his bear nature, an inner power that could transform or consume him. The call to story is thus a response to some profound force within, as well as to the awe inspired by a sacred place.

Critics agree that *The Ancient Child* enacts a process of individuation: exploring identity—shedding an old identity and growing a new, specifically

Indian one.[4] The novel's use of myth ensures that this process will be symbolic and sacred. Beyond this it's tempting to see *The Ancient Child* as Momaday's amplification of his own journey to integrate elements of his identity. Like Grey, Momaday has a Kiowa father and a Navajo mother, and Grey borrows the title of her chapbook of poems about Billy the Kid from a younger Scott Momaday. Grey's connection to the land and tradition, her struggles as a writer, and her fascination with cowboys as well as Indians represent one aspect of her author. Set's success in the art world, his international achievement, represents another. It is almost as if one part of Momaday were telling the story of another, more mysterious, less conscious part. Craig Frischkorn calls the Kiowa bear myth, used repeatedly by Momaday, "a personal myth of the imagination, one which is part of a continual search for personal identity."[5] However, one cannot read *The Ancient Child* as autobiography without diminishing the mythical power of bear energy; equally, one cannot read it as myth without losing the richness of reference to Momaday's engagement with the land and with the sacred.

Wild and Harnessed Energies: The Bear and the Horse

Reconnecting with bear energy is at the heart of Set's individuation. The quality of this energy is indicated in the cast of characters, where Momaday identifies the bear with "wilderness." While there is widespread agreement that in traditional Native cultures the concept "wilderness" did not exist,[6] Momaday nonetheless finds this a useful and indeed powerful term, using it as the complement to "civilization" throughout *The Man Made of Words*. For example, in "Revisiting Sacred Ground" Momaday is on his way to the Medicine Wheel, a sacred place, when he says that "something wonderful happened: we crossed the line between civilization and wilderness. Suddenly the earth persisted in its original being." In the same passage he calls the place a "sphere of wildness," "an equation of man's relation to the cosmos." As he leaves, he sees a coyote, "a wild being." As I read Momaday, such uses of *wild* suggest a state in which someone exists according to the laws of his or her own ("original") being, outside the spheres of commerce or utility. Seen this way, people too can be "wild." Likewise, "wildness" suggests an interior, spiritual or psychological, energy that is not domesticated; it has overtones of danger. Momaday specifically links wildness, wilderness, and sacredness in a number of places; for example, of the Wichita Mountains he says, "It is a consecrated place, and even now there is something of the wilderness about it."[7]

I belabor this issue of defining *wilderness* because it is central to understanding the bear in *The Ancient Child* and because Momaday seems to use the term in ways similar to, but not identical with, conservationists' use of *wilderness* to designate land set aside, protected from human interference. Momaday appreciates places that are free from the desecrations of commercial culture, but he does not imply that "wilderness" is separate from humans. Since humans are part of the land, related to all beings, there is no such division in his view. His representation of sacred places echoes that of Vine Deloria Jr., who calls them "places of power and significance" that "[require] respect and human self-discipline." Such places are often at the center of a particular tribe's spatial universe, "set aside by the higher powers as a sanctuary for the birds and animals."[8] Momaday characterizes sacred places as those sanctified by sacrifice—offerings of song and prayer, ceremony, even life: "Acts of sacrifice make sacred the earth." He visits and revisits these places, both literally and in his writing. His stories pay homage to their power; they are celebrations and offerings of relationship. Finally, he says, the sacred "transcends definition. The mind does not comprehend it; it is at last to be recognized and acknowledged in the heart and soul." He stands in awe before cave drawings of animals, saying that they "extended [the artist's] human being to the center of wilderness, of mystery, of deepest life itself." In this notion of "deepest life," Momaday also links wilderness and human instinct—human "wildness": "Like the wilderness itself, our sphere of instinct has diminished in proportion as we have failed to imagine truly what it is."[9]

Gerald Vizenor provides an interesting riff on the bear. Writing about the presence of words in the oral tradition, Vizenor speaks of the "unsaid presence in names" found in tribal stories. He quotes Luther Standing Bear regarding the similarities between bears and humans, then goes on to say: "The bear is a shadow in the silence of tribal stories; memories and that sense of presence are unsaid in the name. Luther Standing Bear hears the shadow of the bear in his memories. . . . The bear he hears, reads, and writes is a shadow of the bear, not the real bear, not a mere concept of the bear, but the shadow memories of the bear. The shadow, not the bear, is the referent, the sense of presence in the name, and the trace to other stories."[10] Vizenor's language here seems to dance with silence, suggesting the struggle both Set and Momaday himself feel in the presence of the bear.

Storytelling, particularly as it inspires awe and celebrates mystery, negotiates between the human and the sacred, amplifying the reader's capacity to apprehend mystery. "Perhaps the central function of storytelling is to reflect the forces, within and without us, that govern our lives," Momaday writes.[11]

For Set these "forces . . . that govern our lives" are imaged in the bear, as a compulsion to transformation that includes a midlife breakdown. His psychological distress reflects his distance from the land and the loss of his wild bear energy. At age forty-four he feels compromised by buyers' demand that he simply reproduce the subjects and techniques that have made his paintings so marketable. Now Set needs to find a new way of seeing; he "would endeavor to save his soul."[12] Thus, the action of the novel is represented as the fulfillment of his identity in his submission to a mythic process that returns him to the land and culture of his ancestors. At the same time, however, the story of the bear exists independently of him. He is its avatar, but he exists as part of it, rather than the other way around. Set *suffers* the transformation, and he does so at first without knowing that he's living a larger story. Time and again he feels that something is taking place through him. In a number of places, we learn of how bear energy has earlier entered his life, through coincidences or inspirations. However, most of the time Set doesn't understand what's going on, so through him we perceive the experience of living out a myth unconsciously. It's as though he's pregnant with the bear. In order to give birth, Set needs "feminine" energy in his life; he needs the energy associated with the fertile land.

Linking Set with the bear locates his instinct, his wildness, and his mystery in the realm of the sacred, setting up this story as an instance of a myth that is larger than Set. But a secondary story threads through Set's narrative—that of Grey. While in some respects Momaday seems to use her in the story primarily as an accessory to Set, he does give Grey enough of himself to make her interesting in her own right. Aligning Grey with the horse establishes her connection to Kiowa history and, like Set, to animal energies. While the horse is different from the bear as Set experiences him, both animals function in the identity processes of Set and Grey and act as internal Others who are compelling and dangerous. In addition, horse and bear link erotic energy with sacred motifs and with the daily lives of animals. Bear energy requires Set to encounter the unknown, while her identification with the horse links Grey with history, what Momaday calls the centaur culture of the Kiowa.

In *The Man Made of Words*, Momaday details his own experiences with a horse, which "became the extension of my senses, touching me to the earth, the air, and the sun more perfectly than I could touch these things for myself." He links centaurs with Kiowa culture and history, speaking of how the horse enabled the Kiowa to "move beyond the limits of . . . human strength." While the horse extended their power, it also "gave [the Kiowa] a taste for danger and an inclination to belligerence. A predatory society is said to bear the seeds of its own destruction." Like the bear, then, the horse poses some danger to humans: too close an alliance can tempt the human to arrogance. As with other profound images, Momaday underscores the mixed blessing the horse confers: again and again he speaks of the sacred, or the powerful, as containing "the equation of fascination and peril," emphasizing the risks involved both in encountering mystery and in storytelling itself, which seems to be a way of coming to terms with compelling images and urges. Because words are powerful, the storyteller has a particular responsibility to himself, to the land, to other humans, to the sacred. In *The Man Made of Words*, Momaday speaks of the centaur as "the centaur complex," suggesting that the power horses give humans, like the power language gives humans, is psychologically thrilling but also dangerous, to be used with restraint. Moreover, he says, it is "popularly, at least, . . . a masculine one."[13]

It's interesting, then, that the character Momaday associates with the horse in *The Ancient Child* is female and a writer. This is a risky move on Momaday's part, an attempt, perhaps, to link his conscious grappling with the responsibilities and power of the storyteller with a less public, perhaps less fully lived, "feminine" part of himself.[14]

Anima and Animus in The Ancient Child

Anima and *animus* are terms Jung used to describe what he called contrasexual aspects of the personality. Jung based his ideas on this subject on the dreams and fantasies of his analysands. From these he developed his theory that dream figures of the other sex represent the "inner masculine" or "inner feminine" potentials of the psyche. Today, many analysts concur with Andrew Samuels that Jung "overlooked the culturally contingent nature of the symbolic communication in the dream or fantasy."[15] Samuels and many others now consider that anima and animus reveal potentials of the dreamer that are so unconscious as to be expressed in contrasexual images. In an individual the content of anima and animus will depend on the family, as well on as the culture of origin. Yet because the symbolic order remains divided today, many qualities of anima and animus will be common. Characteristically, because they are elements of the personality that have been consigned to the unconscious, anima and animus are projected onto others. Projection of the positive anima/animus often occurs in falling in love. The negative anima and animus can also be projected, resulting in the perception of a woman as, for example, suffocating or a man as ruthless.

Anima and animus appear in dreams as characters of the other sex and in culture as figures of inspiration, such as the Muses. Celebrities attract anima and animus projections. Jung calls anima and animus the "soul" of the personality, the guides for the ego into the unconscious. The anima and animus thus play a crucial role in individuation. Michael Vannoy Adams remarks that for the archetypal psychologist the goal of soul work is not individuation but "animation," a process in which the ego deepens into a soul.[16] If the individual can identify this split-off energy as part of the self, the anima or animus can act as a guide and mediator in assimilating unlived potentials.

Grey seems to have easier access to her animus energy than Set does to his anima. We learn that the first time Grey saw the horse, she "determined to have it . . . at the disposition of her will, to the extent that the creature would allow it, to have it in her hands and between her legs, to count it among the things that defined her."[17] The horse named Dog is thus associated with Grey's youthful erotic energy. She patiently trains herself to pick up a folded dollar bill from the ground while riding Dog, welding her will to Dog's grace in a female version of the centaur. This self-discipline reflects her conscious dedication to the task of harnessing her own "masculine" energy in service of a difficult goal, bringing it into conscious use. This effort bears fruit in the work Grey does in her imaginative relationship with Billy the Kid.

Several elements in the novel cast Grey as an idealized, anima figure for Set. He spies her first as a boy in the shadows, suggesting her association with the bear myth, and she comes to him in a dream, as a fate; she "spoke in riddles in the night, in a darkness in the light of the moon, in a darkness that comprehended the galaxies." Her "feminine" credentials are established before the story begins, in her alliance with the old grandmother Kope'mah and with the land. Almost all of Set's interactions with Grey carry a romanticized quality; even when they're together daily, he is "enthralled" and sees her as "naïve."[18] At the same time Grey's association with both horses and dogs carries masculine coloration: in *The Way to Rainy Mountain*, Momaday writes that before the Kiowas had horses, they "had need of dogs." Moreover, the principal warrior society of the Kiowas was called the Ka-itsenko, or "Real Dogs."[19]

Momaday establishes the central link between Grey and Set early in the novel, announcing it through a powerful character, the old grandmother. Immediately after the passage in which Grey decides she wants the horse "between her legs," the grandmother Kope'mah whispers to her, "The bear is coming." Grey then dreams of sleeping with a bear; the dream is intensely erotic and "full of wonder."[20] Grey thus carries Set's projections of an idealized "feminine," but she also responds sexually to his dark bear energy. She calls Set toward the bear, and she represents a potential for development that is not yet part of Set's consciousness. That is, she embodies his cultural heritage, as well as his unconscious "feminine," especially in her association with the earth. Indeed, much of the narrative prose that surrounds Grey also seems gauzy, as though even Momaday himself were in love with her. Her rape occurs in the interval between Grey's visit to the sleeping Set and his awakening, almost as if the rape were his dream and Dwight Dicks his shadow, a projected version of the violence of the bear.

Bear and Shadow

For Set the bear energy is terrifying. Opening the Bear bundle precipitates his breakdown, which can be seen as a descent into the unconscious. Momaday presents the experience as mortifying: "Set had the terrifying conviction that when the beast drew near to him, within reach, it would crack open with pain and all its shining, ulcerous insides, its raveled strings and organs, its slime and blood and bile would fall and splash upon him, and he would dissolve in the hot contamination of the beast and become in some extreme and unholy amalgamation one with the beast."[21] The language here communicates precisely the revulsion and disgust experienced when the ego sees the shadow as part of the self. Set is divorced from the land not as a choice but because he was orphaned. His allegiance to land and culture is in shadow for him, as an unlived potential. Thus, while Set has done nothing immoral or unclean, he feels contaminated. The predatory violence of the bear expresses the terror of discovering oneself at the mercy of unconscious forces.

The bear connects Set with powerful shadow forces for which he is unprepared. He feels himself in "the presence of the darkest power—until this moment he would have named it 'evil'—he had ever known." However, confronting shadow also permits a release of energy. Set finds his bear power tonic, and he begins a creative period in his painting. "Disturbing visions . . . impulses to violence and pain" alternate with "periods of great calm and creativity." At this point the bear possesses him: "It was *his* bear power, but he did not yet have real knowledge of it."[22] His courage in staying with depression and disorientation is further testimony to the power of the bear. James Hillman points out that for archetypal psychology the paradigm of psychopathology is depression: "pathology is the most palpable manner of bearing witness to the powers beyond ego control and the insufficiency of the ego perspective."[23] The gods, Hillman notes, enter human life mainly through wounds. To be the mouthpiece of the god is to be humbled, to have the ego break down. This is the crisis of midlife, when, according to Murray Stein, "the psyche explodes, and the lava from this eruption forms and reforms the landscapes of our psychological lives."[24] Such a crisis, as Stein demonstrates, may inaugurate the process of individuation.

Nothing in his world helps Set navigate the pit into which he has fallen. In the hospital he is assured that such breakdowns happen all the time. His psychiatrist, Dr. Terriman, trivializes Set's experience: he "knew wonderful stories, gleaned from the annals of folklore and witchcraft and medical mythology, but he did not tell them well, and without sensitivity or shame he made crude and intolerable invasions into Set's mind."[25] Just as Terriman is explaining away the bear, Set smashes a vase into his face. Terriman (the simulacrum of an earth-man) can only offer what Western culture has available to Set (who must not have had an HMO, because they kept him in the hospital for six weeks).

In order to survive, Set needs Grey. Grey gives him access to culturally specific ways to contain shadow and guides him in the process of individuation, which requires a ritual to enable him to absorb bear energy into his life. Grey thus arranges a centaur for Set: Perfecto Atole, on horseback, preys upon Set, who is on foot. Atole chases and finally strikes Set in the throat with the bear's paw. This ritual allows Set to experience bear energy as both subject and object, predator and prey, thereby providing him a basis for containing that energy. He comes to own the internal Other as part of himself. His ability to act ethically, that is, depends on his experience of being the object of his own violence.[26]

The nurturing Set receives from Grey, the everyday small attentions and reconnection with the maternal he experiences at Lukachukai, are crucial to his emergence from depression. Grey's intervention allows Set to settle in to domestic life, to see the stars, to run. He paints strong, simple images and attunes himself to the land. Yet he knows that he is still "sick" because "the bear stands against" him. After he marries Grey, he develops a personal ritual with the bear bundle: "He felt the power of the bear pervade his being, and the awful compulsion to release it," which he honors by raising the paw, "huge and phallic on the stars."[27] In the Sioux poem with which he introduces the final section of the novel, itself entitled "Shadows," Momaday links the bear with warrior energy.

Bear, Myth, and Transformation

In the novel's final chapter, Set travels to Tsoai to undertake a vision quest. There he enacts the story of the bear, running, slowing, staggering. His smell and hearing sharpen; he loses his human voice: "And there came upon him a loneliness like death. He moved on, a shadow receding into shadows."[28] His imitation of the bear constellates a set of associations so powerful and complex as to suggest an encounter with the Self, a force controlling his life that awes and humbles Set. In the myth the bear is violent and menacing. First it takes over the body of the boy, causing him to lose his human voice, and then it pursues his sisters, who disappear from their families. Still, because of the generosity of the stump, the sisters are transformed into stars, linking the Kiowa with the land and the cosmos. In aligning himself with the bear, Set invests himself in the land and incorporates it into his imaginative being. Momaday has expressed this relationship as one of "reciprocal appropriation," calling it "a matter of the imagination . . . which is moral and kind. I mean to say that we are all, I suppose, at the most fundamental level what we imagine ourselves to be."[29] To imagine himself as bear is also to imagine himself into the land. It is, moreover, to imagine himself as myth. Just as Grey's poems of Billy the Kid make him part of *her*, as they Indianize the outlaw, Set's participation in bear energy grafts him to myth, and myth to him. It thrusts Set into the landscape.

Momaday concludes his story with an epilogue paragraph that appears in the same typeface as earlier accounts of Koi-ehm-toya (also Grey's Indian name), the grandmother who witnessed an earlier iteration of the bear story, who saw the seven sisters and the eighth child disappear and grieved for them. In the epilogue we learn that "*Koi-ehm-toya's great-great-grandson became a renowned maker of shields. He never saw Tsoai, but he knew Tsoai in himself, its definition in his mind's eye, its awful silence in the current of his blood.*"[30] This ambiguous ending, with its suggestion of myth enacted, is represented as the climax of Set's soul-making.

Perfect Freedom

In *The Ancient Child* animals link humans with the natural world. In *House Made of Dawn*, Momaday celebrates a series of animals that are native to the land—hawks, rattlesnakes, coyotes, foxes, bobcats, lions, bears, wolves, eagles, even deer, even humans. These, he says, "have tenure in the land." By contrast, "other, latecoming things," such as the horse and the sheep, the dog and the cat, "have an alien and inferior aspect, a poverty of vision and instinct, by which they are estranged from the wild land and made tentative."[31] In *The Way to Rainy Mountain*, Momaday writes, "There is a perfect freedom in the mountains, but it belongs to the eagle and the elk, the badger and the bear."[32] "Perfect freedom" is the terrain of wild things, the eternal youth, and the outlaw. Living in community requires restraint, and so does the land. Humans are not free to despoil, to rape, to upset natural balances. Nor are they free to flee responsibility, to live without ties.

This is not to say that humans don't desire "perfect freedom": images of "perfect freedom" are powerful and tantalizing. But "perfect freedom" is the lure of commercial culture, the condition of eternal youth, and it is incompatible with such adult images of desire as artistic achievement or family life. Such maturity, Vine Deloria Jr. argues, is "in the American Indian context . . . the ability to reflect on the ordinary things of life and discover both their real meaning and the proper way to understand them when they appear in our lives."[33] In *The Ancient Child* Momaday explores bear energy in part as a way of acknowledging the power of the desire for "perfect freedom," as well as the terror such freedom entails. Perhaps its sacrifice is what sanctifies domestic life at Lukachukai. In this respect, while it does not present a story of the healing of the land, it does address the cultural values that permit exploitation and provide an alternative.

Individuation and the Symbolic Life

Individuation, like maturity, entails a reconciliation of consciousness and instinct or, on a larger scale, of culture and nature. In *The Ancient Child* the process is compressed and symbolized. In his use of the phrase "he would endeavor to save his soul," Momaday brings to mind James Hillman, who uses "soul" to indicate the individual, personal experience of *anima mundi*, the soul of the world, which "is already there with the world itself."[34] All of nature has soul, and psyche (sometimes referred to as "anima") exists independent of individuals. Hillman uses *soul* almost as a verb, calling it "an imagining activity." Soul "makes meaning possible," and *soul* also refers to "the *deepening* of events into experiences."[35] Hillman proposes that soul-making requires active engagement with images from dreams or the imagination, letting them have priority and speech. He advocates that analysts working with dreams stay with the image and avoid interpretation. Allowing the images to speak sidesteps the ego's willfulness and allows it to be nourished by psyche's richness. At the same time it keeps the ego from identifying with forces larger than itself.

As a result of staying with the image, the artist is able to draw on new spiritual and natural powers. After he receives the bear bundle, Set begins to produce images that he must study and understand, such as the "dark figures" that appear in his new work, which he sees as self-portraits, "for they expressed a certain reality in me." He paints quickly, feeling that "something seemed to be taking possession of me." He produces a watercolor, "the likeness of a man on a horse, but the image was indistinct, subliminal. . . . The image was that of the horseman passing from time into timelessness." The gallery owner calls it a centaur, and Momaday describes Set studying the painting for a long time, "trying to see . . . what deepest part of me I had imaged."[36] Momaday also does this in all his own work, as he imagines and reimagines the bear and the horse and uses art to give voice to images. Momaday has spoken of his personal experience of bear energy as lending strength, intensity, agitation, and even recklessness to his work and his life.[37] Grey undergoes a similar process in writing about Billy the Kid. Both Grey and Set allow the images an independent life (as fantasy, as inner experience, in dialogue), but both must ultimately give the images form, give them public life. As Catherine Rainwater puts it, "Set's spiritual development reveals the task of the artist: to confront the mysterious 'black infinity' and to wrest out of it the forms and images that lead through contemplation to knowledge and wisdom."[38]

Momaday muses on the complex responsibilities that language imposes on humans in *The Man Made of Words*: "Because of language we are, among all the creatures in our world, the most dominant and the most isolated. Our dominance is supreme, and our isolation is profound. That equation is the very marrow of story." The compensation for loneliness is that language and imagination allow humans "to realize a reality beyond the ordinary . . . to create and to re-create ourselves in story and in literature."[39] The crafted narrative is the work of soul, the collaboration of history and myth, consciousness and the unconscious. While some readers see the end of *The Ancient Child* as a plunge into inhuman loneliness, I believe it can be read more symbolically. The bear's paw, silhouetted against the sky, represents a symbol for Set in the same way that the leaping fish does for the narrator of *Surfacing*. It brings together the mythic and the literal, shadow and consciousness, iconically, as story does for Momaday. Language, Momaday says, sets humans apart from other creatures, making us "the most dominant and the most isolated." Telling stories is a way to acknowledge and contain a cosmic (ursine) loneliness.

The title of *The Ancient Child* refers, of course, to the boy in the myth, who is ancient, by virtue of his storied existence, and at the same time a child.

Kope'mah, too, as she approaches death, enters a "boundless state of mind . . . as wholly contained in her nature and innocence as on the day she was born . . . in which time had no function."[40] The paradox implied in "the ancient child" suggests a quality of mind Momaday offers as exemplary, a capacity to contain myth and history, male and female, instinct and spirit, not as oppositions but in dialogue. Each entity is part of something greater, and each also exists in time, in a community that is both human and nonhuman, historical, particular, and sacred. Thus, while *The Ancient Child* does not dwell on Set's reinhabitation, it explores the kind of consciousness necessary to live ethically with the land.

CEREMONY: *THE POWER OF STORY*

In Leslie Marmon Silko's *Ceremony*, individuation involves a recovery of health for the land as well as for the protagonist. Story itself plays a central role in this process, providing the framework within which characters determine the meaning of events. Silko intersperses the story of Tayo, a World War II veteran who returns home to the Laguna pueblo suffering from shell shock, with several related but independent verse narratives drawn from Pueblo culture that provide images of how health can be lost and recovered, comment on Tayo's condition, suggest the ways in which Tayo acts for the community, and link humans with the land. These narratives also provide a ceremonial structure, taking Tayo through a year, beginning and ending with sunrise. In *Ceremony* coming home is the first step toward Tayo's recovery of his own health and, with it, that of the land.

Tayo is a culture hero, whose realignment with the stories of his people will ultimately heal himself and the land. In the traditional Laguna story, "Tayo" is the name of a character who, as Edith Swan notes, "flies on wings of eagles, sings in Hopi and lives with Spider Woman."[41] At the outset of Silko's narrative, however, Tayo returns to a land choked by drought. He believes he has caused the drought by his urgent prayers for an end to rain on the Bataan Death March, understanding even in his distress the intimate relationship between human thoughts and the natural world.

Throughout the novel competing stories vie for Tayo's allegiance. At the outset his mind is a stewpot of voices, "Japanese voices . . . Laguna voices . . . fever voices . . . women's voices . . . a language he could not understand." These mingle with the stories told by science books, the army recruiter, the doctors at the VA hospital, and the school—stories of personal achievement, patriotic duty, and success. Tayo's veteran friends sound variations on these themes. They gather in bars where they "repeated the stories about good times in Oakland and San Diego; they repeated them like long medicine chants, the beer bottles pounding on the counter tops like drums."[42] These stories try to persuade Tayo that his land is worthless and his culture superstitious. They cast him in shadow and situate him at the margins. Gradually, through the ceremonies that give the novel its title, Pueblo stories displace these narratives of despair, centering Tayo in the land and culture and returning his mind to balance. Psyche and land, anima and *anima mundi*, are not separable here. Recovery entails psychological, ecological, and cultural healing.

Shadow: Cultural, Archetypal, and Personal

To return to health, Tayo must deal with shadow at three levels: cultural, archetypal, and personal. First, he has to reject the cultural shadow projected onto him, which we hear in the stories told by Emo, Harley, and Leroy, obscuring connection and eroding hope, producing a numb and isolated mind. In a drunken ritual they tell stories about the white women they screwed and the respect they commanded in the uniform of white America. They deny the power of the land and the value of the people's culture. Their stories expose the pain that results from shadow projected onto Indians. During the war, in uniform, Tayo's friends felt like they belonged in the United States. People respected them; they made good money. But afterward they discovered that nothing had changed: "First time you walked down the street in Gallup or Albuquerque, you knew. Don't lie. You knew right away. The war was over, the uniform was gone. All of a sudden that man at the store waits on you last, makes you wait until all the white people bought what they wanted. And the white lady at the bus depot, she's real careful now not to touch your hand when she counts out your change." These stories are a ritual meant to keep the good times alive, but this requires that they accept a "white" view of what's important. As Emo says, "You know . . . us Indians deserve something better than this goddamn dried-up country around here. Blowing away, every day. . . . What we need is what they got. I'll take San Diego." The barroom ritual medicates the pain of self-hatred, sucking Tayo in to passivity and shame. While Tayo never assents to their despair, the stories mix with the alcohol; they numb him, dull his feelings. He staggers and retches and sinks into cynicism. In the end always they talk about killing: "Emo grew from each killing. Emo fed off each man he killed."[43]

These men all suffer from the U.S. military's distortion of their traditional warrior role. According to Eduardo Duran and Bonnie Duran, the American Indian male's loss of his warrior role results in repressed feelings of loss and rage that manifest in alcoholism, intratribal violence, and suicide. For most of the novel, these men are Tayo's only peer group, warriors who turn their self-hatred against one another because they cannot turn it against the power that has devastated their land.[44] While Tayo doesn't actively seek their companionship, his friends show up, dragging him into their cars to go on joyrides he can't seem to resist. Often, they are the only company he has. As long as he buys into their stories, Tayo will not be able to act for himself or for the people. Silko acknowledges the power of the counternarrative through its persistent ability to confuse Tayo, right up to the end of the novel, even as he participates in the ceremony and grows into a greater harmony with the land. Tayo's first challenge is to align himself with the stories of his own culture, so that he will have a grounded center from which to view his experiences.

Archetypal shadow, or evil, is represented in the figure of the witch. Silko has Betonie account for the origin of the current crisis facing the people in his story of the "long time ago" conference of witches. The existence of these witches predates the arrival of white people in the world, ensuring that the Laguna culture cannot now ground itself in a victim's posture but must take responsibility for its own evil. Betonie explains that witchery works through its own stories, the worst of which is a story about the coming of white people who view the world as dead, without soul: "*They fear the world. / They destroy what they fear. / They fear themselves.*"[45]

Further, while his friends and their stories represent issues of cultural shadow that Tayo endures, they also suggest his personal shadow, his own capacity for violence. More than any other character, Emo attracts Tayo's rage; indeed, at one point he almost kills Emo in a bar fight. Silko amplifies his power by associating Emo with the Ck'o'yo gambler who steals the rain clouds and fattens himself at the people's expense. By making Emo, a full-blooded Indian, the embodiment of evil, Silko implicates Pueblo culture in archetypal as well as personal evil. When Tayo finally confronts Emo at the end of the novel, then, he confronts personal, cultural, and archetypal shadow.

In *Ceremony* witchery, or shadow, has many faces: it is most persistently alcohol, despair, self-hatred, envy, and boozy oblivion that bewitch and destroy men's souls. Witchery erodes hope, "so that the people would see only the losses."[46] But it is also insensibility, lack of feeling. Witchery divides the people, setting full-bloods like Emo against half-breeds like Tayo, compounding Tayo's misery with ostracism. But it also makes them blame whites for all evil, accounting themselves only victims. Silko makes clear that witchery is something that happens to you, but it is also something that exists in you and in the world. If all of nature is animate and ensouled, then perhaps even nature has its shadow side, figured in the yellow veins of uranium that are the witch's mirror image of pollen. Shadow acts upon the soul to shape what people see and how they feel. The witch in the story does not grind his evil into powder or tie it in bundles. All he does is tell a story, and as he tells it, it begins to happen. Thus, evil too works through language and story, eroding and corroding the mind it constructs, the world it brings into being.

The verse narratives Silko interlaces into her story add other images of shadow. Two strands of verse tell stories of the disappearance of fertility from the land. In one of these a Ck'o'yo medicine man seduces the people with his magic, luring them away from their observances at the corn altar. One of his tricks makes water pour out of a wall and fools the people into believing that his magic "could give life to plants and animals."[47] As a result Our Mother, Nau'ts'ity'i, takes the plants and grasses and departs. In the other Corn Woman scolds her sister Reed Woman for spending the day splashing in the river, and Reed Woman leaves, taking the rain with her. Both these stories indicate human attitudes that compromise fertility. In the first a fascination with gadgets, easy answers—to insert a contemporary term, technological fixes—distorts the people's understanding of appropriate attention to the land. In the second self-importance and self-righteousness have the same effect. Both these stories encode culturally central understandings of the causes of ecological devastation.

Shadow, Shame, and the Negative Mother

The strongest emotion connected to shadow is shame. For colonized people, particularly men who have lost their role as warriors, shame is powerful and deeply corrosive: shame that they were unable to protect the land and the people from the violence of the conquerors, shame that their powerlessness is revealed for all to see, shame that they cannot restore the culture and the community. The experience of shame is "a burning, gnawing . . . which makes one wish that the ground would open and swallow one. . . . One seems to be on the verge of psychic annihilation and to be kept alive nevertheless."[48] Silko dramatizes this condition in Tayo's frequent bouts of vomiting, the white smoke he feels himself to be in the VA hospital, the eviscerating self-doubt that plagues him. Colonial conquest causes shame, which Duran and Duran call "existential death."[49] While Tayo's response to shame is self-destructive, people like Emo identify with the powerful. Since they cannot be white, they feel shame, but shame cannot be allowed into consciousness in a warrior culture, so they drink themselves stupid and project their shame onto half-breeds like Tayo.

Tayo's shame began in his childhood, with his auntie. This aunt is a complex character. While she shames Tayo for being her sister's half-breed child, she is herself compromised by her Christianity, which "separated the people from themselves." In more subtle ways than Emo and Leroy, Auntie has also internalized shadow, projecting it onto Tayo. While she felt shame that her sister "went with" white men and Mexicans, she also blamed herself because she failed to get her sister back. As a result she kept Tayo at a distance, "close enough to feel excluded," but raised him nonetheless, garnering praise for her Christian kindness.[50] Tayo doesn't understand the complexity of Auntie's responses to him, however, believing that she looks down on him because he is himself shameful, set apart from others by his fair skin and hazel eyes. Like Corn Woman, Auntie is self-righteous, and her pride rests on the shame she projects onto Tayo. Silko makes it clear that shame, a powerful form of self-loathing, is itself a deadener, part of the witchery.[51]

Because of Auntie's contamination, and the absence of Tayo's biological mother from the narrative, Tayo suffers a lack of positive feminine energies in his soul, the personal version of the damaged mother earth. Auntie is an image of the negative mother, what Marion Woodman calls "the old petrifying mother . . . a great lizard lounging in the depths of the unconscious. She wants nothing to change. If the feisty ego attempts to accomplish anything, one flash of her tongue disposes of the childish rebel."[52] The verse narratives make it clear that the damaged land, in the absence of Reed Woman and Our Mother, reflects distortion of feminine and maternal energies. As a consequence Tayo believes himself responsible for Rocky's death, for Josiah's death, for the drought.

The shame that Auntie has inculcated in Tayo, his sense of personal failure, is reinforced every time he sees Harley, Leroy, and Emo. Their repetition of the stories of the colonizer feeds his weakness and erodes the power of the stories of the land. So powerful is the American mantra of booze, babes, and bitterness that even as he gains in grounded wholeness, Tayo backslides again and again into self-doubt, which is what Joseph Henderson calls the personal shadow.[53] Sucked into seeing himself from the point of view of the colonizing culture, he sees only failure, inadequacy, impotence.

Memory and the Healing Process

Healing cannot occur if memory is lost or denied. But memories like those Tayo plays over and over again at the novel's beginning—memories of the forced march through jungle rain—only torture him with feelings of guilt. Tayo needs stories that provide a different framework for making sense of his memories. By juxtaposing Tayo with the stories of Reed Woman, Corn Woman, and the Ck'o'yo gambler, Silko alerts readers to the interpretive context necessary to understand Tayo's story.

The first step in his healing has already taken place: he has come home. Reconnecting with the land itself helps Tayo resist once again becoming white smoke, which "had no consciousness of itself." Shortly after Tayo arrives, his grandmother summons the Laguna healer Ku'oosh to perform the Scalp Ceremony. Ku'oosh describes a deep lava cave that Tayo knows, and Tayo pushes himself up from the bed frame to listen: "He knew the cave. The rattlesnakes liked to lie there in the early spring, when the days were still cool and the sun warmed the black lava rock first; the snakes went there to restore life to themselves."[54] The memory of the place stirs him out of his despair. Ku'oosh explains that each word in its place carries a past, a story, a value, and we see this enacted as the lava cave brings to Tayo's mind a detailed image of a place with restorative power. Simply naming the place evokes its rich presence in Tayo's mind. Because words are webbed with the world, stories can foster spiritual health and align people with the land.

Tayo begins to gain strength as he recovers healing memories of particular places that connect him both to his own past and to the powers of the spirit beings associated with these places. He tells himself a story about a time during an earlier dry spell when he went to the spring in the canyon to construct a ritual of his own for rain. He watched as first a spider and then a frog emerged from their hiding places to drink from the pool, and he remembered the old stories, how "Spider Woman had told Sun Man how to win the storm clouds back from the Gambler so they would be free again to bring rain and snow to the people." In his next thought, though, the battle in his mind recurs: "He knew what white people thought about the stories. In school the science teacher had explained what superstition was, and then held the science textbook up for the class to see the true source of explanations."[55] But the white people's theories pale when he remembers "the feeling he had in his chest" when his grandma told him about the time immemorial. Land and stories restore his feelings, reanimate the numbness. Linda Hogan remarks that in creation stories "life was called into being through language, thought, dreaming, or singing, acts of interior consciousness."[56] In this passage Silko illustrates Tayo's attempts to call his own life into being and harmony through just such an act of interior consciousness. Creativity, then, includes self-creativity.

Remembering this moment helps calm Tayo down so he can enter a state of mind in which the stories and the land can work on him. As Tayo recalls how the spider, the frog, and finally the dragonfly came to the pool, Silko remarks, "Everywhere he looked, he saw a world made of stories, the long ago, time immemorial stories, as old Grandma called them." Finally, the hummingbird comes to the pool, and Tayo thinks, "as long as the hummingbird had not abandoned the land, somewhere there were still flowers, and they could all go on." The hummingbird's message is both literal and symbolic: hummingbirds need flowers, so the hummingbird is a true signifier of hope. The "world made of stories" is not only what we see: "It was a world alive, always changing and moving; and if you knew where to look, you could see it, sometimes almost imperceptible, like the motion of the stars across the sky."[57]

Silko links the "world made of stories" with the mythic experiences of the people. At the same time the "world made of stories" *is* what we see with the naked eye. Throughout Silko's work nature forms the bridge between the everyday and the world of patterns that gives the everyday meaning. Because in the everyday we don't slow down enough, don't know how to look, we need the mindfulness produced by ceremonies and stories so that larger patterns—archetypal, cultural, and ecological—can come into focus for us. When Tayo went to the spring and observed all the tiny creatures, he exercised his power of vision through "the greatest possible intimacy and communication with the world [he] inhabits." Louis Owens calls this "knowledge that enables not just a culture but a world to survive. It is a moral vision and a holy one, truly a vision of great medicine."[58] Thus, when Tayo remembers going to the spring, the words of his memory reconstitute the experience and allow him to restore vision, if only temporarily.

The Scalp Ceremony helps Tayo recover and reorder important memories, allowing him to function well enough to go alone to the ranch, where we find him at the novel's beginning. There, he recovers his memories of the Mexican cattle and of Night Swan, both of which prove to be part of the larger ceremony in which Tayo finds himself an actor. However, the Scalp Ceremony can't cure Tayo: the evil that is gripping him is too strong. Healing requires a stronger ceremony, performed by the Navajo Betonie. From this point on

Tayo begins to rebraid memories as he acts in the world to reclaim his uncle's stolen cattle. Recovering them will provide him a livelihood, so this action has practical as well as symbolic value, and it is one goal of the ceremony he undertakes with Betonie.

Silko locates Betonie's home just above the city of Gallup, where we see scenes of profound depression and degradation. Here is the home front of the war—the shanties, drunks, prostitutes, feral children; the commercial Gallup Ceremonial, organized for tourists; the despair. For Tayo healing means recovering life-affirming memories, but it also requires that he, and the reader, acknowledge painful memories. Retrieving shadow entails bringing to consciousness the pain that one has locked away. In *Decolonizing Methodologies* the Maori theorist Linda Tuhiwai Smith includes the following among twenty-five "indigenous projects":

> Remembering . . . a painful past. . . . While collectively indigenous communities can talk through the history of painful events, there are frequent silences and intervals in the stories about what happened after the event. Often there is no collective remembering as communities were systematically ripped apart, children were removed for adoption, extended families separated across different reserves. . . . This form of remembering is painful because it involves remembering not just what colonization was about but what being dehumanized meant for our own cultural practices. Both healing and transformation become crucial strategies in any approach which asks a community to remember what they may have decided unconsciously or consciously to forget.[59]

Silko's scenes of Gallup, where a small boy waits at the feet of his prostitute mother, do not directly engage the narrative, but they do act as part of a collective remembering, a refusal to ignore the painful consequences of dispossession. Tayo needs this object lesson of a particular place that carries the culture's pain and shame as he begins the healing ceremonies.

Ceremony, Feeling, and Skill

Ceremony creates the conditions for healing, but conscious human action, aided by many powers resident in the land, brings it about. This is a crucial insight. Throughout this book I have been speaking of the value of other ways of knowing and the importance of connecting with energies from the unconscious, often aided by ritual. However, the work of individuation, like the work of environmental healing, entails consciousness. Shadow must be confronted, but until it is absorbed into consciousness, it cannot become the basis for restraint and moral behavior. Because this is a protracted struggle in real life, it is often difficult to comprehend and sustain. Fiction can provide compressed images of the process so that its contours are visible. In this way fictions offer inspiration and hope.

In this novel's central ceremonies, Betonie acts as healer in a number of ways. Before the ceremony Tayo pours out his history to Betonie, who adds information, reframes events, and explains the larger story of which Tayo is a part. Betonie names the witchery for Tayo and tells how it began. After the ceremony Betonie tells Tayo the story of its origin and its continuation through generations. Again, Tayo is reassured that he is not alone, that he does not act for himself only. The history surrounds Tayo with forebears and descendents, for whom his actions will have consequences, and this increases his burden, but seeing himself as part of a larger pattern allows him to share this burden with others. The remembered and mythical contexts relieve his isolation and provide a way for him to make meaning of his life. They offer him a standard against which to judge his success that is more substantial than the impossible images of commercial culture.[60]

The primary ceremony that structures *Ceremony* is the white-corn sand painting performed by Betonie, assisted by a young man who acts the bear. This ceremony recounts the story of a retrieval of spirit. The night after it takes place, Tayo dreams of his uncle Josiah's speckled Mexican cattle; when he wakes, he recognizes the mountains around him as those in the ceremony's sand painting and realizes that "there were no boundaries; the world below and the sand paintings inside became the same that night. The mountains from all the directions had been gathered there that night."[61] The ritual has aligned his vision and the world.

While Silko describes the ceremony itself, she is more interested in the actions Tayo must perform afterward to bring about healing. Ceremony, in other words, creates the conditions for healing, but conscious human action, aided by many powers resident in the land, brings it about. The remainder of the novel thus traces Tayo's pursuit of the speckled cattle and his final show-down with Emo. In this pursuit he encounters two supernatural beings who aid him—Ts'eh Montaño and the hunter, Mountain Lion—but he must ac-complish the final victory over Emo on his own power.

Ts'eh, whom he meets first on Mount Taylor, offers Tayo love and comfort, her ranch picking up the colors of the sand painting. Here, Tayo recognizes the pattern of stars Betonie showed him and the mountain of his vision. Ts'eh, like Night Swan and Betonie and Tayo himself, has ocher eyes that "slanted up with her cheekbones like the face of an antelope dancer's mask," making her look like a kat'sina. She wears a blanket woven in patterns of storm clouds and lightning: "Suddenly Betonie's vision was a story he could feel happening."[62] In Ts'eh Tayo encounters again what Robert Nelson calls "a form of the spirit he seeks to reestablish within himself."[63]

Ts'eh is an earth-based anima, and when Tayo makes love with her, as many critics have pointed out, she seems to merge with the earth itself: "He eased himself deeper within her and felt the warmth close around him like river sand, softly giving way under foot, then closing firmly around the ankle in cloudy warm water."[64] In men who are estranged from the feminine as radically as Tayo is, the anima "may become autonomous and therefore extraordinarily real, as if it had a body."[65] In this narrative the anima mediates not only the unconscious (or mythic) dimensions of Tayo's story but also the earthly, physical energies he needs to access in order both to succeed in his mission and, afterward, to live in the land. Here and in his later meetings with Ts'eh, anima acts as guide and mediator for Tayo, strengthening him for his encounter with the final incarnation of shadow in Emo's killing ritual. She gives him access to feelings, which help to combat the anesthesia that characterizes the veterans. Having told his stories to Betonie, Tayo no longer needs to repress his feelings to mask his shame, and his joy in Ts'eh nourishes his recovery.

As he pursues the speckled cattle, Tayo experiences ritual time and space. He recalls the traditional language, with its single, present tense that contains both past and future: "The ride into the mountain had branched into all directions of time. . . . The ck'o'yo Kaup'a'ta somewhere is stacking his gambling sticks and waiting for a visitor; Rocky and I are walking across the ridge in the moonlight; Josiah and Robert are waiting for us. This night is a single night; and there has never been any other."[66] Acting within ritual power, Tayo concentrates all time in this time, and nothing is lost. It is an ecstatic moment, but success requires practical knowledge and courage as well: you must have faith *and* skill.

So, when his search for the cattle is not immediately rewarded, Tayo falls prey to shadow: his nerves falter, and he nearly loses heart: "What ever made him think he could do this? The woman under the apricot tree meant nothing at all; it was all in his own head. When they caught him, they'd send him back to the crazy house for sure. He was trapped now, tricked into trying something that could never work."[67] Silko's attention to the vagaries of consciousness anchors Tayo's quest in the familiar world, where old stories don't lose their power just because you've heard a new one. An encounter with shadow provokes oscillations of consciousness as the ego struggles to integrate the new.

He has been introduced to the feminine energy of connection, but Tayo also needs courage and stealth: he is, after all, "stealing" cattle in the eyes of the cowboy and the Texan. At his low point he encounters another mountain spirit, the lion, a creature of the wilderness: "Relentless motion was the lion's greatest beauty, moving like the mountain clouds with the wind, changing substance and color in rhythm with the contours of the mountain peaks: dark as lava rock, and suddenly as bright as a field of snow."[68] Nelson argues that the mountain lion is a "shadow-self in this shadow-place, an animal 'helper' figure" for Tayo, and Silko's language foregrounds the liminal qualities of the lion, its trickster capacity to blend with the land.[69] The lion offers a kind of animus energy that had been lost in Tayo's shadow but is now available to save him from his captors, and he makes his escape by imitating a deer, lying in a shallow depression covered with leaves until he regains his strength.

As he trails the cattle southeastward down the mountain, Tayo encounters a hunter, presumably Ts'eh's husband, who is explicitly associated with the mountain lion. Snow—brought on by Ts'eh, who hung her storm blanket out—covers his tracks, as well as those of the lion. The natural-supernatural quality of these two characters suggests the way that ceremony works to infuse the ordinary with the numinous. Louis Owens, in *Other Destinies*, says that this portion of the novel echoes a story from Pueblo mythology in which Yellow Woman (Ts'eh), the wife of Winter (the hunter), meets Summer (Tayo) and invites him to sleep with her. In the conflict that ensues, an agreement emerges that Yellow Woman will spend part of the year with Winter and part with Summer.[70] Robert Nelson, by contrast, understands Ts'eh and the woman Tayo meets at the mountain cabin as two distinct avatars of the same "'spirit of place,' a more-than-human being who represents the land's own life, who knows How Things Work and who is willing to share this knowledge with the People."[71] Whether we see her as one person or two, as anima or as *anima mundi*, the text insists that we acknowledge her reality, her power, and her affection for Tayo. When Ts'eh appears to Tayo the following spring, first in his dreams and later at the ranch, where the earth is greening, Tayo realizes he has lost nothing: "The snow-covered mountain remained, without regard to titles of ownership or the white ranchers who thought they possessed it. They logged the trees, they killed the deer, bear, and mountain lions, they built their fences high; but the mountain was far greater than any or all of these things. The mountain outdistanced their destruction, just as love had outdistanced death."[72] As Henderson points out, anima "in a mature man is an aspect of the feminine that simply allows him to view life differently than he ordinarily would . . . viewing [conscious values] in accordance with nature and in an enjoyable spirit."[73] Faith counteracts the stories of destruction and envy that consume Leroy and Harley. Tayo's mind has returned to a right relation with the land.

It also seems significant to me that Silko creates a story in which Tayo encounters a *couple*. Paula Gunn Allen writes about the "feminine landscape" of *Ceremony*, speaking of Tayo's quest as a search for a mother. He certainly does need to reconnect with anima energy. As Ts'eh explains, the witches "destroy the feeling people have for each other"; in her words Tayo recognizes his own numbness, his fear that the deaths of Rocky and Josiah meant the loss of his feelings for them, and theirs for him.[74] Ts'eh, like Night Swan earlier, offers him a way to reconnect to the flow of feelings, the feminine tide of sensations. However, Tayo also needs courage and hardiness, qualities connected with the masculine and the north, the direction in which he encounters the hunter. These are powerful and sometimes dangerous qualities, as Tayo seems to acknowledge in his reverent response to the lion.

For Tayo, as for the culture, hunting has shadow elements that are honored and contained in ritual. Remembering hunting with Rocky for deer, Tayo contrasts the responses of Josiah and Rocky to the kill, the former celebrating the deer with cornmeal and turquoise, the latter embarrassed at his family's unscientific methods. Shortly after he has this memory, when Tayo is about to attack Emo in the bar, he "moved suddenly, with speed which was effortless and floating like a mountain lion. He got stronger with every jerk that Emo made and he felt that he would get well if he killed him."[75] Because Silko is so deliberate in her placement of avatars and images, I believe that the mountain lion represents a capacity for violence necessary to the hunter and warrior. When this quality is in shadow, it is acted out unconsciously, as when Tayo attacks Emo. The ceremony intervenes between his attack on Emo and his reverence toward the mountain lion, suggesting that Tayo is learning to access and control his own shadow qualities, maturing toward his ultimate capacity to recognize, contain, and use shadow potentials.[76]

Silko does not spend much time laying specific historical blame on white people for the condition of the land, but on the mountain, as he is searching for the cattle, Tayo has an insight that is important to understanding Silko's representation of personal, cultural, and world-historical shadow. He listens to his thoughts and understands that he has been bamboozled by "the lie" whites have perpetrated in the practice of racism, the lie that "only brown-skinned people were thieves; white people didn't steal, because they always had the money to buy whatever they wanted." He thinks: "If the white people never looked beyond the lie to see that theirs was a nation built on stolen land, then they would never be able to understand how they had been used by the witchery.... The lies devoured white hearts, and for more than two hundred years white people had worked to fill their emptiness."[77] The lie comes from the shadow that white culture has projected onto "brown-skinned people." But by denying that all the land was stolen, by putting history into shadow, individual white people make themselves hollow, unable to face their own shadow, unable therefore to heal. Witchery isn't just the theft of the land: witchery—shadow—destroys by denying its own existence. Therefore, the first step toward combating it is consciousness, witness.

Shadow in Time: Myth and History Collide

Tayo's final confrontation with the witchery must happen in historical time. Tayo has to come face to face with Emo and with the friends who betray him, Harley, Leroy, and Pinkie, to make sure that the story does not end the way the witches want it to. He has to remain conscious, carefully remembering "the feeling the stories had," so he will not succumb to his friends' power to shape his reality. He has to confront fear. He has to understand his vulnerability. He does all this at the site of a uranium mine, which gathers to itself the evils of war, long-distance killing of unthinkable proportions, and desecration of the earth—a place where "human beings were one clan again, united by the fate the destroyers planned for all of them." Silko calls the mine "witchery's final ceremonial sand painting," echoing the theme that both good and evil have stories, rituals, and action. The uranium is powdery yellow, the evil shadow of pollen. Tayo sees "the pattern, the way all the stories fit together—the old stories, the war stories, their stories—to become the story that was still being told."[78] Seeing the pattern lets Tayo reclaim his own power, the rightness of his own vision. Moreover, the pattern underscores the insight that the story is ongoing and that healing is social, not just personal.

Silko's repeated use of patterns to structure the novel suggests that they function as symbols that contain the tension of opposites. In her construction of the novel, these patterns of story, circularity, and image bring together the linear and the mythic, giving the novel itself a ceremonial quality and animating the transcendent function in the reader. Tayo sees that "for each star there was a night and a place; this was the last night and the last place, when the darkness of night and the light of day were balanced. His protection was there in the sky, in the position of the sun, in the pattern of the stars."[79] The pattern of stars, illustrated in the novel and echoed in the story of Sun Man and the Ck'o'yo gambler, acts as a symbol that unites history and myth. Tayo knows that his is just one part in the ceremony, and the stars are always there to give him guidance and call him back when his faith ebbs, to keep him conscious so he does not fall into shadow, which is never conquered, only acknowledged.

In this final act of the ceremony, Tayo's challenge is to refuse to kill Emo, for this would be to surrender to shadow. He must have the courage to witness without taking revenge. Emo represents both personal and archetypal shadow. At the personal level, if Tayo's conscious sense of himself is as a warrior, then his shadow contains fear and shame. Leroy, Pinkie, and Emo taunt Tayo as they torture Harley, calling on his desire not to be thought frightened or weak, but he resists. Tayo's witness disables the power of Emo's witchery. In a poem inserted into the narrative, Silko concludes, "Ck'o'yo magic won't work / if someone is watching us."[80] Here, Emo is explicitly linked with the Ck'o'yo witchery. As Tayo has gained in strength, Emo's shadow quality has transformed from the personal to the universal, so that what Tayo battles is not just his personal demons but those of all. Evil—call it witchery or shadow—gains power when it is denied, when it is carried out in the name of something else, God or nation or justice or vengeance. Acting unconsciously, as if what one is doing is good or just, one can be savage and vicious. Shadow is what we cannot see, what we tell ourselves is not there. Once shadow becomes conscious, once it is known to the ego and to others, it loses its capacity to compel.

Shadow and Consciousness

Joseph Henderson argues that wrestling with shadow reveals something not only about the strength of the ego but also about the relationship between ego and Self. When a person confronts the personal shadow, the opportunity arises to witness pain and harness impulses. Personal shadow also contains other potentials, and bringing shadow slowly to consciousness can release new energy. When one confronts the archetypal shadow, one also discovers its opposite, the Self. In *Ceremony* Emo carries archetypal shadow, the destructive negative of the ordering, integrating Self. Struggling with this more-than-personal shadow, Tayo understands that at the uranium mine the pattern of the ceremony is completed. This gives him a momentary apprehension of the Self: "He was not crazy; he had never been crazy. He had only seen and heard the world as it always was; no boundaries, only transitions through all distances and time."[81] Tayo has developed the ego-Self axis. He can access the energies of the Self without becoming identified and consequently inflated. Ceremony and story have given him symbols and sites for this capacity. Robert Nelson points out that the various spirit beings Tayo learns to count on need to be visited at very specific places: the spirits of the land require a manifestation of mindfulness that they both prompt and reward. When self-doubt strikes, when feelings are too frightening, Tayo can now visit any one of a number of sacred places in order to reconnect respectfully with the spirits that animate both place and person. As he does so, he also regains his deep knowledge of the healing powers of nature and the Self.

Silko's sense of spirits in places brings together the psychological and the ecological healing in this novel. Place and psyche reflect one another. Tayo's process illustrates many of the dynamics of a journey of individuation. At the end of the novel, Tayo is initiated, assuming a place as one member of a complex community of humans and the land. In reinhabiting the land, he is also restoring his culture's stories, ceremonies, and ways of knowing. In this consciousness the individual is not alone, and the present is not all there is. One life is part of a larger story, past and present coexist in mind, and action takes place in and for a community. This consciousness embraces "the capacity for remembering, and so our lives become stories that can be told."[82] This is a mindfulness that forms the basis for a right relation with the land, the animals and plants, and the community. It is the prerequisite to living sustainably. The land depends on the people, and the people depend on the land.

Silko recovers what Joseph Henderson calls the cultural unconscious, "an area of historical memory that lies between the collective unconscious and the manifest pattern of the culture. . . . It . . . promotes the process of development in individuals." By representing "the archetypal, preexistent, timeless continuum of ancestral lives whose thoughts, feelings, and behavior patterns are always with us if we look into the imaginal world," Silko reinhabits culture not only for Tayo but for all her readers.[83]

ANIMAL DREAMS: *SHADOW AND LOSS*

Louis Owens analyzes Walt Whitman's poem "Facing West from California's Shores" as a text that "illuminates America's self-imagining." He argues that Whitman's "I" constitutes "a great universalizing narcissism that subsumes everything in its tireless, inquiring quest after its own image," claiming that

Whitman also "registers the ultimate, haunting emptiness the colonizing consciousness faces at last, once it is forced to confront a world emptied of meaning outside of itself."[84] In *Animal Dreams* Barbara Kingsolver creates a character, Doc Homer, whose hobby is producing photographic images that distort an object to make it resemble something else, based on a picture in his mind. The technique he uses is called "dodging."[85] In one incident he manipulates an image of two men sitting on a wall, removing the traces of their hats to make them look like rocks. Homer's hobby thus is an instance of the narcissism Owens deplores, and the novel explores the petrifying implications of such deliberate effacing of the past. *Animal Dreams* is a novel of reinhabitation in a much more realist vein than either *The Ancient Child* or *Ceremony*, but like them it aligns a psychological trauma with a damaged land and traces a narrative of recovery.

Like Tayo and Set, Codi Noline has lost her mother, a condition that produces the intrapsychic complement to the loss of connection with the earth. Like Tayo, Codi is a trauma victim, one who suffers amnesia and anesthesia, and just as in *Ceremony* the action here entails a renewal of the capacity to feel. While the political threads of Kingsolver's novel cannot altogether be teased apart from the personal, I will focus on the loss of the mother as an image for estrangement both from the land and from healing energies in the psyche. Reinhabitation here, as in *Ceremony* and *The Ancient Child*, requires a reconciliation with maternal energy, an opening to feelings and receptivity, and a recovery of memory.

Since this novel is by an Anglo writer, the option available to both Momaday and Silko—of representing a return to a culture with an active mythology and ritual life—is not possible. Roberta Rubenstein identifies the mythic stock of *Animal Dreams* as a combination of the Homeric return of Odysseus and the grail-quest story of the renewal of a parched land and its wizened king. I agree that these resonances lend depth to the narrative, but Kingsolver has invented a local myth that provides her primary roots: the story of the Graciela sisters, the orchards, and the peacocks. In this way she both problematizes a return to the land and suggests that myths of origin may also inhere in nonindigenous settlements.

Krista Comer has criticized this novel as a "fantasy topography," charging that Kingsolver's "wilderness plot" is a distortion of the realities of life in the Southwest, where the critical environmental issue is "how to live with the heat."[86] In a sense, however, this misses the point: the story *Animal Dreams* tells is only partly environmental. Comer is right that most people don't have a "Grace, Arizona," to return to, and Kingsolver does resolve the environmental dilemma with the equivalent of a "magic baby" solution to the damming of the river, but Kingsolver seems to me principally interested in exploring the relationships among psychological growth, intimacy with place, and political activism. Activism requires narratives of hope, both personal and political. Kingsolver makes this clear in *Animal Dreams*, braiding Codi's story with accounts of the efforts of the community to save its river and of Codi's sister Hallie's experiences working in Nicaragua while the U.S. government is funding the Contras. The ecological story of the poisoned river celebrates the community of Grace, which, led by its women, is able to raise enough money to prevent the mining company from diverting the river that waters its orchards. This is an activist narrative with a contrived resolution in the designation of Grace as a historic landmark, but it allows Kingsolver to underline the analogies between the land's memory and the people's and to offer political action as both effective and celebratory.

Animal Dreams is structured around three more or less analogous actions. Codi has lost her mother and her child, but through the women of the town, she learns to access the energy of the mother archetype. The land has been violated and the river polluted, but through creative collective action the women of the town find a solution to restore it to health. The third strand, in which Kingsolver suggests that the entire nation has had its memory distorted through government policy and a press that reports the news very selectively, does not resolve so well. While Kingsolver can't remake history to achieve a happy ending in Nicaragua, she does suggest through the character of Hallie that the pursuit of simple justice is an end in itself: if the personal is political, the political is also personal. This is the message Hallie sends to Codi. Moreover, through the narrative device of having one sister leave and one return home, Kingsolver suggests that Hallie carries the parts of Codi that she thrust into shadow to protect herself from the pain of her losses: her optimism, her enthusiasm for life, her compassion, her activism.

The Lost Mother

Stories of alienation from the land often include an absent or dead mother, as we have seen in these three novels. Sheryl Stevenson has written about the problems of memory generated for Codi by her traumatic losses of both mother and child. She notes that Codi experiences gaps in memory, cynicism, guilt and self-criticism, and a hypervigilant need for safety. These are also symptoms of disconnection from the archetypal energy of the mother.

Codi's father further estranges her from the maternal line, so she lacks ancestors. Moreover, in losing her baby, she has lost the opportunity to practice mothering. She talks about her time in Grace as being "bracketed by death": the deaths of a mother and of a child.[87]

As in *Ceremony*, personal trauma is reflected in the land. *Animal Dreams* also suggests the violation of mother earth through the activity of mining, which results in contamination—here, in the river's death from leaching with sulfuric acid. The land receives the toxic waste that is a byproduct—and the shadow—of consumer culture. In this way the loss of the personal mother is mirrored in the degradation of the mother earth, a condition that the Jungian analyst Fred Gustafson says has produced "collective grief" as "the dominant unexpressed feeling" in the Western world.[88]

All archetypes contain opposites. The child whose mother dies may experience primarily the negative potential of the mother, as the mother appears to withdraw from the child. Lynn Davidman studied people whose mothers died when they were adolescents. Many of those she spoke with almost immediately began nurturing others, siblings and fathers. The lost maternal energy seems thus to be restored in part by being given, where it can no longer be received. In *Animal Dreams* Kingsolver describes Codi as trying to care for Hallie in this way, but when she loses her stillborn infant at the age of fifteen, the trauma compounds the loss of her mother and provokes her to repress her abilities both to connect in a meaningful way with others and to receive their love. In Davidman's study many families maintained silence around a maternal death; like Ruthie and Lucille in *Housekeeping*, children were not allowed to grieve and told not to cry.[89] The mother's death may also result in an unconscious negative self-mothering that comes from repressing feeling. Indeed, many of Davidman's respondents reported experiencing shame at the loss of the mother, as though her death had somehow stigmatized the family. In such cases the need for nurture may be consigned to shadow and then felt as contaminated. As a result an individual may develop a diminished emotional life and disconnect from others, always feeling different. The trauma of the mother's death, accompanied by a conspiracy of silence, may also produce loss of memory in order to avoid again experiencing the enormous pain. Healing requires the individual to remember, which demands suffering the pain of loss again.

An interesting perspective on this is provided by Ashok Bedi, a physician and Jungian analyst who writes about the Hindu Kali. Bedi's work with trauma survivors has led him to the conclusion that early trauma may activate the negative mother, or Kali, archetype. Bedi describes Kali this way: "Kali . . . is described as having a terrible, frightening appearance. . . . She has four or more arms and wears a necklace of freshly-cut heads. Children's corpses serve as her earrings, and serpents as her bracelets. . . . Kali is the feminine aspect of *kala*, or time. She is the origin and the end. She represents the energy of time and stands on the corpse of the cosmos, Shiva himself."[90] All these qualities give symbolic expression to the experiences of rage, grief, and fear, and the shame of pain, betrayal, and abandonment. They are the face of trauma. A victim with a weak ego, such as a child, may be overwhelmed by the archetypal energy, which can leave both psychological and somatic scars. As the ego recovers from the initial shock, the scars remain in the form of complexes. The Kali energy may subsequently be constellated by any iteration of loss, or it may be so terrifying that it is banished into shadow, where it is inaccessible to consciousness, projected or acted out compulsively. Possessed by Kali, a person can be destructive to self and others; deprived of Kali, he or she will lack life energy; feel depression and alienation; and perhaps suffer physical symptoms as well, such as insomnia.

Loss and Shadow

In Codi's case loss has rigidified her, cutting her off from the energies she's denied along with the memory of her childhood. She has become a poster child for American rootlessness. She returns home in an alienated and distorted consciousness, as though her ego experience were totally cut off from her psyche. Hers is also an ironic, postmodern persona, which becomes one of the ways of locating the narrative historically.

Both Grace and Hallie carry shadow for Codi, positive possibilities she has repressed. Barbara Kingsolver once remarked to an interviewer that, of all the characters in the novel, Codi is

> the least like me. . . . Hallie would have been easy because Hallie is me. If I didn't have a family, I would have been helping build a new society somewhere. . . . Codi's motivations mystified me, and her personality scared me because she's so detached; she's so wounded and she's so cynical. Her cynicism is frightening because I feel it's always walking along beside me; and if I ever once turned and embraced it, I couldn't let go. So I didn't like Codi much, and I didn't want to get close to her. But I knew that if I couldn't understand her the story wouldn't work. And the only way to force myself to understand her would be to write the book mostly from her point of view.[91]

This underlines the impression that Codi and Hallie are shadow and persona for one another: Codi carries shadow for Kingsolver, and her transformation in the novel provides Kingsolver with a way of working on her own impulses to cynicism.

The novel suggests that it was not the loss of her mother that traumatized Codi so much as the loss of her child. She had imagined that a baby would love her absolutely, would make her "someone important and similar to others." However, the mother archetype is not all Eros. Pregnant at the age of fifteen, Codi had mixed feelings about her condition. Like Tayo, she later believes that her thoughts caused her loss: "I was lured and terrified. I couldn't help but think sometimes of escape: the thing inside me turning to blood of its own accord, its bones liquefying, leaking out. And then one evening my savage wish was granted."[92] When she miscarried, she felt consumed with shame and fear, and this pain drove her to excise her maternal feelings. The conspiracy of silence that shrouded her miscarriage denied her an outlet for the rage and grief she felt, so the restorative energy of the dark feminine, along with the nurturing capacity of the beneficent mother, was cast into shadow. She became numb, leaving medicine when she could not attend a breach delivery. Codi clearly has lost access to Kali energy.

Recovery and Feeling

Although *Animal Dreams* explores the causes of Codi's problem, it is more concerned with her healing than with her dysfunction. As the personal, environmental, and international stories unfold, we see that many problems are rooted in an absence of memory, the denial that is characteristic of shadow. People forget, but "the land has a memory," and it holds in the earth the scars of human thoughtlessness. Nicaraguan children die because the U.S. press colludes with the government to cover up the truth. One of the most chilling moments in the novel comes when Codi reflects on her own response to press silence on the murders of three Nicaraguan girls. When the story finally appears, distorted to deny the role played by the U.S. military, there is no mention of the girls' deaths. Codi comments, "I knew it was a lie, but I was comforted."[93] Her bitter honesty about the comfort afforded by denial exposes the narcissism that Louis Owens remarks: Americans prefer present pleasure, ease, and convenience, denying the costs, the price that others in the world pay for these indulgences. This is a form of anesthesia, a failure of compassion, and the novel links recovery of the ability to feel with memory. Like Tayo, Codi needs to reconnect with her feelings, to suffer through the most painful ones, in order to remember and to live. This is part of retrieving shadow from unconsciousness. *Animal Dreams* suggests, in linking the personal and the political, that like Tayo and Codi, everyone needs to feel—to feel Kali, to feel the rage of the dispossessed, to feel the pain of the Other—in order to remember and to live consciously. Kingsolver links Codi's anesthesia with her denial, and the plaiting of stories suggests that common estrangement from the mothering energy of the earth has also produced a general anesthesia.

As her return home links her with the mother earth, Codi's recovery of memory occurs primarily through her relationships with the "fifty mothers" of Grace, especially Emelina. In reconnecting with the women she grew up with, Codi encounters people who remember a different person than the one she feels in the present. Their love for her slowly begins to reshape her experience. The novel depicts key moments in Codi's recovery—when she saves Emelina's baby, when she goes to the cemetery with Viola Domingos, when she cleans Homer's house with Uda Dell—but these "aha!" moments are no more important than her daily breakfasts with Emelina and her boys. Through Codi's relationships Kingsolver navigates the complications of home.

Codi's recovery of feeling takes place largely through her relationship with Loyd Peregrina, a gentle animus figure who introduces her to Pueblo places, people, and culture. A well-mothered son, he contains nurturing maternal energy. He is what Annis Pratt calls a "green world lover," who corrects for Codi's brittle animus, just as Emelina offers a rich version of the nurturing mother.[94] If he is a pilgrim, as his name suggests, he is also a kind of Penelope to Codi's Odysseus. On several occasions Loyd takes Codi to places on the reservation where she finds a healing quality in the ancient land. These places are liminal, "improbable and dreamlike" but real, and they allow her to enter a space where she need not be so invested in her defenses.[95]

Codi's recovery of energy develops in her response to the kidnapping and murder of Hallie. Her sister's peril unleashes Kali energy in Codi, who alternates between manic rage and inertia. Kingsolver shows how Codi captures and channels her rage into political action, but none of her letters and phone calls produces more than one biased news report in the business section of the Tucson paper and a spate of identical responses from Washington that "the matter bears investigation." Like her father, the government fosters denial. At another level the novel suggests that Codi's individuation requires the sacrifice of Hallie, the idealized Other against whom she has measured her cherished inadequacy, so that she can be incorporated into Codi's new, more balanced sense of self. At a symbolic level the two sisters represent the split in consciousness that results from the loss of the mother and the subsequent estrangement from the land and the self.

In other myths besides that of Kali, the mother is linked with death as well as birth and with annual cycles of fallow and fertile fields. The Mesopotamian goddess Inanna descends into the earth in an effort to usurp her sister Ereshkigal, Queen of Hell but also Mistress of Life. According to Karen Armstrong: "Inanna goes down into the world of death, to meet her sister, a buried and unsuspected aspect of her own being. . . . Ereshkigal too is a Mother Goddess, depicted as constantly giving birth. In order to approach her, and gain true insight, Inanna has to lay aside the clothes that protect her vulnerability, dismantle her egotism, die to her old self, assimilate what seems opposed and inimical to her, and accept the intolerable: namely that there can be no life without death, darkness and deprivation."[96] In psychological language this is a meeting with shadow, the Other within. For Codi this descent occurs through the ordeal of Hallie's kidnapping and extends to her leaving Grace, so depressed that she cannot see in color.

To recover, Codi must give up the emotional protection that her isolation has given her. She opens herself to the full experience of grief, not only for Hallie but also for her lost mother and her lost baby. Much of the power of *Animal Dreams* comes in its evocation of Codi's grief. As everything contains its opposite, experiencing grief makes hope possible. This is the sacrifice— the renunciation of armor—that makes it possible for Codi to feel again. It is a "symbolic relinquishment of a certain aspect of one's psychic life," which, according to Ashok Bedi, is necessary for someone to move from trauma to health.[97]

Ritual and Transformation

Like Momaday and Silko, Kingsolver recognizes the crucial role played by ritual in psychological transformation. The rituals surrounding the Day of the Dead demonstrate that love can survive loss. Later, they offer a container for Codi's grief and allow her to connect with the energy of the mother through careful tending of the family gravesite. This she does alongside all the others who are performing their ongoing relationships with dead relatives. Community elders oversee these ritual functions to ensure that the energies constellated in the performance are contained and channeled. In the graveyard communion with the spirits is both sacred and joyous, serious and fun. Rituals link the living through the ancestors to the mythic/historical origins of the town. The spirits conjured are those of personal and community connection, both to family and to the earth.

Whereas the rituals in *The Ancient Child* and *Ceremony* are embedded in deep cultural traditions, some of those in *Animal Dreams* have to be invented. Crucially, Codi must create a ritual, in the memorial service she holds for Hallie, that will allow her to express, share, contain, and transform her grief. This ritual enables her to let go of her pain, not only at the loss of Hallie but at all her losses. Robert Moore argues that "humans need to participate in mythological narratives and ritual enactment to gain adequate containment for the archaic numinous libidinal energies natural to the deep self that everyone struggles to locate, regulate, and channel adequately in a life-enhancing manner."[98] While she is clinging to her pain, her difference, Codi has no access to these libidinous energies. She is depressed and cynical, afraid of being overwhelmed by pain. The ritual she constructs for Hallie permits her safe access to her grief, allows it to flow through her, to be shared with others, and to be released. This does not mean that grief then goes away. It does mean that Codi has experienced its power and knows that she can do so again without being damaged. Ritual makes her feel safe enough to risk. The space she chooses for her ritual, in the orchards where she and Hallie played as children, is already sacred, not only to her but also to the town. Moreover, it literally represents both the fruit of their labor and the root of their struggle against the mining company to save the river. Codi's ritual is homemade, but it contains key ingredients: sacred space, symbolic objects (such as the black and red afghan that represents the devotion of the fifty mothers), and powerful language. In the course of the memorial service, Codi feels memories rushing back, and her grief washes over her, but in the company of Emelina, Loyd, and the women of Grace she incorporates Hallie into herself: "Everything we'd been, I was now."[99] Reclaiming positive shadow, she reinhabits her life.

THE PROBLEM WITH HOME

Advocates of wilderness argue that life demands places that are set aside from human activities, places where natural processes can go on isolated from human agendas. Humans' need for such places should not be the sole reason for protecting them; rather, these places deserve protection for their own sake, in accordance with a land ethic. They have their own intrinsic right to exist. In narratives of reinhabitation the land has a different relation to the human. In such narratives the land is habitat. It's home, it's where people face the challenge of living sustainably. Ralph Metzner defines *reinhabitation* as a political and ethical reorientation to the land:

> The bioregional approach advocates replacing the man-made, historically arbitrary political boundaries of nations, states and counties. Instead it suggests using natural ecosystem features, such as watersheds, mountain ranges and entire biotic communities as the defining features of a given region. The primary values, from a bioregional perspective, are not "property rights" and "development," but the preservation of the integrity of the regional ecosystem, the viability of the biotic community, and maximizing economic self-sufficiency within the region. Political control should rest with the community of people actually living in the region.[100]

Judith Plant argues that bioregionalism and ecofeminism are allied through common interests in caring, nurturing, and attending to process rather than product.[101] In these novels nothing has been conquered, solved, or tamed, but relationships have been established that are characterized by compassion and restraint. These works are not didactic, nor were they written by people who have adopted a bioregional agenda. However, they do offer alternatives to the stories that dominate and construct the alienated and cynical postmodern consciousness.

Reinhabitation implies that once there was a time of habitation, that someone left the land and is now returning. In one respect, in the Americas at least, this can only be true of indigenous people. Worldwide, however, many people have left the land. Agribusiness and world trade policies have made small farms less and less viable. Famine, war, and poverty have forced many millions of people into exile. For recent emigrants, and especially for refugees, there is little hope of return. Exile from home lands is poignantly a loss of culture and an immersion in the unfamiliar. "Home" is almost certainly not what it was, and return to the land may not be possible for most people. One of the shortcomings of the reinhabitation movement is that it assumes a financial capacity to leave wage employment. Today, however, returning to the land may mean a near-poverty job at Wal-Mart.

The Western myth of the individual propels people from home to seek fame and fortune. "Progress" implies that children should fare better than their parents. Increasingly, cities are filled with people whose only shared memories are of TV shows and films. Wherever they go, they'll find Pizza Huts and *Law and Order* reruns. They are at home everywhere and nowhere.

And exile itself is not just loss: For gays and lesbians the city may mean community and safety. For refugees survival requires exile. Exile implies crossed boundaries, consciousness that things one had believed universal truths are only the constructions of culture. Acknowledging loss, the exile can also bring new points of view to the adopted land. Exile can promote a critical consciousness, because the exile knows that what was true at home may not be true now: nothing is sure, everything is contingent. This way of life is often an uncomfortable one, and we can see resistance to it in the growing power of fundamentalist ideologies.

We are left then with a dilemma. Only a few people can literally afford to go back to the land, and a traditional, mythic, or tribal consciousness seems unavailable to most people schooled in Western institutions. It appears that the most prevalent alternative to postmodern global consumerism is a frightening fundamentalism. Further, the power of capital to shape thought has few fault lines: nothing is wild today, everything is manufactured. In order to realize Aldo Leopold's vision of a land ethic, an increasingly urban population, largely divorced from community or roots, must come to see, feel, understand, love, or have faith in a complex living system that depends no less on its fungi than on its top-level carnivores. But how is this possible? Must we bow to road rage, consumerism, and the prison-industrial complex? Like Tayo lying in his bed at night with scraps of language shredding his consciousness, competing narratives vie for our faith, both personally and culturally. The overwhelming message of the media should engulf us, but, like grass growing through pavement, stories like *The Ancient Child*, *Ceremony*, and *Animal Dreams* persist or spring up, stories of memory and hope, history and imagination.

7

The Chippewa Novels of Louise Erdrich
Trickster and Restoration

> We need new stories, new terms and conditions that are relevant to the
> love of land, a new narrative that would imagine another way, to learn
> the infinite mystery and movement at work in the world.
> —Linda Hogan, *Dwellings*

THERE'S ONLY SO MUCH story can do. It cannot transport people to the
land. It cannot give them the time, money, and political savvy to ensure
that forests can burn, wetlands can flood, and no one builds in the hurricane's
path. But story can depict alternatives to the narratives that lock people in a
brittle and hopeless antagonism to nature. In this chapter I look at the Anishinaabe novels of Louise Erdrich as a performance of the restoration of culture and land. I hope to bring together here all the strands of my study: the
land, story, and consciousness. This chapter considers the likenesses among
restoring natural areas, restoring culture, and individuation; it examines the
narrative strategies Erdrich uses to restore culture; and it investigates power
in her characters and her use of the trickster as a force for restoration and
increased consciousness.

Stories of individuation are not heroes' journeys of dragon slaying and
triumph. Rather, the hero occupies the first part of life. Individuation, or animation, is the work of later life, and its stories involve suffering, descent, and
return or re-membering. A collection, or re-collection, of potentials accompanies this return, and the knowledge of shadow deepens both humility and
compassion. In Erdrich's evolving portrait of Anishinaabe life, such recollection is cultural. Some characters confront shadow and initiate a more mature
life, but the overall emphasis is on the retrieval of community rather than on

any one individual. Trickster figures often bring shadow to light for the culture, the comic mode underlining the work of restoration, which is natural, communal, and cultural. In her still-growing saga Erdrich details a community so filled with tangled roots, diverse characters, matters of chance, fires and floods, love and sacrifice, that it comes to mirror a land community restored to biological health. In the struggles Erdrich recounts—internal, intratribal, and international—we can see the complexity of the challenge of returning both people and the land to wholeness. The comic vision that shapes these stories offers hope for reconciliation.

In *Four Souls* John James Mauser, a developer who has deforested the north woods and stolen the land of countless Indian people, laughs at the idea that the land might be restored. "I could hardly make restitution," he says, "to a people who've become so depraved. I know the folly of those people up there now! The old type, the old warrior type, they are gone. Only the wastrels, the dregs of humanity left, only the poor toms have survived. . . . The reservations are ruined spots and may as well be sold off and all trace of their former owners obliterated. That's my theory. Let the Indians drift into the towns and cities or subsist where they will. Thinking their tribes will ever be restored is sheer foolishness. There's nothing left!"[1] Louise Erdrich's novels are the rejoinder to Mauser's cynicism. Erdrich begins her series of novels with the disappearance of June Morrissey, one loss that becomes an emblem of all that has been lost: families, culture, land, language, religion, and ways of knowing. In her interwoven stories she offers both a postmodern appreciation of multiple points of view and an enactment of traditional ways of knowing and relating. Her world is local and specific, land based and traditional, but it is not parochial or removed from history. The restoration Erdrich performs requires her characters to find a way to live with both shadow and their dependence on the fertility and wildness of the unconscious. In the process she offers a powerful alternative to despair.

NATURAL AREAS RESTORATION

The previous two chapters looked at novels in light of the conservation strategies of wilderness protection and bioregionalism, or reinhabitation. Their focus was on individuals, whether coping with initiatory experiences, healing, or individuation. In this chapter I use the conservation strategy of natural areas restoration as a lens for examining Louise Erdrich's saga. The focus shifts from the individual to the community, as Erdrich's goal is the restoration of a culture. In arguing for a land ethic, finally, individual growth is not enough. Like other species, humans live in relationship with other humans and with the land. To preserve any species, we must preserve its habitat. Culture and land are the habitat of humans. Without community individuals founder.

When conservationists consider what land to restore, they generally choose to acquire, protect, or begin with land that has not been totally degraded: forests that have been strip-logged, agricultural fields, parking lots, and landfills are poor candidates partly because the land has lost the associations of below-ground organisms that foster a healthy ecosystem. Instead, restorationists will choose a railroad right-of-way or a cemetery where native plants have survived, a forest that has not been clear-cut, a stream that still sustains life. There is a deep sadness about this.

However, value can be found in even fragmentary restoration. Introducing native plants saves or brings back their pollinators, which in turn provide food for other species, gradually returning biological diversity to an area. Bringing in seed from a nearby natural area ensures that species are a native genotype. In some places neighbors are reclaiming vacant city lots; in others they are planting native gardens around schools, nursing homes, hospitals, railroad rights-of-way, municipal buildings, even corporate campuses. The efforts of thousands of volunteers and land managers are transforming weedy forests, eroded streams, and areas that have been overgrown as a result of fire suppression into biologically diverse habitats for creatures that have long been absent. The resulting restoration will not be perfect, but it will be better than leaving the sites degraded. Restoration of habitats must also consider reanimation of varieties of cultures, the knowledge of the land that is encoded in their languages and stories. This kind of restoration is part of what Erdrich achieves in her series of novels. The stories themselves are like the seed bank that waits to germinate, the potential for life that even boarding school can't destroy.

CULTURAL RESTORATION IN NARRATIVE THEMES AND TECHNIQUES

The theme of loss permeates Erdrich's work; indeed, recognizing and honoring loss are central to the work of restoration. As Stephanie Mills says of ecological restoration, "Restoration is about accepting the brokenness of things, and investigating the emergent property of healing."[2] The death of June Morrissey contains the brokenness of things, and Erdrich's stories move backward and forward from this moment, not as the cause of anything, but rather as a primal loss and a living memory. As they have evolved, the novels enact an achronological condition that imitates nature itself, a tangle of past and future that resembles the narratives of dreams. Michael Dorris described it this way: "Basically this is the story of the reverberation of June's life even though she is the one character who does not have her own voice. Bringing her home is finally in fact resolving her life and death in balance."[3] Various writers have noted the value in Erdrich's work of "present absence," or "the play of absence and presence."[4] Shadow lives in loss, and losses are everywhere in Erdrich's work—in the absences of June, of Gerry in prison, of Henry Lamartine, of Fleur for Lulu. Mothers are often absent too, as in other novels we have examined, but in Erdrich's work the community steps in to mother lost children. Moreover, the reappearance of all the lost ones, from novel to novel, both in person and in memory, holds out the promise that some restoration is possible.

What is restored is the tangle of roots and relationships that constitutes an ecology of the culture. Throughout her saga Erdrich uses a diversity of characters and points of view to underline the central place of community in her vision. As in a natural ecosystem, connections and relationships—predation as well as mutualism—permeate the stories. Her characters appear and reappear; they run roots and stolons and tendrils into each other's lives, and from book to book. This collection of humanity includes old growth like Fleur and Nanapush, young trees like Lyman and Lipsha, and even toxic weeds like Pauline. As with biodiversity in an ecosystem, this "organization of individuals into a wide-ranging field of allowable styles creates the greatest possible social stability because it includes and encourages variety of personal expression for the good of the group."[5] As Lipsha explains, in describing his relationship with Lyman: "His real father was my stepfather. His mother is my grandmother. His half brother is my father. I have an instant crush upon his girl." These "tangled bloodlines" knot the novels together and help to keep the community stable, just as the tangled connections of wild land do.[6]

The shifting point of view does not pretend to objectivity so much as it leads to humility; we no sooner finish hearing one version of a story than we understand from another participant that the first teller could see only part of the whole. Susan Perez-Castillo argues that her use of multiple narrators allows Erdrich "to recover the collective perspective which characterized traditional Chippewa oral narratives and simultaneously to highlight the spiritual fragmentation of her tribe."[7] Every history is contested, and each amplifies the other. There's a humbling quality in understanding that others inevitably experience the world differently, but the truth-value of each person's world is seen in relationship, rather than as absolute. To the extent that characters are able to listen and expand their vision, they thrive.

Another of Erdrich's narrative techniques involves a condition of paradox or doubleness in the novels. Catherine Rainwater outlines the intertwining of Catholic and traditional religions, of Western and Native time, of ideas about family and notions of identity. She points out that Erdrich refuses to resolve the tension in either direction, a resolution that would be patently false, given her own mixed Ojibwa-German heritage.[8] This doubleness is also a figure for the condition of the land, which although subjected to logging and farming still maintains its wild potentials. Doubling gives the novels a liminal quality, a holding of opposites in tension. Sometimes these opposites are given a fake synthesis, as in the tomahawk factory or Lipsha's store-bought love medicine. Sometimes they lead to a genuine symbol, such as the dandelion, which is both "a nuisance" and "a globe of frail seeds that's indestructible."[9]

As the series has developed, Erdrich has increasingly used untranslated words from the Anishinaabe language. In the endnotes to *The Last Report on the Miracles at Little No Horse*, Nanapush, telling the story of the name Little No Horse, concludes:

> If we call ourselves and all we see around us by the original names, will we not continue to be Anishinaabeg? Instead of reconstituted white men, instead of Indian ghosts? Do the rocks here know us, do the trees, do the waters of the lakes? Not unless they are addressed by the names they themselves told us to call them in our dreams. Every feature of the land around us spoke its name to an ancestor. Perhaps, in the end, that is all that we are. We Anishinaabeg are the keepers of the names of the earth. And unless the earth is called by the names it gave us humans, won't it cease to love us? And isn't it true that if the earth stops loving us, everyone, not just the Anishinaabeg, will cease to exist? That is why we all must speak our language, nindinawemagonidok, and call everything we see by the name of its spirit. Even the chimookomanag, who are trying to destroy us, are depending upon us to remember. Mi'sago'i.[10]

Restoring language, then, and stories, is a form of restoring the land itself. In her interdependencies and woven tales, Erdrich demonstrates that there are as many chambers in the heart as there are food webs in the wild woods and lakes.

ECOLOGY: COMEDY, CHANCE, AND CHAOS

Erdrich also mirrors the natural world through narrative in her use of chaos and her comic worldview. According to Gerald Vizenor, Native American Indian literatures "are unstudied landscapes, wild and comic rather than tragic and representational, storied with narrative wisps and tribal discourse."[11] Vizenor is at pains to locate tribal discourse in a comic mode to suggest the traditional manner of cocreating the world through language, rather than placing tribal literatures exclusively in the Western historical context, in which the expected ending is tragic, the vanished Indian.

The ecocritic Joseph W. Meeker argues that biology itself is fundamentally comic: cyclical, community oriented, self-renewing. He associates the tragic mode with Western culture, which "assumes that man exists in a state of conflict with powers that are greater than he is." Comedy, on the other hand, demonstrates human adaptability, resilience, and renewal: "Literary comedy depicts the loss of equilibrium and its recovery. Wherever the normal processes of life are obstructed unnecessarily, the comic mode seeks to return to normal."[12] Erdrich echoes this pattern repeatedly in the novels, creating comic chaos and restoring order. The result is extremely funny. Sometimes chaos is more fruitful than it is at other times: when a riot erupts at the tomahawk factory, participants feel "a kind of organized joy" at destroying this simulacrum, and their actions are cleansing and clarifying.[13] When Lyman and Lipsha fight at the Dairy Queen, the potential violence is tempered by the comic images of flying sundaes, and the aftermath, as they lick syrup off their arms in the car, is "almost joyful."[14]

Not all chaos is comic, however. When King and Lynette smash the pies that Marie, Zelda, and Aurelia spent the morning baking, the chaos is simply part of a dysfunctional marriage. Albertine thinks, "Once they smash there is no way to put them right."[15] Some chaos, too, is terrifying and deadly: the epidemic that has wiped out most of the band at the beginning of *Tracks*, as Lawrence W. Gross points out, is apocalyptic, "the end of the world as the Anishinaabe had known it."[16] And the "blizzard of legal forms" that Nanapush laments at the end of this novel accompanies the loss of Matchimanito.[17]

Chaos is related to chance, another recurring element in Erdrich's work that is also crucial in ecology. Restoration strives to render an ecosystem able to sustain processes of natural selection found in wild, self-regulating places. Biodiversity provides the conditions for evolution: a rich variety of species and genetic diversity are the foundations of natural selection. By chance genes cross in ways that improve adaptation, and the selection of fitter individuals for reproduction ensures the vigor of the species and sets the stage for the gradual appearance of new species. Ecology is rife with chance. By chance this oak falls and leaves a light gap just here; by chance this seed germinates and produces a viable plant; by chance this tadpole does not get eaten by a bird. Erdrich weaves games of chance and the experience of luck throughout her novels, particularly *The Bingo Palace*, where chapters bear titles like "Redford's Luck" and "Shawnee Ray's Luck."

John Purdy argues that in Erdrich's work chance is never really chance, but rather the recognition of patterns and motifs. To be lucky, like Lipsha, is a blessing. Fleur and Lulu are more than lucky. They are observant and sly. Fleur distracts the district agent with her child at the card table, and Lulu dresses in full traditional garb to steal attention from Gerry's getaway. Such conscious focus is a practice of science, and it is necessary for an ecological consciousness too: events in nature are related not just by linear cause and effect but also by patterns, multiple interactions, and chaotic repetitions. Success in games of chance—as in navigating change in general—increases with self-knowledge, family and cultural memory, and an understanding of "human nature as revealed in the stories of the long history of life on this continent."[18] In foregrounding the role of luck, Erdrich builds her story on a natural foundation. In appreciating the role of the crafty, she acknowledges the value of consciousness. Erdrich's complicated bloodlines, confusing stories, and decentered perspective imitate a natural area where species coexist, mutually dependent in ways both seen and unseen. In maintaining family likenesses, in tracing recurring patterns, Erdrich mirrors the work of DNA.

Despite the enormous losses experienced by her characters, Erdrich manages to keep her tone comic. Most of her deaths occur "offstage," and each of the novels ends on a note that can be considered hopeful: Lipsha delivers Gerry to Canada; Dot comes to understand the value of Celestine's love and embraces her Indian identity; Lulu returns to Nanapush and Margaret; Zelda goes to Xavier Toose; Gerry escapes to Canada again; Agnes/Damien rejoins Fleur and Nanapush in a chosen death; Fleur goes off to cleanse herself in Margaret's medicine dress. The storyteller becomes the trickster who keeps the culture, the land, and hope alive. The comic chaos renews a relationship with wildness, while the stories preserve a relationship with meaningful structures of experience. In this way the novels model the absorption of the fruitful unconscious into a stable ego.

From a psychological point of view, the comic vision acknowledges that passions and the potential for inflation are always present, that each person has a shadow side, and that community is a conscious choice and tradition necessary to regulate a human nature that is as wild as that of the world around us. To see from the point of view of nature is to care about preserving a system; to see from the point of view of the individual is to care about preserving control. Nature sees from the Self, and individuals see from the ego. In Erdrich's vision much comic chaos results from ego inflation: Wallace Pfef in *The Beet Queen* imagines that he'll redeem himself in Dot's eyes by throwing her a luau or making her a beauty queen. Sita fantasizes about operating a fancy French restaurant. Celestine plots revenge on Mary with her hardware Jello. In other cases cycles of hostility and revenge have serious potential, except that people keep intermarrying. As Nector remarks just before the tomahawk factory blows up: "Lipsha Morrissey was a combination of the two age-old factions that had torn apart our band. His mother was a Morrissey, but I was his half uncle, and that gave the two of us the same descent, the Pillager background."[19] So what could be tragic becomes comic instead. Indeed, the scope of Erdrich's storytelling ensures that her vision will be comic and restorative, as each generation sees the previous generation's tragedy as a story.

CREATION AS RESTORATION

Finally, Erdrich's work resonates powerfully with the creation story of the Anishinaabe, itself a restoration narrative. Basil Johnston, an Ojibwa ethnologist, tells this story as follows: Kitchie Manitou has a vision or dream in which he sees sky, stars, earth, plants, and animals, as well as time, stories, weather, and passion. From this vision he makes everything out of nothing, beginning with rock, water, fire, and wind—the four elements—breathing into each "the breath of life." But a great flood takes away all life on earth. When the rain stops, the lone creature, a spirit woman, begs Kitchie Manitou for company, and he sends a spirit to be her consort. She conceives, and her consort leaves. She bears two children, one all spirit and the other all matter, who fight and destroy each other. Again Kitchie Manitou sends her a consort; again she conceives, and he leaves. The sea creatures respond to her loneliness, persuading a turtle to raise its back so that she may rest on it. After all the others have tried and failed, the muskrat, the lowliest of creatures, succeeds in bringing back some soil from the bottom of the sea. The spirit woman paints it on the turtle's back and breathes life into it, and it grows to cover the turtle's back, forming an island that grows and becomes repopulated. She gives birth, this time to twins who are a compound of spirit and matter, one male and one female. They are called "Anishnabeg" because they are not made of rock, fire, water, or wind. They are "spontaneous beings."[20] Like Feather Woman in the Blackfeet story, then, the Anishinaabe first mother experiences excruciating loneliness. Chaos and struggle are part of her story, but compassion is what saves the world. The Anishinaabe story also shows the shared responsibility of humans and other animals for the world that both inhabit and reassures humans that life can reappear after a disaster.

FLEUR AND THE POWER OF NATURE

Erdrich structures many of her narratives around a contest between different kinds of agency, with Fleur Pillager standing throughout as an exemplar of traditional forms of power. Many characters in the novels regard Fleur with suspicion, seeing her as both powerful and dangerous, even a witch. She is identified with Misshepeshu, the creature in the lake who figures in Anishinaabe mythology, and she shares some qualities with the trickster, such as her skill at gambling, but her power is also identified with the place she inhabits. In a sense, if the trickster can be seen as the power of *human* "nature," then Misshepeshu, and by association Fleur, can be seen as the power of *all* nature.

Erdrich's descriptions of the woods around Matchimanito suggest Fleur's association with nature's power and danger: "Those woods were a lonely place full of the ghosts of the drowned and those whose death took them unaware, like Jean Hat. Yet we couldn't resist hunting there. The oaks were big and the bush less dense, the berries thick and plump, the animals seemed fatter and more tender. People went here although they didn't want to meet the dead or the living." Early in *Tracks*, when Nanapush is counseling Eli against courting Fleur, he says: "Those trees are too big, thick and twisted at the top like bent arms. In the wind their limbs cast, creak against each other, snap. The leaves speak a cold language that overfills your brain. You want to lie down. You want to never get up. You hunger.... That was no ordinary doe drawing you out there."[21] The darkness and danger of the woods are linked with their fertility, and with Fleur's particular power, which is both real and a function of the projections she receives from others.

MISSHEPESHU

Erdrich also uses traditional Anishinaabe stories, particularly those of Misshepeshu (or Micipijiu), to locate characters in relation to the culture and to reframe tradition so that it speaks to contemporary threats. Misshepeshu, the creature of the lake, confers great power on Fleur. Pauline remarks of him that he is "neither good nor bad but simply had an appetite."[22] However, according to the Anishinaabe scholar of religion Lawrence Gross, Misshepeshu "has incredible strength, but can be extremely dangerous."[23] He is part of what Jace Weaver calls "numinous landscapes where every mountain and lake held meaning for [the people's] identity and their faith."[24]

According to Victoria Brehm, the character of Micipijiu has transformed several times since the arrival of European fur traders disrupted the traditional life of the Ojibwe. An underwater figure with catlike or leonine features, he was one of the most powerful *manidog*, or spirits, in the Ojibwa world. To encounter him in a vision quest was to gain great power, for both good and ill. He was the guardian of the waters, the spirit who needed to be placated in order to ensure a safe passage across the dangerous Lake Superior. The master of the game, he controlled the supply of prey and regulated the commons, so that supplies were not depleted by greed. Later, he was a gateway to the shamanic Midewiwin. "His role in the creation myths," Brehm tells us, "was to enforce wise use of renewable resources to prevent their exhaustion; in the late Midé ceremonies he was reinterpreted to reinforce culturally sanctioned means of gaining power and economic security. . . . In his role as guardian of resources he is immortal, reappearing to punish anyone who attempts to upset the balance of eco-social relations."[25] Brehm recounts a version of the flood story in which Nanabozo (Wenabojo), who has been adopted by a family of wolves, tricks Micipijiu, kills him, and causes the world to be flooded. He survives by climbing a tree and sends the muskrat for mud to re-create the middle world. In this story Micipijiu has Wenabojo's wolf companion killed because his greed is endangering the community. In retaliation the trickster reveals his appetitive nature in outwitting Micipijiu. Brehm comments that the myth of Micipijiu may be a postcontact story that changed to meet the people's new need to conserve what was fast becoming a scarce resource.[26] This draws attention to the role of stories as well as rituals in mediating human disputes and promoting the capacity to contain and channel appetitive energies. The value of Erdrich's restoration of traditional stories in contemporary form rests partly in their ability to suggest one's power and obligation to regulate one's relation with the natural and human worlds that are home, sustenance, and community.

Her relationship with Misshepeshu gives Fleur power and natural vitality, but it is not a power that can withstand the relentless drive of white land policies. The triumph of the lumber companies and the government is also a kind of deicide: the desecration of Matchimanito represents the displacement of Misshepeshu and the transformation of the people's way of life from its traditional, bioregional economy to a cash and paper nexus. The clear-cut ensures that the land will be devastated. Some losses can be transcended or retrieved; some, such as the desecration of sacred places or the loss of species or language, are tragic.

Erdrich magnifies and comments on Fleur's power by making her the object of talk, not the speaker. Like the woods and the lake, she is seen and projected onto, but we do not have access to her thoughts. In *Tracks* Pauline distrusts and competes with her, while Nanapush loves and protects her. In *The Beet Queen* she appears as an itinerant, and in *The Bingo Palace* she has assumed mythic proportions. In *The Last Report* she is a friend to Damien, and in *Four Souls* we learn about her origins and see her shadow in her pursuit of revenge at the expense of her children. Like *Tracks*, *Four Souls* uses Nanapush to tell one part of Fleur's story and another woman to tell another part. Here, though, the envious and devious Pauline is replaced by Polly Elizabeth, whose own life becomes more robust through her association with Fleur. Joni Adamson argues that the two narrators' readings of Fleur in *Tracks* are a function of their different relationships to tradition and authority: "Like the oral tradition itself, Fleur becomes the object of continual telling and retelling."[27] This is also true in *Four Souls*, where the authority of the Church in Pauline's life is replaced by that of Miss Hammond, the authority on respectability for Polly Elizabeth. Even the repeated sounds of their names suggest some continuity between the two characters.

At the end of *Tracks*, Fleur has lost some of her power because she acted out but did not acknowledge shadow. Nanapush calls her "a different person than the young woman I had known. She was hesitant in speaking, false in her gestures, anxious to cover her fear." As Nanapush says: "Power dies, power goes under and gutters out, ungraspable. . . . I never made the mistake of thinking that I owned my own strength, that was my secret. And so I was never alone in my failures."[28] Erdrich is stuck with history: the land is really lost, too many people have died, too many have sunk under the bottle. If, as a writer, she wants to restore the culture, to repair some of the relationships, she needs to recognize her own limits. As a writer, she tells us here, she cannot count on her own power, cannot presume access to the wild places that make her writing vital.[29]

Erdrich never altogether strips Fleur of her power. In *The Beet Queen* Fleur reappears to heal Karl Adare, who has jumped from a train in despair. She is pulling the cart she took from Matchimanito, peddling "mismatched plates, mended cups, and secondhand forks," and trading lace from the nuns for berries.[30] She pulls her cart along the railroad tracks, which at that time would have been the principal right-of-way across the countryside but which also retained some of its wild creatures, ducks and muskrats, skunks, coons, bitterns, hawks, reeds. Fleur occupies liminal territory; she trades in remnants, inhabits borders, clings to stretches of the land that are least damaged. Later in *The Beet Queen*, she is living with Eli and Russell on the reservation. In *Four Souls* Erdrich deepens her portrait of Fleur, adding to her shadow, pointing out Fleur's arrogance and self-pity, the single-minded pursuit of revenge that causes her to betray Lulu, acting as the negative mother in her identification with the ancestral land. However, Fleur's power allows her to take revenge on John James Mauser, who logged out the forests at Matchimanito, and to return to win back her land from Tatro, the Indian agent. In *The Bingo Palace* Fleur, at the end of her life, retains an awesome power as she passes the Pillager mantle on to Lipsha.

The achronological development of Erdrich's stories also means that power is never gone forever. Characters who are lost at the end of one narrative reappear as younger people in the next, a sleight of hand that emphasizes the indestructibility of nature itself. The theme of resurrection, too, begun with Gordie Kashpaw, replays as the "rebirth" of Fleur's grandmother, Under the Ground; the revival of Agnes after her ordeal in the Red River; and the comic returns of Nanapush at his wake. What seems lost is not truly gone. As Erdrich recasts traditional stories, the ethical burden they bear is to restore a culture that will promote and support a mindful relationship among the human, the natural, and the spiritual. Cultural restoration also reanimates the beliefs that can promote a restoration of the land, providing the structure within which individuals can realign themselves to heal from the dislocations of mind enforced in schools and towns.

PAULINE AND THE POWER OF DENIAL

In the character of Pauline, Erdrich illustrates the toxic power of a denial of nature. As much as she identifies Fleur with the land and with wild nature, Erdrich links Pauline with a brutal, and often comic, notion of the body-hating spirit. Pauline is also a shape-shifter with considerable power. Like Fleur, she is associated with a spiritual symbol, Jesus, whose power she wishes to appropriate. This pairing lets Erdrich play with images, ideas, and points of view. In particular, questions of consciousness and self-consciousness are foregrounded, narrators seeing the same events in very different ways.

One way of understanding consciousness is to view it as an oscillation between seeing from within oneself and seeing oneself from some outside point of view. Seeing from within can lead to a grounded self-knowledge like that of Nanapush, or it can produce the narcissism of a character like Wallace Pfef. Seeing from without can generate empathy, like Marie Kashpaw's, or it can condemn someone, like Sita in *The Beet Queen*, to perpetually trying to measure up.[31]

The most toxic example of a character who sees from outside is Pauline, who "saw through the eyes of the world outside of us" and "wanted to be like [her] grandfather, pure Canadian." Because she sees through outside eyes, she seems to believe the persona she constructs for the nuns. She cannot accept as her own those impulses the Church calls sinful, so she denies them in herself and projects them onto others, mostly Fleur, who becomes her shadow. Because Pauline identifies Misshepeshu with sexuality and death by drowning, her drive to defeat him comes from her ego-based need to control both. Because ambition occupies shadow for Pauline, Fleur's power looks menacing: "Some say she kept the finger of a child in her pocket and a powder of unborn rabbits in a leather thong around her neck. She laid the heart of an owl on her tongue so she could see at night, and went out hunting, not even in her own body."[32] Invested in her fantasies, Pauline projects onto Fleur what she herself practices, as we see her later turn into an owl and go out hunting for souls. When we do actually see Fleur's supply of medicines, they are roots and the leaves of plants. Pauline blunders through the storehouse, unable to distinguish one from the other, likely costing Fleur her infant.

If Fleur is a force of nature, Pauline is a force of death throughout the novels. Working with Bernadette Morrissey, Pauline attends the dying. However, even here her self-perception is flawed. She identifies with the owl and calls herself the "merciful scavenger." In any ecosystem scavengers and detritivores perform an essential function. Life cannot go on unless some force transforms fallen leaves, dead squirrels, corn husks, fish bones, and human remains into humus: *earth* and *human* have a common root. But the owl is not a scavenger. It is a predator. The death of Mary Pepewas may not have been natural. Just as Pauline never quite accepts responsibility for closing the latch on the meat locker and causing Lily's and Tor's deaths, she "understood" that Mary "wanted to be gone." Moreover, Mary's death frees Pauline from her nightmares. As an owl she gains an aerial view, seeing the people below her as "stupid and small" and rationalizing her predation on them. Afterward, Pauline accepts an inflated view of herself as "devious and holy, dangerously meek and mild."[33]

It is never clear how fully conscious Pauline is of her deviousness. Her persona is wholly holy, her denials devious, and her ambition dangerous. Because she denies her sexuality, Pauline also rejects her pregnancy. As it proceeds, she identifies her lover, Napoleon Morrissey, with Satan and tries to abort her fetus. In childbirth she wills the baby to stay within because "if I gave birth . . . I would be an outcast, a thing set aside for God's use, a human who could be touched by no other human." But why would she be an outcast? This is a self-imposed exile, the product of great loss (her parents and siblings died in the epidemic), self-loathing, and shame. Identifying with the Church and the white world has led her to construct a monstrous shadow that denies her very bodily existence. But this shadow is the counterpart to a hideous inflation, an identification with godhead. She wishes herself spirit, but the more she tries to martyr herself, the more her inflation grows. She rejects her child, her body, and nature itself, remaking herself in her conversations over the stove with Christ, who she says turns to her in "His great need."[34] Thereafter, her comic acts of self-scourging exaggerate the inflation of her "vocation," culminating in the hilarious scene in which Nanapush takes the piss out of her.

But the consequences of her inflation are disastrous for others. Because Pauline bumbles and flops, Fleur miscarries. Pauline sets out to combat Misshepeshu, thinking, "it was I who was armored . . . I with the cunning of serpents. . . . I would be His champion, His savior too."[35] From seeing herself from without, she has turned here to imagining herself rescuing Christ. She murders Napoleon Morrissey in a descent into unconsciousness provoked by her inflated identification with the Self. Thereafter, she becomes the monster she would kill, a Roman Catholic in garb only, dedicated throughout the opus to an inflated desire for sainthood.

In *Love Medicine* Pauline, now Leopolda, tortures her daughter, Marie, and later lies dying, utterly unconscious of her own shadow. In her case seeing from outside has resulted in the psychic death of her soul, the denial of her Anishinaabe identity. She too persists in the narratives, the question of her potential sainthood—a result of certain miraculous cures attributed to her—forming the pretext for *The Last Report on the Miracles at Little No Horse*, an investigation carried out by Father Jude Miller from *The Beet Queen*.

In a sense she becomes shadow, losing the psychological individuality of her earlier life in her single-minded pursuit of religious power. "Leopolda," the name she assumes on entering the convent, calls to mind King Leopold of Belgium, who authorized the conquest of Africa in the name of the *mission civilatrice*. As Fools Crow does, Leopolda sees the future, a vision of surveying crews, land divided, and the young "blinded and deafened" by government schools. Unlike Fools Crow, however, she will be the instrument of destruction, bringing souls to Christ, whose only injunction is to "fetch more."[36]

TRICKSTER AND THE GROWTH OF CONSCIOUSNESS

Central to Erdrich's restoration of culture is the figure of the trickster. Erdrich weaves trickster stories into her novels to acknowledge the appetites, the innocence, the foolishness, the cunning, the self-importance, the impulsiveness, the unconsciousness, and the instincts of the human animal. In many ways these are the qualities cast into shadow by the process of socialization. Tricksters represent a cultural acknowledgment of the persistence of shadow energies. By showing us trickster, by laughing at and with trickster, and by embracing trickster, Erdrich encourages the reader to reflect on trickster as a means to increased consciousness.

Erdrich's novels contain many trickster moments, but three characters in particular are identified with trickster: old Nanapush; his namesake, Gerry Nanapush; and Gerry's son, Lipsha Morrissey. In these three we see three stages or manifestations of trickster: as a storyteller and verbal shape-shifter; as a rebel, the spirit of the people that can't be contained in prison; and as a developing consciousness, the comic trickster character embodied in Lipsha.

Just as reclaiming shadow can provide new access to energy, restoring trickster, particularly in his role as storyteller, results in the revitalization of culture. Where trickster lives, the polarities are contained in a creative tension. Trickster expresses the liminal, the capacity to hold in tension tradition and change, sacred land and the bingo palace. Gerald Vizenor emphasizes this multiple quality of the Anishinaabe trickster Nanabozo, who gives his name to the Nanapush family. Vizenor calls Nanabozo

> the compassionate woodland trickster [who] wanders in mythic time and transformational space between tribal experiences and dreams. The trickster is related to plants and animals and trees; he is a teacher and healer in various personalities who, as numerous stories reveal, explains the values of healing plants, wild rice, maple sugar, basswood, and birch bark to woodland tribal people. More than a magnanimous teacher and transformer, the trickster is capable of violence, deceptions, and cruelties: the realities of human imperfections. The woodland trickster is an existential shaman in the comic mode, not an isolated and sentimental tragic hero in conflict with nature.
>
> The trickster is comic in the sense that he does not reclaim idealistic ethics, but survives as a part of the natural world; he represents a spiritual balance in a comic drama rather than the romantic elimination of human contradictions and evil.[37]

The trickster story is found in cultures throughout the world. The Greek Hermes is an image of trickster, as are Hanuman (India and other areas), Loki (Norway), and many others. Karl Kerényi calls trickster *the spirit of disorder, the enemy of boundaries.*[38] The trickster myth speaks to the natural experience of being human, the bodily and psychological realities of being an animal. Thus, we can see trickster as a figure for human "nature," or the instincts and capacities coded into humans at birth. Trickster is sometimes confused with shadow, since in Western culture bodily experience is often denied and repressed. The frequent identification of trickster with an animal, whether coyote, raven, or wolf, suggests the correspondence between human animality and animal wisdom. Like all of nature, trickster contains opposites.[39] Stories of trickster remind people of our common lust, foolishness, ingenuity, treachery, and impulsive kindness. Stories like Erdrich's, then, can be seen as restorative. Recovering trickster, like acknowledging and bringing shadow to consciousness, is part of a restoration of ourselves to a fully human condition, a psychological parallel to using human ingenuity to return land to biodiversity.

In the Winnebago stories trickster begins in a state of almost total unconsciousness. His left arm fights against his right arm. Sometimes he is duped, as when he spots a log across a lake and believes it is a person pointing at him; sometimes he dupes others, as when he persuades ducks to dance for him with their eyes closed so he can wring their necks. He must learn to control the size of both his intestines and his penis. He fashions an elk's liver into a vulva, attaches it to himself, and impersonates a woman, then marries a chief's son and has several children. He converses with foxes, skunks, and nits, among many others.

But occasionally, something happens that suggests a change: trickster becomes self-conscious, or he turns stupidity into good. Paul Radin notes that the character seems to evolve very gradually from "an amorphous, instinctual and unintegrated being into one with the lineaments of man and one foreshadowing man's psychical traits."[40] According to Basil Johnston, "Nanabush had much to learn about the nature, extent, and limitations of his powers. Not only had he to learn what they were, he had to develop them, and foster their growth." Trickster becomes socialized, differentiated: as he becomes conscious of himself, he integrates conscious knowledge of shadow impulses and becomes capable of ethical behavior. Among his powers is the ability to change his shape, to assume the form of a human, a plant or animal, a pebble or gust of wind: "Whatever form or shape he assumed, Nanabush had also to accept and endure the limitations of that form and nature."[41]

This is not to say that as he matures, he loses his trickster qualities, any more than a person can eliminate the shadow, but rather that he gains some conscious control over them. In this way the trickster can be seen to model one aspect of the journey of individuation. Near the end of the cycle, trickster leaves his wandering ways, which are antisocial and inappropriate, and returns to home and family. In entering into relationships with others, trickster begins to develop compassion.

Erdrich demonstrates the slow growth toward maturity in many of her stories. In *Tracks*, for example, after the episode with Sophie, Eli performs a reconciliation with Fleur that demonstrates a process of growth. He has behaved stupidly, and he comes to Nanapush, deflated, defeated, full of longing and remorse. Nanapush teases him, plays with him, but finally takes pity on him and guides him to a moose that he kills so that both the men and Fleur can have food during the severe winter. Nanapush gives Eli something concrete to do that will cure his doldrums and do some good. He also gives him mindfulness, patience, and knowledge of his prey. This hunt is an initiatory process for Eli, one in which he must trust and persist. He was listening to his penis in the episode with Sophie. Now he must listen to Nanapush, who acknowledges this by telling him on his return, "You're my son . . . you're my relative." Nanapush observes in him "a young man who . . . was lost in the spirit, and both disgusted with his betrayal and desperate for Fleur."[42] In his remorse Eli gains both self-knowledge and humility; he has seen his shadow at work, and he knows its presence in his life.

It would be a mistake to overemphasize psychological development in looking at the character of trickster. He is a bundle of contradictions: divine, human, and animal; cunning and stupid; appetitive, reactive, mean-spirited, and kind. If he develops, he also remains the same, and his function is to re-mind us of what we wish to forget, "to add disorder to order and so make a whole, to render possible, within the fixed bounds of what is permitted, an experience of what is not permitted."[43] Toward the end of the story cycle, trickster's behavior becomes more socially beneficent, reflecting a gradual diminution of the shadow energy as it is made available to consciousness. Al-lowed into consciousness, welcomed into social ritual, trickster can transform into a sage, a healer, a source of grounded connection. This is not to say that any of us will ever escape making stupid mistakes. For me it's useful to think of trickster this way: trickster is the enemy of the perfectionist. As a character he models consciousness's direction toward completeness, but as a symbol he retains his paradoxical, instinctual energies. Trickster may transform, but the transformation is never permanent. In this respect the character of Nanapush is probably the most fully developed trickster in literature, and the revenge story he recounts in *Four Souls* is as funny and pigheaded as any trickster folly.

TRICKSTER AS HEALER

Trickster is also sometimes a healer, and trickster and shaman have thus often been identified. Gerald Vizenor defines a shaman as "a person who dissolves time, establishes an ecstatic relationship with the spirit world, and learns to speak the languages of animals, birds, and plants. . . . The cause of most dis-eases is understood to be an imbalance in the individual and the world. Sha-mans . . . seek to balance the forces in the world through ecstatic experiences: music, herbs, dreams and visions, and ceremonial dances."[44] Both shaman and trickster can change shape, speak with other species, and bring balance to the culture. Because he is close to instinctual experience, the trickster is "comfort-able with chaos."[45] This allows him to mediate between nature and culture, chaos and order. As trickster moves toward self-awareness, he moves in the direction of the healer: just as a small dose of poison can be medicinal, appre-hension of the forbidden, awareness of one's own shadow capacities, can help to cure inflation and control pride. As Jung puts it, "the sufferer takes away suffering."[46] This iteration of trickster energy is close to the one Erdrich draws on in creating characters like Nanapush, Gerry, and Lipsha.

In Nanapush trickster energy is so evolved that through his storytelling he becomes a healer. His knowledge of shadow comes both through his own trickster episodes, his outbursts of rage and jealousy and lust, and through the suffering he has seen and endured. In the stories Gerald Vizenor relates, Nanabozo sought to avenge his mother's abduction, just as Nanapush plots to avenge Margaret's humiliation by Clarence Morrissey and Boy Lazarre. Nanabozo must confront an evil gambler in order to find his mother, outwitting him and "stopp[ing] evil for a moment in a game."[47] This too has resonance in Erdrich's work, where gambling has a significant role, and where the best one can do, sometimes, is stop evil for a moment in a game.

Is this enough? In their psychotherapeutic work Eduardo Duran and Bonnie Duran report that general cultural amnesia about the genocide of Native Americans is "one of the stumbling blocks to the healing process of Native American people."[48] Unacknowledged, suffering descends into shadow; becomes a source of shame; and generates depression, despair, and alienation. In trickster the pain of humiliation is given form and consciousness. Telling the old stories, telling the history, exposes the suffering and brings pain back to mind, where it can be felt and honored. Telling also uncovers lies and, in doing so, perhaps stops evil for a moment. While Gerry Nanapush is not as fully developed as Nanapush and Lipsha, he seems to stand for a spirit of opposition and resistance that can be imprisoned but not held, bent but not broken. In Lipsha Erdrich suggests something more like the developmental process by which trickster becomes the healer.

NANAPUSH'S TRICKSTER NARRATIVE

Nanapush's narrative provides the antidote to Pauline, who calls him "the smooth-tongued artificer." This echo of Joyce suggests the labyrinth of stories into which Erdrich is leading us. In Nanapush, the self-identified trickster, Erdrich creates a narrator who can demonstrate the alternative to Pauline's self-hatred. Nanapush speaks, he says, "both languages in streams that ran alongside each other, over every rock, around every obstacle. The sound of my own voice convinced me I was alive." His fluency derives from the streams and rocks themselves, as well as from his willingness to use both tongues. Stories, he tells us, are "all attached, and once I start there is no end to telling because they're hooked from one side to the other, mouth to tail." Like Erdrich's novels, his stories remember, connect, and embody, one leading to another, as the complex elements of an ecosystem exist in interdependency. But the stories aren't just entertaining or instructive; they're also healing and propitiatory: "During the year of sickness, when I was the last one left, I saved myself by starting a story. One night I was ready to bring to the other side the doll I now gave Eli. My wife had sewed it together after our daughter died and I held it in my hands when I fainted, lost breath, so that I could hardly keep moving my lips. But I did continue and recovered. I got well by talking. Death could not get a word in edgewise, grew discouraged, and traveled on." Nanapush's voice, the living breath, appears as the opposite of the sterile spirit Pauline peddles. Talking gets him through sickness, and later in the novel he sings, "calling on my helpers, until the words came from my mouth but were not mine, until the rattle started, the song sang itself." Later still he sings "cure songs" all night to the frostbitten Lulu, keeping her from stumbling into death.[49] He heals her then by talking, hoping this long talking to Lulu in *Tracks* will inspire her to visit her mother and restore their relations.

In bringing memory to consciousness, Nanapush makes it possible to absorb the grief that would otherwise be lodged in shadow. He models the capacity to accept shadow by acknowledging and laughing at his own rage, lust, and despair. In Erdrich's restoration the absence of a heroic point of view and the centrality of community suggest that familiarity and time can foster the withdrawal of projections, as we see with Lipsha and Lyman, with Marie and Lulu, with Nector and Eli, and with Polly Elizabeth. Equally important, a living culture provides images in story and tradition that recognize shadow and celebrate the fullness of human experience.

Power plays on people's blind spots, and trickster is often the butt of the joke. Because Eli, Margaret, Nanapush, and Fleur herself did not take seriously enough the threat posed by development and government intrusion, they lost the Pillager land. They were willing to ignore the power of the Other, and this made them less than conscious about protecting themselves. Nanapush recoils in disgust from Clarence Morrissey, seeing the "depth of their [the Morrisseys' and Lazarres'] greed." Had he been more mindful, he might have saved the land, but he could not imagine thinking like a Lazarre. It's left to Nector to ask "the questions a small adult might ask, not a boy of nine. He wanted to know how land was parceled out, what sorts of fees were required. ... Nector took the worry inside himself."[50] Nector saves his mother's land because he is willing to take responsibility by acting in ways that carry shadow in his family. It's ironic, then, that in *Four Souls* Margaret falls prey to a new shadow affliction: greed. She trades half the land for a linoleum floor, and Nanapush's prompt desecration of her consumer shrine seems like a natural consequence of her lust for acquisition.

The double perspectives of *Tracks* and *Four Souls* bring to the forefront the question of story. Clearly, story has power, but as in *Ceremony*, this power can be used for ill as well as good. Nanapush tells stories that restore connection. His songs guide and heal. Pauline tells stories that infect and deny connection. In juxtaposing Pauline's narrative with Nanapush's, Erdrich contrasts two ways of constructing knowledge. Pauline embraces the hierarchical, patriarchal, scriptural method of the Church, while Nanapush's stories celebrate what Paula Gunn Allen calls "gynocracy," along with myth and the sacred sense of place central to traditional life. Obliterating language and stories was an important component of the U.S. government's strategy for deracinating tribal life and imbuing native people with capitalist and Christian values. Erdrich uses Pauline to expose the destructive consequences of this enterprise for her people.[51] However, Pauline's is not the only voice of Christianity in Erdrich's work. In *The Last Report on the Miracles of Little No Horse*, Erdrich makes sure that her saga includes multiple ways of understanding religion, as well as history. In this way readers are cautioned against simplifying and projecting shadow. An ethical consciousness, Erdrich implies, is careful, self-critical, and specific.

THE GROWTH OF CONSCIOUSNESS: LIPSHA AS TRICKSTER

If Nanapush is trickster in his verbal metamorphoses, and Gerry is trickster as a spirit of political resilience, Lipsha gives us trickster as adolescent energy, particularly adolescent male energy. The experience of appetites is often confusing, making young people feel foolish and self-conscious. The adult world seems to have its appetites under control, but Erdrich's stories expose the extent to which this appearance is a mask. Since stories with an active trickster provide an image for the reader's or hearer's experiences, they can reassure him or her that impulses are normal and that mastery of them is often an illusion. Gerald Vizenor calls trickster a "comic healer and liberator in literature; the *whole figuration* that ties the unconscious to social experience."[52] In Lipsha and Lyman Erdrich illustrates how the young person in the throes of appetite both admires and scorns the adult, who seems imperturbable. At the same time trickster stories offer object lessons in the desirability of mastering appetites through cultural and religious means, trickster's transformations mirroring the plasticity of psyche. The maturation of trickster, from Lipsha to Gerry to Nanapush, suggests the creativity of instinct when it is embraced in consciousness.

Lipsha is an adolescent amalgam of Fleur's healing touch and trickster's possession by his penis.[53] The description of him offered by the anonymous "we" of the first chapter of *The Bingo Palace* explicitly links him with the trickster stories: "Spirits pulled his fingers when he was a baby, yet he doesn't appreciate his powers. His touch was strong but he shorted it out. Going back and forth to the city weakened and confused him and now he flails in a circle with his own tail in his teeth. He shoots across the road like a coyote, dodging between the wheels, and then you see him on the playground, swinging in a swing, and again he has made himself stupid with his dope pipe."[54] Like trickster, Lipsha does not settle down; he sabotages himself, behaves childishly, even stupidly, but he has the touch. For most of *The Bingo Palace*, he is led around by lust. He plays tricks on others, and they come back to bite him; he loses focus and almost wrecks things. His anima possession makes him persistent and annoying and prevents him from really seeing Shawnee Ray, at least until she blows up at both Lipsha and Lyman. But his willingness to submit to love seems preferable to Zelda's rejection of Xavier Toose, which leaves her inflated, manipulative, and dry. Moreover, as the story develops, so, gradually, does Lipsha's consciousness, giving him greater control over the instinctual energy that makes him powerful.

As a trickster character Lipsha repeatedly encounters his shadow. A border guard finds one seed of marijuana in Lipsha's car and, while he has Lipsha and Shawnee Ray in custody, casually drags the eagle feather from Nector's pipe on the floor. Afterward, Lipsha reflects: "The wrongness, the brush of heaven to the ground in dust, is part of our human nature. Especially mine, it appears."[55] Lipsha's humility lets him acknowledge shadow, "the brush of heaven to the ground in dust." We see the alternative to this later on, in Lyman's gambling, when the pipe is not simply desecrated but hocked. While addicts deny shadow, consciousness requires that one confront it over and over again. There is no cure, only growing awareness and control. In Lipsha's case the process entails a reconciliation of his adolescent male energy with the female energies represented in his great-grandmother Fleur, his mother, and his lover.

Fleur offers Lipsha a traditional female model for his power, his healing touch. He is afraid of Fleur, but so is everyone else. She lives alone at Matchimanito, an old, old woman. Not surprisingly, what drives him to overcome his fear is his desire for a love medicine, so he carries her groceries up to Matchimanito, where Lyman wants to build his bingo palace. As they walk, Lipsha enters a different sort of space. He thinks "the woods go all silent as she passes, the birds choke on their own songs . . . roads and gravel turnoffs . . . get us closer to earth, narrow, sift to dirt. . . . I knew the reservation inside out, I thought, but it turns out I knew it by car, not foot. Now it feels like we're lost, off the radar." He has left ordinary reality and entered something closer to "a spirit place." He has entered a different psychological space as well, becoming weak and dizzy as he examines the powerful objects in Fleur's home. Erdrich obscures the encounter: Fleur serves Lipsha tea and food, and he zones in and out of ordinary consciousness, but once he has asked for the love medicine, Fleur "broadens, blurs beyond my reach, beyond belief. Her face spreads out on the bones and goes on darkening and darkening. Her nose tilts up into a black snout and her eyes sink. I struggle to move from my place, but my legs are numb, my arms, my face, and then the lamp goes out. Blackness. I sit there motionless and my head fills with the hot rasp of her voice."[56] His request allows Lipsha to see Fleur in her bear form, which here as elsewhere is an image of her power. Whatever Fleur offers Lipsha here, she offers directly into his unconscious; either that, or it can't be represented in ordinary language.

Erdrich follows this chapter with a flashback to Fleur's return to the reservation, narrated, like a few other episodes, by a nameless chorus of residents full of belief in Fleur's power. This story turns on Fleur's gambling with Tatro, the Indian agent who then owned the Pillager land, and the trick she plays to distract him. In one assessment "Fleur had studied the situation and kept track of time, calculated justice, assessed possibilities."[57] Her gambling has little to do with luck, but this story, midway through the novel and without obvious connection to the main narrative, has a mythic feel: the car, the boy, the card game in which she wins back her land and exacts retribution—all confirm her power as the spirit of the land and of the people. Energy gathers around Fleur, and her power manifests in the ways she inhabits people's consciousness. For Lipsha she becomes a source and a model for the uses of power.

As June's son, Lipsha carries her pain, the pain of his own abandonment, the consciousness of her loss. This is a piece of himself that Lipsha has to reclaim. Throughout *The Bingo Palace* the reader senses that June's absence is a determining void for Lipsha. Yet loss and strength are intertwined: June brings Lipsha luck. After his apparently disappointing vision quest, he travels back in time to the moment when June tried to drown him: "I lie there on the bottom of the slough all the rest of the night and the next day too, crying. It is like my whole body has been filling all of these years with a secret aquifer, a sorrow. I remember the sensation I spent my whole life trying to forget. The quick tug, the stones that tumbled, the deep of dark. I hear my mother's voice, feel her touch, and by that I know the truth. I know that she did the same that was done to her—a young girl left out to live on the woods and survive on pine sap and leaves and buried roots."[58] As he embraces the shadow and allows the anguish of his infant betrayal into consciousness, Lipsha learns compassion. He reflects that those who have learned pain will cause pain.

As he sinks into this feeling, he enters into relationship with the unconscious, just as the narrator of *Surfacing* and Ruthie do. In his descent he remembers being saved by Misshepeshu: "Darkened and drenched, coming toward me from the other side of drowning—it presses its mouth on mine and holds me with its fins and horns and rocks me with its long and shining plant arms. Its face is lion-jawed, a thing of beach foam resembling the jack of clubs. Its face has the shock of the unburied goodness, the saving tones. Its face is the cloud fate that will some day surround me when I am ready to die. What it is I don't know, I can't tell. I never will. But I do know I am rocked and saved and cradled." Lipsha has what is clearly a religious experience of a force—located under water, in the unconscious, but also in his culture—that has *already* saved his life. From this point on he understands that the future "is so ordinary and so demanding all at once that at first I can't understand it."[59] This move is characteristic of Erdrich's work: whenever transcendence threatens, or characters have a peak experience, she insists on the ongoing force of ordinary reality. Transcendence isn't the point; transformation is.

Erdrich links Lipsha's insight with a reminder of the message of the skunk that visited him on his vision quest, telling him, of the land, "*This ain't real estate.*"[60] In *The Blue Jay's Dance*, Erdrich describes her experience as a teenager sleeping alone on a football field in early spring. A skunk wanders up and snuggles next to her. Both sleep; both dream: "Perhaps that night the skunk and I dreamed each other's thoughts or are still dreaming them." In the rest of this essay, Erdrich muses on a stretch of private hunting land in New Hampshire, where a patch of wilderness has been managed for the pleasure of rich hunters. On the one hand, this is a pen where animals are kept as "game" for hunters; on the other hand, "it is the source of flocks of evening grosbeaks and pine siskins, of wild turkey, ravens, pileated woodpeckers, and grouse, vireo, of Eastern coyote, oxygen-rich air, foxes, goldfinches, skunks, and bears that tunnel in and out." Erdrich concludes with a meditation on the skunk: "If I were an animal, I'd choose to be a skunk: live fearlessly, eat anything, gestate my young in just two months, and fall into a state of dreaming torpor when the cold bit hard. Wherever I went, I'd leave my sloppy tracks."[61]

The skunk carries a kind of wildness—a stinky kind—that thumbs its nose at the commodification of the rich. He is a homely totem, but he keeps Lipsha grounded, and what follows is a negative vision of the new casino, obscene in its details of "bulldozers scraping off wild growth from the land like a skin, raising mounds of dirt and twisted roots." Lipsha sees blackjack tables on Pillager graves. As if he is trying to return the skunk to shadow, he argues that the casino will serve his personal greed, but the reality to which he awakens is, as he predicted, ordinary, political, and complicated rather than split: "It's not completely one way or another, traditional against the bingo. You have to stay alive to keep your tradition alive and working." Yet Lipsha is also convinced that the bingo life is the "wrong direction . . . luck fades when sold."[62]

TRICKSTER, ANIMA, AND LOVE

In order to come into his power, Lipsha also has to deal with his anima possession in relation to Shawnee Ray. He carries around her picture, taken from a newspaper: "I hold the newsprint so often to my lips that the ink smears onto me, indelible, fading to silver her graven image." This combination of sex obsession and idolatry is comic. Like trickster, Lipsha appears to carry his penis around with him in a bag. Shawnee Ray asks him to try on a vest she's sewing for Lyman, and he starts to take off his jeans. He thinks, "I know I'm making a fool of myself, that this is dangerous, stupid, but I speak softly to her now as I work the tight buttons of my shirt apart one by one." Lipsha doesn't have any notion of Shawnee Ray as a person with her own perceptions. Erdrich writes that she "folds her arms and then gives herself a shake, unclenches her hands, and turns to her sewing machine . . . slams her hands down on the table of her sewing machine," and so on, but Lipsha doesn't respond to either her words or her body language in his desperation to make love to her.[63]

Erdrich's treatment of Lipsha's passion is also compassionate. He's not an object of contempt, and like Shawnee, the reader succumbs to his charms in the end. To Lipsha's instinctuality Shawnee Ray offers consciousness and ambition. Each needs something of the other. Without Lipsha Shawnee Ray could become as cold and controlling as her aunt Zelda, and Lipsha needs to move past idolatry and pure instinct if he wants a real woman in his life.

After he visits Fleur, Lipsha has an insight that's crucial for the development of his consciousness: he remembers Fleur's saying, *"Admit your love . . . take it in, although it tears you up."* To "admit" love is not to surrender to it, but to join consciousness with the irresistible impulse. When Lipsha does this, he realizes that "part of my emotion for her is all mixed up with the love that she has for her little boy." Shortly afterward he understands that "Lyman sees himself as Redford's father and I see myself as Redford's competition." The motherless Lipsha, tossed in the lake in a sack by June Morrissey, needs to withdraw the projected mother image from Shawnee Ray before he can see the woman herself and develop a mature consciousness. This process begins on the way to the sweat lodge, when, in an urgency of desire, Lipsha asks Shawnee to marry him. She's shocked and angry, and Lipsha sees a different Shawnee, "not my sweet Shawnee, not my tender airbrush picture. Suddenly she shows the undertone, the strokes of which she is created. Her hair flows like snakes, shaking down, and in her cornered anger she is jiggling Redford so fast that his cheeks bounce."[64] This shadow Shawnee has to percolate awhile in Lipsha.

Several times Erdrich links Lipsha's idea of love with plant images. Of Shawnee Ray's anger Lipsha says:

> For my love is larger than it was before she blasted it with fire. It was a single plant, a lovely pine, but now seeds, released from their cones at high temperatures, are floating everyplace and taking root on every scraped bare piece of ground. My love before she got so mad was all about what was best for Lipsha Morrissey. Since those endless moments of truth and rage in Zelda's yard, I have reconsidered. If my love is worth anything, it will be larger than myself. Which is not to say I don't dream about motels, her body moving, and read sex books and thrillers and my Gideon's for more inspiration.[65]

The fire imagery here is interesting, especially coming as it does on the heels of Lipsha's memory of not drowning. Fire, as Lipsha knows, permits the germination of some seeds and protects herbaceous plants and even trees from being shaded out by competitors. Fear of fire has led to its suppression, causing U.S. forests to degrade and leaving them prone to terrifying blazes that take lives. Human culture has largely coevolved with fire. Stephen Pyne, a historian of fire, claims: "Remove fire from a society, even today, and both its technology and its social order will lie in ruins. Strip fire away from language, and you reduce many of its vital metaphors to ash."[66]

Likewise, people need anger. Imprisoned in shadow, anger loses its power and transforms into self-pity or depression. Like fire, anger can burn away the underbrush of lies and release the germ of new growth. But anger needs to be restrained by consciousness, or it will burn out of control. If, at the end of *The Bingo Palace*, some hope is hinted at in Gerry's escape and Lipsha's fierce protection of the infant, this new hope has been generated at least in part by Lipsha's encounter with Shawnee Ray. Her fiery outburst has led him to withdraw from her some of his anima projection, which in turn has allowed him to reconsider his own infant experiences and reaffirm his ability to love. While Erdrich makes clear that Lyman's energy is also necessary to the community, Lipsha's values are much more communal than Lyman's, and it's for Lipsha that Fleur is willing to trade her life.

Passion without consciousness is dangerous, but it is also the human lot. Reason without passion has its own hazards. Near the end of *The Bingo Palace*, Zelda has a minor heart attack. In its wake she understands how she has tried all her life to hold love at bay, to control passion so that she won't be subject to its burning rages. Never, like her father, Nector, would she set her lover's house ablaze: "She could do it because she willed it. She could live in the shell of her quilt as the cold night lengthened, and she could let a man's fires flash and burn, flash and burn, until they disappeared." As the Pillagers gravitate to water, the Kashpaws live by fire. When Zelda wakes, she thinks of her father's pipe, which early in the novel is desecrated by the border guards: "She didn't need to see it, to hold it, but she pictured it there on her counter. Earth and heaven, connecting, the fire between that burned in everything alive. . . . A holy fire exists in all we touch, she thought, even in the flames that fed my father's heart. Framed and finished in the anguish, she felt her own face take on his depth."[67] She lets go of an image of self-sufficiency that she has used to distance herself from her own nature and goes to Xavier Toose. Somehow, her thaw unfreezes Shawnee Ray as well, and as the novel ends, she is at the university, beading a shirt for Lipsha and dreaming of his kiss.

THE ANDROGYNOUS TRICKSTER: AGNES/FATHER DAMIEN

The Last Report on the Miracles at Little No Horse offers the character of Agnes/Father Damien as a religious counterbalance to Pauline/Leopolda. But Agnes also serves as a Catholic version of Nanapush, her teacher, whom she more and more resembles: shape-shifting, verbal, and subject to foible. The qualities Erdrich develops in Agnes represent a "feminine" take on both Catholicism and trickster; she becomes Erdrich's "agnes dei" in her compassion, mercy and forgiveness, receptiveness, and humility. Erdrich makes clear that these womanly qualities must be clothed in the "masculine" priest's garb for the character to be effective within the institution of the Church. At first this is a persona issue for Agnes, who issues herself the splendid list of "Rules to Assist in My Transformation," including "Make requests in the form of orders" and "Give compliments in the form of concessions."[68] But she becomes more and more absorbed in her new identity, bringing her female compassion to the role and absorbing a degree of authority from it, until at the end she is utterly androgynous.

Agnes's story is also a study of individuation. Agnes embarks on the role of Father Damien as the result of a flood of mythic proportions, which she understands as a kind of death and rebirth.[69] In the flood she briefly loses her memory, and the miraculous appearance of Jesus confirms in her a sense of mission. The priest's garb affords her some protection, and she comes to adopt it as persona. This experience is a kind of vision quest for Agnes, a wilderness sojourn like those of the young characters in *Surfacing* and *Housekeeping*. It initiates her into a new identity. But just as she brings androgyny to her ministry, she also absorbs, gradually, an Anishinaabe way of knowing and revering the land, and she incorporates more and more Anishinaabe religion into her theology.

In Agnes's passion for Gregory Wekkle, Erdrich introduces consciousness into the experience of eros. Agnes, as Father Damien, does not scorn the desires of her flesh, but she has chosen a path that asks something else of her. After Gregory leaves, Agnes suffers greatly. His absence exposes her to a thorough immersion in shadow: "Not quite of the body, yet not entirely of the soul, pain closed like a trap on Agnes and held her tight. Some nights it was a magnetic vest drawing blood to swell tightly just under her skin. Agnes wanted to burst from the cassock in a bloody shower! Other nights a shirt of razors slit and raked her and left no mark. Her womanness crouched dark within her—clawed, rebellious, sharp of tooth." Here, shadow is not unconscious; Agnes has chosen the priesthood consciously. Her renunciation of her womanly flesh agonizes her. She attempts to poison herself and travels in her sleep "deep into the country of uncanny truth," from which she is rescued by the devoted Mary Kashpaw.[70] In a section entitled "The Sacrament," Nanapush prepares a sweat lodge for Father Damien, which returns her from despair. She moves from the sexual into a different kind of embodied love.

After this encounter with shadow, Agnes moves gradually toward individuation. She resumes playing the piano, builds her church on a rock, charms snakes, commissions a statue, and learns from Nanapush how to beat the devil. Day by day she becomes native to the place. Erdrich presents Agnes as an instance of an utterly successful blending—or crossbreeding—of the two cultures that make up Erdrich herself. The novel ends with one of the most moving scenes in all Erdrich's work, as Agnes chooses her death and Mary Kashpaw preserves her dignity. Of all Erdrich's novels this is both the one that most suggests the potential for absorbing traditional ways into the dominant culture and the most fully developed narrative of individuation.

CONSCIOUSNESS AND LOVE

In Erdrich's work the movement away from the ego focus on narcissism, greed, or pride is a softening to love, a vulnerability that touches virtually every character. Love medicines, in various guises, offer the semblance of a quick fix, but the love that heals individuals and binds communities is deliberate, sometimes difficult, requiring work and sacrifice. This love links humans with nature, the unwilled, appetitive, generative power of life, and provides the immediate experience on which a land ethic can be based. Love can be denied, controlled, or suppressed; it can be as temporary as the wind or Karl Adare, or as addled as Lipsha's blind addiction to Shawnee Ray. Love can be as serial as Lulu, with her fertility and her power to bewitch a parade of lovers, or as old as Nanapush and Margaret. It can be the passion of Fleur and Eli, or the harmony that unites Lulu's boys in "the simple, unquestioning belonging-ness of part of one organism."[71] Love can be as faithful as Marie is to Nector or as Dot is to Gerry Nanapush through all his years in jail. It can be the great maternal hunger that drives Marie Kashpaw. Love can be the reconciliation of Marie and Lulu after Nector's death, their partnership in tribal life, their management of Lyman. It can be Agnes's passion for Gregory Wekkle or Mary Kashpaw's devotion to Father Damien. Love can be Margaret's ministering at Fleur's and Marie's childbeds or June's miraculous gift of the lucky bingo cards to Lipsha.

Love, finally, is a force of nature. Erdrich uses the image of the dandelion a couple of times to represent both love and power, the touch that is itself compassion. Both of these passages are attributed to Lipsha, one in *Love Medicine* and one in *The Bingo Palace*. In the first he is digging dandelions, a favorite pastime of his uncle Nector, who has just died because Lipsha faked the love medicine. But Lipsha has confessed to Marie, and he's feeling humbled but at peace: "With every root I prized up there was return, as if I was kin to its secret lesson. The touch got stronger as I worked through the grassy afternoon. Uncurling from me like a seed out of the blackness where I was lost, the touch spread. The spiked leaves full of bitter mother's milk. A buried root. A nuisance people dig up and throw in the sun to wither. A globe of frail seeds that's indestructible."[72] Lipsha sees himself in the dandelion, both a weed and a prize. The deep taproot of the dandelion makes it difficult to remove, a trophy when it's dug up intact, the ambiguity of the metaphor suiting the complexion of the insight. Lipsha connects the healing touch with the feelings that touch him—Marie's love and compassion for him, her passion for Nector, his grief at Nector's death—and he connects these with the pleasure of digging in the earth. The seed of this feeling falls in his lost blackness. Whether we call this blackness shadow or hurt or the unconscious, it forms a rich soil that nourishes the buried root, the bitter leaves. Love and compassion can be a nuisance, but they are also indestructible.

In *The Bingo Palace* Lipsha says: "Love is a weed, a dandelion that you poison from your heart. The taproots wait. The seeds blow off, ticklish, into a part of the yard you didn't spray. And one day, though you worked, though you prodded out each spiky leaf, you lift your eyes and dozens of fat golden faces bob in the grass."[73] Here, although Lipsha doesn't identify as explicitly with the dandelion, he is still clearly glad for its survivance. Whereas the former passage, its language evoking "the blackness where I was lost" and "leaves full of bitter mother's milk," suggests a force that is scarier and more powerful, more primitive, this passage rejoices in the hardiness of love. The ordinary, everyday image of the dandelion here carries a lighter weight. The seeds are "ticklish" and take root not in inner blackness, but only in "a part of the yard you didn't spray," sidestepping the vigilance of rational control we all exercise in order to function in the world.

I will close this study with the image of the dandelion, of its trickster survivance. Lipsha says, "Love is a weed that you poison from your heart," but you don't control its seeds, and it germinates and grows again. The image of the weed that persists suggests the comic point of view: American colonialism may have tried to weed out the Anishinaabe, or turn them into daylilies and hostas, but effort has failed. Erdrich suggests that Lipsha himself feels a bit like a weed, but in restoring vitality to the culture, the land, and the psyche, she generates a rich diversity that ensures that there is room for everyone. Love for a person, or a place, or a people, may feel some days like a burden, the pain of caring more than can be endured. But love is what gives us all life—the connections, the underground associations, taproots, mycorrhizae, worms, and bacteria. It is the soil of life.

In an interview Katie Bacon asked Erdrich, "If one thing could be said to tie your work together, would it be the myriad forms of love?" Erdrich replied, "I wouldn't mind that being said, although one could also point out that the work is also tied together by the unity of place, or by the failure of love to solve people's lives, or by the desperate wish to be back in our parents' arms, or to be home, or by the dreadful and persistent longing to know why we are on earth."[74] Love and the failure of love, place, home, and purpose are themes woven throughout this study. Aldo Leopold argued that we must come to know and love the land before we will extend the ethical circle to include it. Caring, loving, empathizing with other humans, other creatures, with the land, is a burden. But it is the beginning.

Afterword

The world is our consciousness, and it surrounds us. There are
more things in mind, in the imagination, than "you" can keep track
of—thoughts, memories, images, angers, delights, rise unbidden. The
depths of mind, the unconscious, are our inner wilderness areas.
—Gary Snyder, *The Practice of the Wild*

I HAVE BEEN ARGUING that a consumer culture that regards the land as
dead also deadens people to their feelings, intuitions, imaginations, and
dreams. I have also put forward the notion that connecting with the land
stimulates people to explore their own subjective wildness and that the energy
thus released fosters growth toward wholeness. That process entails encounters with shadow that are frightening and shameful. Sustaining it, therefore,
requires courage, support, and containment, or a feeling of safety. Through
the difficult engagement with shadow, people gain access to feelings, intuitions, and new potential. The capacities to give and receive love grow. The
ethical sense deepens.

In writing of the land ethic, Aldo Leopold said, "We can be ethical only
in relation to something we can see, feel, understand, love, or otherwise have
faith in."[1] Leopold addresses a serious problem in extending the ethical circle
to include the land: Why should one behave well in relation to the land?
What will motivate moral action toward dammed rivers and lost habitat?

One of the prevalent discussions in ethics today has to do with the ad-
equacy of the Western model, which is based on the ideal of justice. Western
ethical theory has not dealt much with love or compassion as the basis for
moral action. Rather, Western philosophers have assumed that human life
involves competition and conflict between equally able independent persons
who are motivated first by self-interest. Thomas Hobbes's argument that the

state of nature is a state of war provides the pithiest rendition of this premise. In this context reason provides the means by which people can be persuaded to constrain their instincts in the interest of self-preservation. Reason alone persuades men to obey laws and treat others honorably, because the alternatives are anarchy or tyranny. This tradition has promoted important ideas, such as that of universal human rights, which have offered crucial protections to the powerless in unjust political systems. But the assumptions on which philosophers have based "universal" moral codes have been Western, not universal.

Today, led by feminist ethicists such as Carol Gilligan, Nel Noddings, Sara Ruddick, Virginia Held, and others, a theory of ethics that is based more in the feeling function is gaining influence. Posed as an ethics of care, or a maternal ethics, this approach addresses itself to transactions between people with unequal power, such as adult and child, doctor and patient, moneyed and poor. It argues that humans do not live in isolation or exclusively in relations of conflict and competition. Humans exist in relationships, and ethics must consider these networks of relatedness, many of which are characterized by caring. Indeed, it is relationship itself that motivates moral action: we are "good" because we care, and we damage ourselves by being "bad." In this model caring motivates ethical behavior, not fear.

Critics of this ethics argue that caring is an adequate motive only in close relationships. People may be motivated to care for those like themselves, but what of Others? What of those whose needs you do not even suspect? Only reason can persuade people to restrain themselves in relation to the distant, the dissimilar, the Other. To this objection advocates respond that what is needed are not rules, but knowledge. When people know others, compassion grows. For this reason they promote the use of narrative as a means to gain empathetic knowledge and as the language of the ethics of care.

This overly simple sketch of the dialogue between justice and mercy feeds into a discussion of the land ethic in a number of ways. The ethics of care is emerging with the entrance of women's voices into the academic debates. Who speaks for the land? The emerging fields of environmental ethics, ecopsychology, and ecocriticism are just beginning to develop theory that can challenge anthropocentrism in ethics. At the same time the flowering of work by writers from suppressed cultures, such as the American Indian and the African, feeds the new ethics with images of assumptions about humans and the human place in nature that are radically different from those of the West.

These narratives in turn enrich the knowledge of readers, thereby moving them to expand their compassion.

Western rationalism has entailed a kind of dismembering, distancing mind from body, but its socializing process has consolidated ego-consciousness and allowed a degree of control over such aspects of instinctual nature as the lust for revenge. Rationalism is the process of the first part of life, or the cultural Enlightenment, when we acquire literacy, learn to use scientific instruments to extend our senses, and develop mathematic and scientific methods to represent organic nature in abstractions and quantities. Now, however, we have reached a point at which this adaptation appears more and more inadequate. On a global level we are suffering a midlife crisis. Technology has solved many problems, but it has addicted us to uses of energy that are depleting our habitat and precipitating devastating wars. Religious hostilities reflect a profound state of splitting and projection. Ecologically, as well as ethically, we need to reintegrate the traditional, the amputated natural, into our culture. We need to acknowledge the shadow of our own greed and carelessness and to practice restraint. Moreover, we need to integrate what has been relegated to the "feminine" and the "maternal." As we have seen, the anima and the mother archetype contain relational and emotional energy that are available to consciousness when they are recognized as part of the self and not projected onto others. I have written a good deal in this analysis about other ways of knowing besides the rational. Probably the most powerful of these is an emotional way of knowing, which opens individuals to make decisions based on compassion as well as utility.

In the novels I have examined, the process of individuation provides a model on a personal level for the development of a land ethic. A breakdown, crisis, or loss initiates the process, and transformation begins in an encounter with shadow. For the process to proceed, the experience of shadow needs to be framed and contained, given images, honored, and accepted in community. In this light fictions and other cultural forms that imagine transformation and individuation offer nourishment to the person struggling with his or her own shadow.

Can stories help heal the rift between humans and the natural world? Can fictions really be, as James Hillman calls them, "healing"? Novels can perform several crucial functions in this regard. They can act as guardians of memory, preserving painful experiences that would otherwise fall into shadow. They can enact a politics of remembering, exposing shadow to light. They can compete with the stories that dominate the culture. They can expose a reader to lifeways that are unfamiliar, expanding the circle of compassion and imagining practices that promote mindfulness. They can provide compressed representations of processes that in life take years, offering readers an image for what in real time may feel amorphous and only confusing. In their complex narratives novels enact what the ethicist Margaret Urban Walker calls an "alternative epistemology for a feminist ethics." Walker argues that an ethics of relationship requires an epistemology that is embedded in narrative history: moral decisions need to be made on the basis of knowledge of individuals that is specific and contextualized. These decisions "require of us very acute attention to the minute and specific, to history and incident, in grasping cases in a morally adequate way."[2] The old universals and abstract actors do not satisfy the need for a morality that attends to particular circumstances and relationships. An attentive reading of complex novels can expand the moral vocabulary of readers.

Art that captures the imagination offers symbols that, while they come from the unconscious of the artist, speak to the unconscious of the age. When the ego receives and interprets a symbol, the knowledge that results is emotionally charged. This leads into one of the key areas of a Jungian aesthetic: when art generates a symbol that resonates with the individual, the knowledge that results from the encounter, mediated by the ego but evoking the unconscious, can produce a kind of practical personal change. Part of the power and delight of literary fiction comes from its being enjoyed in tranquility, allowing the mind to wander, stimulated by the symbols offered by the narrative. Reading, then, provokes active imagination, and a reader can return from a fantasy and identify the mood and trigger that propelled the fantasy. An engaged reader of fiction creates living symbols from the text, allowing it to stimulate his or her own imagination, emotions, and intellect, so that a novel changes the reader, and the reader's interpretation changes the culture in which the text continues to be read. The reader must be both receptive (initially) and critical (in response to the emotion generated by the symbol). When significant numbers of people respond to the symbols presented in novels, these stories can begin to reframe a culture's self-awareness. Annis Pratt argues that "the novel performs the same role in women's lives as do the Eleusinian, dying-god, and witchcraft rituals—a restoration through remembering, crucial to our survival.... The restorative power of women's fiction consists in a dialectical relationship between novel and audience" because "the synthesis . . . does not occur within the individual novel, or even in the field as a whole, but in the mind of the reader, who, having participated in the narrative reenactment, must put its message into effect in her own life."[3] The relationship between reader and novel, then, has a trickster quality: it is both contained and unpredictable. Because the trickster is present in the relationship, no one will ever have the last word.

Communities and activities that allow individuals to enter into relationship with the natural world also can nourish transformation by endorsing the value of nonrational nature. Organizations like Outward Bound incorporate solo expeditions in wilderness as part of the experience they offer—often to adolescents, for whom they work as a rite of passage. In wild places, where human industry has not imposed its version of order, one can have glimpses of the numinous. This apprehension of a force that transcends will—the awe one feels beside the ocean, beneath the cathedral canopy of a great forest, or at the peak of a mountain—stimulates new ways of understanding oneself and the world. The numinous, as Rudolph Otto understood it, comprehends both the terrifying and the alluring, and nature's destructive power may equally be a source of experiencing the numinous. For Jung the Self is numinous, and it manifests in consciousness through symbols. Such experiences are unbidden, but they may be sought, in nature and in certain ritual practices such as dancing, fasting, chanting, and sweating. Once touched by the numinous, people reorient themselves in relation to the universe. When Jung described the numinous as the real therapy, he suggested the transformative power of the experience of the Other.

Wilderness is the traditional site for encountering the numinous, but a wilderness experience is by its nature temporary. Most people cannot afford to move "back to the land," nor do most people in the United States have cultures waiting to embrace them. Anyone, however, can work politically for clean air and water, limits on development, energy conservation, and the protection of land and species. And almost anyone can participate in natural areas restoration.

While there is value in restoring land for its own sake, the practice of restoration also offers the opportunity for city people to reconnect with nature. Volunteers develop a relationship with a particular place, returning to it regularly, learning its processes, its moods, its preferences, its pace. Working with nature affects people in many ways: nature's timetable slows us down and calms our driving wills; nature's proportions remind us that we are not the center of the world. We are one species, albeit a very powerful one. But we are not alone, and we depend on a diverse, sometimes violent, sometimes sheltering, nature in order to exist. Nature's shapes and colors, with their variety, their irregularity, their whimsy, provide a different mirror for the condition of our souls than do the rectangles and glaring neon of the city. Nature's webs remind us of our dependency, our need, our connections, of those we nourish and those who nourish us. All this implies a mindfulness that does not happen automatically.

When restoration—or any closer connection to nature—assists in expanding consciousness, the experience of nature often feels sacred, transcendent, or religious. In many of the novels I have studied, engagement with the natural world is enriched by myth and ritual. These induce the mindfulness that promotes moral behavior and assuages the loneliness humans feel when they are cut off from nature. Myth and ritual underline the sacred in nature and in humans. I have argued that these emerging stories of connection and hope can help to reframe attitudes toward nature and human nature. But where, today, can people find communities and rituals that will sustain them through time?

William R. Jordan III, writing in *Restoration and Management Notes*, regularly argues for the value of ritual in the practice of restoration so that it may be "undertaken in a spirit of love and sacrament." "Indeed," he says, "the act of restoration provides a most striking parallel to the rituals by which archaic peoples ... sacralize the world. ... It is experienced as a way of renewing the vitality and spiritual energy of the world."[4] Christopher Norden says restoration may provide "the basis for rituals and narratives needed to negotiate the relationship between nature and culture." He points to the challenge "to develop restoration as a community experience—a ritual of relatedness to both human and biotic communities."[5] In a more modest tone, Lisa Meekison and Eric Higgs look to anthropological literature on the value of ritual in generating *communitas*. They caution, however, that rituals cannot be imposed on participants, reminding advocates that many people associate ritual with deeply held religious beliefs. As an alternative they suggest adopting Albert Borgmann's term *focal practices*, referring to events that call for emotional, intellectual, and physical engagement, drawing us deeply into their context.[6] Practices that foster "emotional, intellectual, and physical engagement" promote mindfulness.

In one of his last publications, an article called "The Ecological Conscience," Aldo Leopold laments the slow pace of conservation: "The basic defect is this: we have not asked the citizen to assume any real responsibility. We have told him that if he will vote right, obey the law, join some organizations, and practice what conservation is profitable on his own land, that everything will be lovely; the government will do the rest." Although Leopold wrote this article in 1947, his summation of the problem holds today. Leopold goes on, "No important change in human conduct is ever accomplished without an internal change in our intellectual emphases, our loyalties, our affections, and our convictions."[7] This is not a simple change of political orientation, nor is it only an expansion of feelings. Leopold is calling for a major transformation in thought as a requisite for the spread of a land ethic. He restates the ideas he presents in "The Land Ethic" in his argument for "an ecological conscience": as ecology is the study of communities, an ecological conscience requires an ethics of *community* life. Moreover, Leopold suggests that a land ethic will require some sacrifice on the part of individuals.

Leopold's insistence that community well-being requires some individual sacrifice echoes what N. Scott Momaday says about the relationship between sacrifice and the sacred: "Acts of sacrifice make sacred the earth."[8] This resonates with the words of Ashok Bedi, who says that sacrifice represents a "symbolic relinquishment of a certain aspect of one's psychic life."[9] Specifically, what must be sacrificed is a sense of entitlement, of individualism at the cost of others. Demands for such sacrifice often meet with anger and resistance, the projection of shadow onto the conservation activists who hold up a conflicting good. What the conservation community needs to impart, then, is the understanding that sacrifice returns a sense of the sacred to the human relationship with land. We sacrifice for those we love, and we love those for whom we sacrifice.

In psychological life too individuation requires sacrifice. The encounter with shadow humbles the ego, which must come to accept that it is puny in relation to the whole of psyche. Individuals have to sacrifice a heroic persona in order to grow toward wholeness. Encountering shadow and assimilating knowledge of it into everyday life means repeated experiences of humility— or humiliation—that can be exceedingly painful until we realize that they are widely shared. One of the passages to maturity comes when people recognize that our common nature is part of what makes us lovable. Here, too, fictions can provide images that promote understanding. If a person is lucky enough to be able to go through this experience, rather than having it medicated out of mind, if that person has resources in family, friends, and community that understand and can mediate the process, then a return to life and a new vitality can emerge. The passage through shadow can open individuals to new ways of being in community.

Individuation is always partial, never finished; it requires the ego to acknowledge its limits, even its tyranny, and to incorporate into consciousness energies from the unconscious. In the course of doing so, the ego becomes more and more self-conscious, alert to the social forces constructing the personality, humble in the face of shadow, and better able to attend to the multiple voices of psyche. To come to consciousness about capitalist relations with the land is to be aware of what capitalists would wish to mask: it is to know social shadow and acknowledge one's own interests in the current relations of power.[10] This requires at least an imaginative capacity to consider the situation from an Other's point of view. Developing a personal practice of a land ethic involves some knowledge of ecology, as well as awareness of the political and economic forces that have been most destructive to the planet. Everyone who lives in advanced capitalist culture, who uses its tools and enjoys its toys, also participates in its relentless pursuit of growth, which means ever-expanding domination of nature. Ecological consciousness therefore requires us to acknowledge our complicity, and living lightly is always an unfinished process. Consciousness is not achieved in splendid isolation in one's study, on the hiking trail, or on the analyst's couch. Ecological consciousness grows from practice in the world, the knowledge gained from labor, failure, reassessment, and reengagement, and individuation only occurs as the person consciously works through new ways of responding to the power of archetypes and complexes. Moreover, knowledge is not possible without community. Jung argues that individuation leads to closer and wider relationships because the person in the process of individuating comes to understand his or her dependence on others.[11] Consciousness is a process without end; it is a matter of imagination, work, discipline, and engagement with the world.

Notes

1. TOWARD A LAND ETHIC: NATURE AND SHADOW

1. Leopold, *Sand County Almanac*, 262, 239. Of course, plenty of natural events disrupt the integrity and stability of natural systems, such as hurricanes, earthquakes, volcanic eruptions, and El Niño years. Humans have learned from such events about the process of secondary succession that follows such disruptions. It seems clear that Leopold is talking about human-induced disruptions, rather than natural occurrences.

2. Vine Deloria Jr., *Spirit and Reason*, 50–51.

3. Leopold, *Sand County Almanac*, 252, 253.

4. Vine Deloria Jr., *Spirit and Reason*, 46.

5. Leopold, *Sand County Almanac*, 140.

6. Leopold, *Sand County Almanac*, 251 (italics mine).

7. See White, "Historical Roots," 9; Shepard, *Nature and Madness*; Harrison, *Forests*, 6–7; Bate, *Song of the Earth*, 25–30; Merchant, *Death of Nature*.

8. Love, *Practical Ecocriticism*, 6.

9. Haraway, *Simians, Cyborgs, and Women*.

10. Bernstein, *Living in the Borderland*, 10.

11. Annette Kolodny demonstrates how the image of the American land as female helped rationalize its domination. See *Lay of the Land*.

12. Roszak, *Voice of the Earth*, 42.

13. Jung distinguished the archetypes of the collective unconscious from the complexes of an individual, which are the personal experiences of archetypal patterns. Family, gender, class, race, and history inflect the experience of the archetypes differently, but the experiences—of mothering or being mothered, of falling in love, of religious awe, of the dark side, of the fearful Other—are common. Antony Stevens, a British Jungian, writes: "A complex is a group of associated ideas bound together

by a shared emotional charge: it exerts a dynamic effect on conscious experience and on behaviour. An archetype . . . is an innate 'centre' or 'dominant' . . . which has the capacity to initiate, influence and mediate the behavioural characteristics and typical experiences of all human beings, irrespective of race, culture, historical epoch or geographical location. A close functional relationship exists between complexes and archetypes, in that complexes are 'personifications' of archetypes: complexes are the means through which archetypes manifest themselves in the personal psyche"(*On Jung*, 28).

14. Roszak, *Voice of the Earth*, 42.

15. Because the terms *symbol* and *symbolic* have multiple associations, to avoid confusion, I will use them only in this specifically Jungian context. *Symbol*, that is, will mean an image presented by the unconscious that has the power of resolving what appears to be an insoluble conflict, an image to which psychic energy is attached and which is capable of transforming libido.

16. Stevens, *On Jung*, 39.

17. Jung, *Collected Works* (CW hereafter), 3: para. 565.

18. Roszak, "Where Psyche Meets Gaia," 14.

19. Jung, *CW*, 10: para. 395.

20. Stevens, *On Jung*, 79–80.

21. Stevens, *On Jung*, 32.

22. Jung, *CW*, 9: II, para. 13.

23. Von Franz, *Shadow and Evil*, 9.

24. Jung, *CW*, 9: II, para. 14, para. 17.

25. Von Franz, "Process of Individuation," 163.

26. Stevens, *On Jung*, 114.

27. Willeford, "Feeling, Imagination," 204.

28. Jung, *Memories, Dreams, Reflections*, 324.

29. Hillman, *Healing Fiction*, 40.

30. Jung, *CW*, 7: para. 121.

31. Stevens, *On Jung*, 52.

32. Hillman, qtd. in Watkins, "From Individualism," 60.

33. Watkins, "From Individualism," 60.

34. Hillman, *Thought of the Heart*, 92–93.

35. Bishop, *Greening of Psychology*, 79.

36. Samuels, *Political Psyche*, 21, 12.

37. Snyder, *Practice of the Wild*, 60.

38. Qtd. in Metzner, "Psychopathology," 59. See also Shepard, "Post-Historical Primitivism"; Glendinning, "Technology."

39. Samuels, *Political Psyche*, 103.

40. The experience of the sublime in nature that drew Wordsworth, Emerson, and John Muir to wild places may now be so mediated by National Park Service regulations, ecotourism, and the destruction of ecosystems, cultures, and people throughout the world, that many people no longer feel as though they are "away." But this presumes that wilderness alone provides an adequate experience of the sublime in

nature. I argue that since humans have never truly been separate from nature—we are animals, we contain "nature" within us in the unconscious—we do not need to imagine *uninhabited* nature (a nature that, if currently uninhabited, is only so because of the removal of the people who used to live there) to experience powers that transcend our historically and culturally inflected egos.

41. Hillman, *Archetypal Psychology*, 26.

42. Hogan, *Dwellings*, 60.

43. Much contemporary theory concerns the power of culture to shape subjective experience. The analysis of postmodern culture explores its depthlessness, failures of memory, and Disneylike substitution of the image for experience. Postmodern critics have focused attention on the drive of commodity capitalism to construct a way of thinking and an experience of self that are organized around capitalism's imperatives. This experience of self is that of a "new being" described variously as schizophrenic, decentered, "utterly without meaning, for it has given over its soul to its objects, and without future, for it cannot imagine one" (Rushing and Frentz, *Projecting the Shadow*, 16). If the *energy* of theory is to understand ideology—its construction, its inscription in culture, its function in institutions, its transmission—the *matter* of theory is often negative, showing that oppressive relations of power are enacted and maintained in ideology and in widely dispersed institutions, that images have replaced substance, that consciousness has been constructed around social roles designated by capitalist relations of production, and that desire has been molded to the profit needs of faceless corporations. Much postmodernist theory denies any distinctions between nature and culture, absorbing everything into culture. Given the overwhelming power of corporate capitalism, what hope is there? The equation of postmodern cultural trends with human consciousness seems to leave little room for either personal or social change. Relations of power are maintained by a complicated nexus of unequal relations, but resistance and subversion surface in multiple forms, from dream circles to demonstrations against globalization. I also argue that any culture's understanding of human nature is in significant part a result of its relations with other-than-human nature. Humans have not transcended nature; as animals we are subject to a "nature" that precedes culture. Many postmodern theorists assert that (human) nature is socially constructed, but this argument itself comes from cultures that are divorced from the nature that forms their habitat and their bodies. It's useful to remember that the word *hermeneutics*—the study of interpretation—derives from *Hermes*, the trickster.

44. Hauke, *Jung and the Postmodern*, 2.

45. Raymond Williams, *Keywords*, 219.

46. To focus exclusively on the social construction of nature, however, suggests that the human capacity to "construct" nature is not subverted by nature's trickster power, as though no autonomous "nature" existed outside our understanding. A focus on the pervasive power of cultural institutions to construct human identity (or to fragment it) obscures the extent to which humans, as animals, participate in a "nature" that is beyond our control. Even with Botox we still age; for all our road rage, we can still be moved by the call of the sandhill crane. Can we conceive that nonhuman

nature also acts from a subject position, as traditional American Indian views held? Perhaps the instability of Western knowledge has resulted from regarding nature as mechanical or inanimate, merely object. Psychologists know that in studying human "nature," the unconscious, they get tricks played on them, just as physicists do when they explore subatomic particles. Is it not possible that other parts of "nature" resist human attempts to know them from something like a subject position?

47. Haraway, *Simians, Cyborgs, and Women*, 187.

48. SueEllen Campbell, an ecocritic, examines methods and priorities that eco-critics share with postmodern theorists, arguing that "both theorists and ecologists . . . begin by criticizing the dominant structures of Western culture and the vast abuses they have spawned" ("Land and Language," 127). The ecological principle of connectedness finds an echo in the poststructuralist understanding of the ways ideas and institutions are interwoven in culture. However, Campbell points out that for poststructuralist theorists theory is itself action, while ecologists generally agree that action entails more: engagement with physical reality, political activism, and scientific research.

49. Watkins, "From Individualism," 58.

50. Glotfelty, "Introduction," xix.

51. Howarth, "Some Principles of Ecocriticism," 79.

52. Campbell, "Land and Language," 133.

53. See Murphy, *Farther Afield*; Armbruster and Wallace, *Beyond Nature Writing*.

54. Said, *Orientalism*, 3, 1.

55. Ashcroft, Griffiths, and Tiffin, *Empire Writes Back*, 2.

56. See, e.g., Vizenor, *Manifest Manners*.

57. Although there is disagreement about whether to call American Indian writers "postcolonial," since they still live in occupied land, their work shares some impor-tant features of postcolonial literatures. Postcolonial literatures often have a spatial rather than a temporal structure, reflecting their intimacy with the natural world and their origins in ritual cultures. As in much postmodernist work, postcolonial theo-rists and novelists contest the power of the political center, shifting focus to regional and historical locations from which to rewrite history from their own perspective. Oppositional literatures also suggest the power of traditional ways of knowing—in particular, direct, narrative experience of the natural world and ritual and myth as ways of accessing states of consciousness that are not limited to ego. The form in which formerly (or presently) colonized cultures speak to the dominant culture is often hybrid. Where the traditional culture was oral, writing—in particular writing in the form of the novel—represents a mixed breed, a new being that brings practices from oral, recursive storytelling to the linear inscription. Postmodern and postcolo-nial theorists like Spivak, Bhabha, Haraway, and Said speak of a "hybrid," "diasporic," or "cyborg" response to both colonial identities and dualistic epistemologies. Postco-lonial theory suggests that as colonized people "write back," their hybrid discourses can combine the revolutionary potential of Western, historical, written culture with the values of traditional, myth-based earth awareness. As Linda Hutcheon argues, postcolonial art and criticism have "distinct political agendas and often a theory of

agency" that take them past deconstructive analysis and skepticism, which she calls "ambivalent" ("Circling the Downspout," 168).

58. Linda Tuhiwai Smith, *Decolonizing Methodologies*, 1.

59. Snyder, *Practice of the Wild*, 61.

60. Bate, *Song of the Earth*, 64.

61. Slovic, "Nature Writing," 362.

62. Rowland, *C. G. Jung*, 62.

63. Horkheimer and Adorno, "Concept of Enlightenment," 44.

64. Vine Deloria Jr., *Spirit and Reason*, 66.

65. Jung, *CW*, 5: para. 113.

66. Vine Deloria Jr., *Spirit and Reason*, 13–14.

67. Haraway, *Simians, Cyborgs, and Women*, 106.

2. THE COLONIAL SHADOW: CONRAD AND PARKMAN

1. Conrad, *Heart of Darkness*, 13. All quotations are from the Norton text. The epigraph may be found in *CW*, 10: para. 103.

2. Said, *Culture and Imperialism*, 165.

3. JanMohamed, *Manichean Aesthetics*, 158.

4. Churchill, *Fantasies of the Master Race*, 13.

5. Achebe, "Image of Africa," 252.

6. Jameson, *Political Unconscious*, 215, 214.

7. Conrad, *Heart of Darkness*, 9–10.

8. Conrad, *Heart of Darkness*, 13, 32.

9. Conrad, *Heart of Darkness*, 36.

10. To appreciate the extent of Marlow's projections, compare Conrad's account with that of Jesuit priest Cristobal de Acuna. Traveling along the Amazon in 1639, he wrote about "healing drugs . . . huge trees that could be harvested for shipbuilding, and fertile riverbanks that could be used to grow manioc, sweet potatoes, pineapples, guava, and coconuts. The river was swimming with fish, the woods were full of game—including tapirs, deer, peccaries, monkeys, and armadillos—and the lagoons were populated by numerous birds. His was a wilderness that was more bountiful paradise than fearsome jungle" (Whittaker, *Mapmaker's Wife*, 181). Whittaker's work includes many other accounts of the Andes and the Amazon from a mission of French and Spanish scientists who spent ten years in South America in the mid-eighteenth century. The scientists' interest in these places, including ecosystems very similar to the Congolese jungle, suggests the complexity of the European response to nature. It appears that fear of nature is exaggerated when adventurers are engaged in an imperial project. When the purpose is to understand rather than to overcome, nature seems less malignant.

11. Conrad, *Heart of Darkness*, 29.

12. Conrad, *Heart of Darkness*, 37.

13. Todorov, *Conquest of America*, 30.

14. Conrad, *Heart of Darkness*, 35, 28.

15. Conrad, *Heart of Darkness*, 48.

16. Conrad, *Heart of Darkness*, 28, 52, 51.

17. Jeffrey Myers points out that Conrad wrote *Heart of Darkness* at a time when there was confusion and anxiety in Europe about the implications of evolutionary theory. If humans are really simply part of nature's vast processes, what happens to the Great Chain of Being? What is the place of the individual ego? Myers claims, "The erasure of their personal subjectivity and anxiety over reincorporation into the body of nature drive the seemingly motiveless atrocities that Kurtz and others commit" ("Anxiety of Confluence," 99).

18. Conrad, *Heart of Darkness*, 49. Adam Hochschild reports that King Leopold told Roger Casement that "'the African climate seemed frequently to cause deterioration in the character'" (*King Leopold's Ghost*, 198).

19. Edinger, *Ego and Archetype*, 14, 7.

20. Conrad, *Heart of Darkness*, 49.

21. Conrad, *Heart of Darkness*, 68.

22. Conrad, *Heart of Darkness*, 29.

23. Christopher Manes points out, "Nature *is* silent in our culture (and in literate societies generally) in the sense that the status of being a speaking subject is jealously guarded as an exclusively human prerogative" ("Nature and Silence," 15).

24. Todorov comments, "In the world of Machiavelli and of Cortés, discourse is not determined by the object it describes, nor by conformity to a tradition, but is constructed solely as a function of the goal it seeks to achieve" (*Conquest of America*, 116).

25. On the subject of American Indian languages and their relation to the natural, social, and spiritual worlds, see also Abram, *Spell of the Sensuous*; Gunn Allen, *Sacred Hoop*.

26. Hochschild, *King Leopold's Ghost*, 294–95.

27. Johanna M. Smith, "'Too Beautiful Altogether,'" 173.

28. Conrad, *Heart of Darkness*, 60.

29. Bishop, "Wilderness as a Victim," 125.

30. Conrad, *Heart of Darkness*, 19.

31. Stevens, *On Jung*, 235.

32. Writing about the experience of shadow in midlife, Murray Stein argues that the midlife crisis entails an encounter with shadow that is liminal and hermetic. He asks, "What do you need to be most critically protected *from* during midlife liminality?" Stein argues that nature itself protects people: "What is to prevent you from running amuck with impulsivity, or from indulging what turn out to be deeply regressive urges, or from succumbing to gross pleasure-seeking and to the 'id' with its proclivity to perversion and its destructive potential?" He points out that this fear springs from a suspicious view of human nature that is encoded in the Judeo-Christian idea of original sin. Freud and Jung both incorporated this anxiety into their psychologies. Stein responds to his own question with the argument that the "taboo against regression is itself archetypal" and that "nature [can] be trusted to treat nature. When a split is created between nature and culture, and culture is seen as mankind's

only protection from destruction, then ego-consciousness becomes our only hope, and we fearfully conclude that without external cultural and legal prohibitions and enforcements individual human beings and the human race as a whole will degenerate and sink irretrievably into regressive attitudes and behavior." According to Stein, the "restraint" of which Marlow is so proud is itself an instinctual, archetypal response to the experience of liminality (*In Midlife*, 84–85).

33. Owens, *Mixedblood Messages*, 44.

34. Conrad, *Heart of Darkness*, 12.

35. Philip Deloria, *Playing Indian*, 64.

36. Vizenor, *Manifest Manners*, 28.

37. Parkman, *Oregon Trail*, 33.

38. Parkman, *Oregon Trail*, 216, 107, 141, 201.

39. Parkman, *Oregon Trail*, 195.

40. Parkman, *Oregon Trail*, 225.

41. Parkman, *Oregon Trail*, 210–11.

42. Parkman, *Oregon Trail*, 317.

43. Parkman, *Oregon Trail*, 440.

44. Parkman, *Oregon Trail*, 430.

45. Parkman, *Oregon Trail*, 187.

46. Parkman, *Oregon Trail*, 338.

47. Parkman, *Oregon Trail*, 339.

3. OUT OF THE SHADOW: *THINGS FALL APART AND FOOLS CROW*

1. Some of these ideas are developed at length in Ashcroft, Griffiths, and Tiffin, *Empire Writes Back*, a cornerstone work of postcolonial criticism. See esp. 65.

2. Owens, *Mixedblood Messages*, 22.

3. Achebe, *Things Fall Apart*, 7. Achebe has said a number of times that *Things Fall Apart* was a response to his outrage at the picture of Nigerian life in Joyce Cary's *Mister Johnson*.

4. *Igbo* and *Ibo* are alternate spellings of the clan, language, and territory; for consistency I use *Igbo* throughout.

5. Achebe, *Things Fall Apart*, 19–20.

6. Bührmann, "Nature, Psyche," 75–76.

7. Achebe, *Things Fall Apart*, 43, 44.

8. Soyinka, *Myth, Literature*, 52–53.

9. Achebe, *Things Fall Apart*, 85.

10. Bührmann, "Nature, Psyche," 77.

11. Shepard, "Post-Historic Primitivism," 44.

12. Achebe, *Things Fall Apart*, 32.

13. Soyinka, *Myth, Literature*, 52.

14. Achebe, *Things Fall Apart*, 138.

15. In *Landscape and Memory* Simon Schama points out that *forest* derives from the Latin *foris*, or "outside the writ of Roman law." Schama recounts Tacitus's ambiva-

lent response to the German forests, "desirably, as well as deplorably, primitive" (83). He describes a "natural religion" found at the heart of the forest that practiced "veneration of divinities that lodged within, and were indivisible from, natural phenomena like great oaks" (84). In writing about a woodland ritual sacrifice, Schama says: "The woodland sacrifice, then, is likely to have been a ritual of collective tribal rebirth. But Tacitus saw only an act of horrifying barbarism" (85). Clearly, the tradition of "civilized" travelers misreading "primitive" cultures antedates the nineteenth century.

16. Achebe, *Things Fall Apart*, 21, 133.

17. Ezenwa-Ohaeto, *Chinua Achebe*, 53.

18. Soyinka, *Myth, Literature*, 14.

19. Eliade, *Myth of the Eternal Return*, 22-28. David Abram reconfigures Eliade's ideas in terms of spoken language, arguing that the regular repetition of a culture's prayers and stories in the places and seasons of their origins binds people to the sensuous cosmos, to place and cycle (*Spell of the Sensuous*, 186).

20. Soyinka, *Myth, Literature*, 26, 18-19.

21. Soyinka, *Myth, Literature*, 30.

22. Soyinka, in *Myth, Literature*, contrasts Yoruba gods to those of the Greeks, pointing out that in Greek myth offending deities do not make reparations to those whom they've injured. The conquering forces of Her Majesty, more Greek than African, have no intention of making reparations; indeed, the issue of reparations for the injuries caused by slavery is still unresolved in the United States.

23. Achebe, *Things Fall Apart*, 59.

24. Achebe, *Things Fall Apart*, 64.

25. Soyinka, *Myth, Literature*, 27.

26. Todorov, *Conquest of America*, 144.

27. Todorov, *Conquest of America*, 145.

28. Adam Hochschild's *King Leopold's Ghost* details the murders, torture, and massacre practiced by European colonizers, adventurers, and merchants in Africa at this time.

29. JanMohamed, *Manichean Aesthetics*, 161.

30. JanMohamed, *Manichean Aesthetics*, 164, 165, 166.

31. Burlingame, "Empowerment," 2.

32. Ngugi wa Thiong'o, *Decolonising the Mind*, 16.

33. Cronon, *Changes in the Land*, 65.

34. Krupat, *Turn to the Native*, 36

35. Vizenor, *Manifest Manners*, 72.

36. Owens, *Other Destinies*, 165.

37. Jung makes this distinction in *Two Essays on Analytical Psychology*. The workaday dream, he argues, comes from the personal unconscious, while the big dream comes from the collective unconscious. Jung writes: "How is a man to know whether his dream is a 'big' or a 'little' one? He knows it by an instinctive feeling of significance. He feels so overwhelmed by the impression it makes that he would never think of keeping the dream to himself. He *has* to tell it, on the psychologically correct assumption that it is of general significance" (*CW*, 7: para. 277).

38. Welch, *Fools Crow*, 85.

39. Welch, *Fools Crow*, 118.

40. Ruoff, *American Indian Literatures*, 2.

41. Driver, *Magic of Ritual*, 96.

42. Welch, *Fools Crow*, 165.

43. Welch, *Fools Crow*, 171.

44. Welch, *Fools Crow*, 119, 124–25.

45. Welch, *Fools Crow*, 125.

46. States, *Dreaming and Storytelling*, 9.

47. Welch does not flinch from acknowledging the difficult lives of women in a polygamous, patriarchal culture, but he does not foreground them. At one point he writes the following about the feelings of Double Strike Woman, Fools Crow's mother, who has persuaded her husband to take her sister, Striped Face, as his second wife: "Striped Face . . . liked to tease Rides-at-the-door, to make him angry and aroused enough to take her into the small lodge, where they would struggle among the robes. The first time this happened, Double Strike Woman had felt strange; not betrayed, exactly, but forgotten, as though she were no longer principal wife but a thing, a cow that suckled the two infant sons. She had felt old, even at the age of twenty-four winters. . . . But when they came back to the big lodge in the morning, she saw in Rides-at-the-Door's eyes that she was still his sits-beside-him woman" (*Fools Crow*, 219–20).

48. Schechner, *Future of Ritual*, 111.

49. Welch, *Fools Crow*, 211.

50. Welch, *Fools Crow*, 352.

51. Welch, *Fools Crow*, 358.

52. Velie, "Indian Historical Novel," 203.

53. Welch, *Fools Crow*, 359–60.

54. Armstrong, *Short History of Myth*, 10.

55. Shepard, "Post-Historical Primitivism," 45–46.

56. Meeker, "Comic Mode," 157–58.

57. Vizenor, *Manifest Manners*, 15.

58. Owens, *Mixedblood Messages*, 26.

4. *TOWARD RECOVERY: SEEKING A PSYCHOLOGY OF RENEWAL*

1. Leopold, *Sand County Almanac*, 251 (italics mine).

2. Jung, *CW*, 10: para. 847.

3. Hogan, *Dwellings*, 51.

4. Gunn Allen, *Sacred Hoop*, 116–17.

5. Armstrong, *Short History of Myth*, 8, 31.

6. Harrison, *Forests*, 26.

7. Harrison, *Forests*, 130.

8. Harrison, *Forests*, 149.

9. Harrison, *Forests*, 6, 7.

10. Harrison, *Forests*, 13.

11. Harrison, *Forests*, 249.

12. Harrison, *Forests*, 124.

13. At the same time, as Schama points out, those who have pursued myth have courted dangers they did not foresee. "Myths," he writes, "are seductive." He goes on to implicate "a long line of devotees of archetypes, from Carl Jung to Friedrich Nietzsche ..., whose embrace of myth fired their hostility to natural-rights individualism, and the democratic politics that protects it" (*Landscape and Memory*, 133–34). Perhaps the "spell" of myth entices people to wish to impose on others ideas or images they have declared universal truth. Such a spell certainly could be said to have enthralled Christian missionaries in distant colonies. This aversion to Jungian ideas about archetypes can be seen in the responses of some American Indian writers who question the notion that their mythic figures are comparable to those of European myths. Pointing to the differences among Indian cultures, they resist the universalizing thrust of European modernism. For example, Gerald Vizenor comments that "to impose archetypes on tribal remembrance and narratives, is to sustain ... the literature of dominance" (*Manifest Manners*, 171). Differences between the origin stories of Western and traditional cultures point to differences in their orientation toward nature, suggesting significant differences in their other myths. However, Spring Journal Books, a Jungian-oriented publisher, will be publishing in the next year a book by Vine Deloria Jr. entitled *C. G. Jung and the Sioux Traditions*. This new book promises to reframe the conversation about Jung and American Indian cultures.

14. Owens, *Mixedblood Messages*, 224, 227.

15. Toelken, "'Seeing with a Native Eye,'" 14.

16. Abram, *Spell of the Sensuous*, 160.

17. Gunn Allen, *Sacred Hoop*, 13.

18. Brown, "Roots of Renewal," 28–30.

19. Meier, *Healing Dream and Ritual*, 29–31.

20. Vine Deloria Jr., *God Is Red*, 81.

21. Silko, "Landscape, History," 887, 888.

22. Vine Deloria Jr., *God Is Red*, 114.

23. Toelken, "'Seeing with a Native Eye,'" 15, 17.

24. Toelken, "'Seeing with a Native Eye,'" 18–19.

25. Rappaport, "Sanctity and Adaptation," 109.

26. Silko, "Landscape, History," 892.

27. Vizenor, *People Named the Chippewa*, 59.

28. Duran and Duran, *Native American Postcolonial Psychology*, 45.

29. Sessions, "Ecocentrism, Wilderness," 98.

30. Devall, "Deep Ecology Movement," 133.

31. Macy, "Toward a Healing," 295.

32. Roszak, *Voice of the Earth*, 303.

33. Cronon, "Trouble with Wilderness," 70, 85.

34. Berg, "Bioregionalism."

35. Berry, *Dream of the Earth*, 166.

36. Metzner, "Place and the Story," 2.

37. Mills, *In Service of the Wild*, 18–19.

38. Coalition organizations like Chicago Wilderness provide a structure for bioregional thinking that is a model worldwide. Over 170 organizations—including local, county, state, and federal government agencies; universities; and NGOs—coordinate research, planning, protection, education, and land management. The magazine *Chicago Wilderness* reaches out to families, educators, and citizen scientists. The *Atlas of Biodiversity*, compiled by Jerry Sullivan, describes the predominant natural areas in the region, including prairie, oak savannah, wetland, dune, and aquatic ecosystems, and presents the principal species of each, with their interactions. It includes a history of the area and introduces readers to the work of restoration. Handsomely presented with high-quality photographs and charts, the *Atlas* is accessible to the Chicago public. The *Biodiversity Recovery Plan* provides more technical information for scientists and project managers on the status and needs of terrestrial and aquatic communities. It also lays out research priorities and key players. The publication *Protecting Nature in Your Community*, by Navota and Dreher, speaks most directly to local officials, planners, and community activists, providing examples of communities that have protected and restored green spaces. Chicago Wilderness also offers outreach, education, and technical assistance to local community officials, planners of corporate campuses, people decommissioning industrial facilities, and many others. Its other publications include family guides; a journal for conservation professionals; material on sustainable development; and Jerry Sullivan's *Hunting for Frogs on Elston*, an illustrated book of essays on the natural wonders of the Chicago Wilderness region. As a model for organizations in other areas, Chicago Wilderness has been studied by teams from around the United States and internationally. See the organization's Web site: http://www.chicagowilderness.org.

39. LaDuke, "Recovering the Land," 16.

40. Qtd. in Judith Graham, "For Tribes, Bringing Back Buffalo a Labor of Love," *Chicago Tribune*, Nov. 3, 2002.

5. WILDERNESS AND VISION: SHADOW AND THE
QUEST FOR IDENTITY

1. Cronon, "Trouble with Wilderness," 70.

2. Spretnak, "Ecofeminism," 6.

3. Cronon, "Trouble with Wilderness," 80.

4. Atwood, *Surfacing*, 5, 118, 122.

5. Atwood, *Surfacing*, 131.

6. Atwood, *Surfacing*, 70, 108–9.

7. Atwood, *Surfacing*, 131.

8. Atwood, *Surfacing*, 143, 144, 145, 146.

9. Jung, *Memories, Dreams, Reflections*, 335.

10. Jung, *Memories, Dreams, Reflections*, 335.

11. Edinger, *Ego and Archetype*, 109.

12. Salman, "Creative Psyche," 64–65.

13. Samuels, *Political Psyche*, 110.

14. Atwood, *Surfacing*, 151.

15. Atwood, *Surfacing*, 164–65.

16. Atwood, *Surfacing*, 172.

17. Atwood, *Surfacing*, 187, 193.

18. Atwood, *Surfacing*, 197.

19. Atwood, *Surfacing*, 198, 199.

20. Wilkins, "Defense of the Realm," 219.

21. Staels, "Social Construction of Identity."

22. Ward, "*Surfacing*," 99.

23. Fiamengo, "Postcolonial Guilt," 141, 143, 150. Regarding *Surfacing* as a manifestation of the 1970s, Peter Wilkins argues that a fantasy of "wholeness" is the personal version of the concept of "sovereignty," which allows Canadians to imagine themselves "a seamless, innocent whole threatened only by outside antagonism from the United States." He makes the case that the novel demonstrates the need to acknowledge inner divisions, both political and personal, in order to act ethically. The absence of First Nations people from the action of the novel allows the narrator to "coopt their position" as an opponent of "American" "civilization" and the reservoir of a spiritual relationship with the land, without confronting her own complicity in their dispossession. See "Defense of the Realm," 209, 215.

24. Howells, *Margaret Atwood*, 21.

25. Atwood, *Surfacing*, 171, 182, 187, 131.

26. In fact, even the "wilderness" in which the narrator submerges herself is not a wilderness but secondary growth, the forest returning where her father cleared it for the house. The lake is treacherous not because it is pristine nature but because of drunken fishermen and old logs "left over from the logging and the time they raised the lake level." The narrator's hallucinatory participation at the end of the novel in a flux of decay and new life, "energy of decay turning to growth, green fire," involves a degree of wishful thinking: nature does regenerate, but degraded nature in this ecosystem requires the passage of time on a nonhuman scale if it is to return to its previous biological diversity. See Atwood, *Surfacing*, 27, 172. By the time she wrote *Wilderness Tips*, Atwood was less optimistic about such regeneration.

27. Atwood, *Surfacing*, 141.

28. Atwood, *Surfacing*, 181, 197.

29. Andrew Samuels sees the narrator as a "female Trickster," suggesting that Atwood uses the common cultural conflation of women and nature to foreground that very association and, by doing so, to create political instability: "Ceasing to be a woman, she cannot be subjugated *like* nature because she *is* nature. But, to the extent that nature threatens people, especially men like Joe, or Americans, as a woman still she acquires nature's deathly powers. . . . But we know it is still an illusion, because men still have the 'real' power, the socioeconomic power, the political power" (*Political Psyche*, 111).

30. Earthday.net has a "footprint quiz" that calculates how much damage one's life

habits incur; according to its figures, we would need over eleven planets if everyone lived as I do (alone, in a house). Driving cars induces guilt; using paper implicates me. My daughter, a vegetarian graduate student, has a lifestyle that would require only slightly over two planets.

31. Robinson, *Housekeeping*, 6, 8.

32. Robinson, *Housekeeping*, 9.

33. Robinson, *Housekeeping*, 41.

34. Robinson, *Housekeeping*, 17, 13.

35. Robinson, *Housekeeping*, 19.

36. Robinson, *Housekeeping*, 25.

37. Robinson, *Housekeeping*, 99.

38. Robinson, *Housekeeping*, 124–25, 113.

39. Robinson, *Housekeeping*, 104, 99, 123.

40. This is an initiation into what Matthew Fox calls the *via negativa*, the approach to spirit through absence. As Fox says, "Without the silence that constitutes the letting go of images, without the emptying and the being emptied that full living brings, without sinking into nameless nothingness, we do not grow" (*Original Blessings*, 155).

41. Robinson, *Housekeeping*, 70.

42. Robinson, *Housekeeping*, 157–58.

43. Robinson, *Housekeeping*, 86, 116.

44. Robinson, *Housekeeping*, 84, 103.

45. Robinson, *Housekeeping*, 91, 92, 96.

46. Like Hilde Staels, who identifies the semiotic with both nature and the unconscious, Kristin King sees *Housekeeping* as enacting a balance of two kinds of symbolic and semiotic discourse. King suggests that while Ruth seems to desire a loss of self, a merging with Sylvie in a womblike oneness, the narrative itself signals her capacity to use language to voice her own identity. See King, "Resurfactings of the Deep." Staels echoes this argument in relation to *Surfacing*: "The narrator gives shape to an experience of shapelessness; she names, thinks, and symbolizes the unnameable and the unthinkable" ("Social Construction of Identity," 28).

47. Robinson, *Housekeeping*, 99, 100, 106, 116.

48. Critics seem to agree that it is important for Ruthie to be alone. Marcia Aldrich says that Sylvie leaves Ruth "to traverse again anger, fear, loneliness, and longing until she herself wishes to be unhoused of her flesh and unsheltered" ("Poetics of Transience," 137). Karen Kaivola sees Sylvie's abandonment of Ruth as a reenactment of Helen's, which "allows Ruth to experience again the feelings of abandonment" ("Pleasures and Perils," 684). Critics disagree, however, on the effectiveness of Sylvie's action: Aldrich sees the initiation as effective in transforming Ruth into a transient, while Kaivola argues that it is not empowering, since Ruth seems eager simply to merge with Sylvie. Keeping in mind that Ruth is a preadolescent at this time, her desire to be mothered hardly seems pathological; as the narrative, written "many years" later, testifies, Ruth makes a successful emergence into a fully voiced adulthood. See Robinson, *Housekeeping*, 213.

49. Whitmont, "Evolution of the Shadow," 16.

50. Robinson, *Housekeeping*, 154, 158, 157.

51. Robinson, *Housekeeping*, 159, 160.

52. Robinson, *Housekeeping*, 162.

53. Robinson, *Housekeeping*, 163, 172.

54. Robinson, *Housekeeping*, 169–70.

55. Robinson, *Housekeeping*, 178, 180.

56. Kaivola, "Pleasures and Perils," 675.

57. Several critics note that Ruth and Sylvie's transience is a form of transcendence. Anne Carter claims that they "symbolically transcend ordinary human boundaries when they cross the bridge out of Fingerbone and into a timeless reality and visionary space" ("Dark Water Grace," 4). Jacqui Smyth calls transience "a metaphor for subversion" ("Sheltered Vagrancy," 282), while Maggie Galehouse says it is "a kind of liberation . . . a dialogue between indoors and outdoors," citing Henri Bergson in support of her argument that Ruth transcends ordinary time ("Their Own Private Idaho," 2). William M. Burke calls *Housekeeping* a "primer on the mystical life, in which the basic accomplishment . . . is the expansion of consciousness through a process of border crossings. . . . The rigors and self-denials of the transient life are necessary spiritual conditioning for the valued crossing from the experience of a world of loss and fragmentation to the perception of a world that is whole and complete" ("Border Crossings," 717). Joan Kirkby calls "becoming liquid and capable of assuming new forms . . . the apotheosis intimated by the book" ("Is There Life after Art?" 100).

58. Robinson, *Housekeeping*, 214.

59. Keats, letter to George and Thomas Keats, Sunday, Dec. 21, 1817, in Abrams and Greenblatt, *Norton Anthology*, 2: 889.

60. O'Rourke, "Moralist of the Midwest," 67.

61. Robinson, *Housekeeping*, 131, 137, 152.

62. Vizenor, *Manifest Manners*, 170.

63. Robinson, *Housekeeping*, 204.

6. REINHABITATION: LAND, MYTH, AND MEMORY

1. Bevis, "Native American Novels," 16.

2. Momaday, *House Made of Dawn*, 131 (italics mine).

3. Momaday, *Man Made of Words*, 16.

4. See, e.g., Heldrich, "Constructing the Self"; Frischkorn, "Shadow of Tsoai"; Rainwater, "Planes, Lines, Shapes"; Jason W. Stevens, "Bear, Outlaw and Storyteller."

5. Frischkorn, "Shadow of Tsoai," 23.

6. Vine Deloria Jr. discusses this in many places; see, e.g., his essay "Kinship with the World," in *Spirit and Reason*.

7. Momaday, *Man Made of Words*, 119–20, 46.

8. Vine Deloria Jr., *Spirit and Reason*, 56.

9. Momaday, *Man Made of Words*, 114, 128, 48.

10. Vizenor, *Manifest Manners*, 73.

11. Momaday, *Man Made of Words*, 169.

12. Momaday, *Ancient Child*, 38.

13. Momaday, *Man Made of Words*, 77, 68, 92, 77.

14. While I am uncomfortable with the assignment of aggression, discipline, and "foreign relations" to the domain of the "masculine," and nurturance, relatedness, and "domestic relations" to the realm of the "feminine," I am using these words as shorthand. All these potentials exist in all people, but they are variously available to consciousness as a consequence of the effects on the mind of a gendered social reality. To acknowledge this discomfort, I am enclosing "masculine" and "feminine" in quotation marks.

15. Samuels, *Political Psyche*, 142.

16. Adams, "Archetypal School," 113.

17. Momaday, *Ancient Child*, 27–28.

18. Momaday, *Ancient Child*, 72, 268. Arnold Krupat reads her as Momaday's "rather embarrassingly fantasized nineteen-year-old woman"; see "Postcolonialism," 81.

19. Momaday, *Way to Rainy Mountain*, 20–21.

20. Momaday, *Ancient Child*, 29.

21. Momaday, *Ancient Child*, 215.

22. Momaday, *Ancient Child*, 115, 214, 216, 213.

23. Hillman, *Archetypal Psychology*, 41, 39.

24. Stein, *In Midlife*, 2.

25. Momaday, *Ancient Child*, 241.

26. Kenneth Roemer points out that this ritual bears a "striking" resemblance to the Shock Rite, a Navajo Mountainway practice directed at healing illness brought on by too close a contemplation of extraordinarily powerful spiritual beings. See "Ancient Children at Play," 107.

27. Momaday, *Ancient Child*, 295, 304.

28. Momaday, *Ancient Child*, 314.

29. Momaday, "Native American Attitudes," 80.

30. Momaday, *Ancient Child*, 315.

31. Momaday, *House Made of Dawn*, 57.

32. Momaday, *Way to Rainy Mountain*, 7.

33. Vine Deloria Jr., *Spirit and Reason*, 13–14.

34. Momaday, *Ancient Child*, 38; Hillman, *Archetypal Psychology*, 16.

35. Hillman, *Archetypal Psychology*, 6, 16. Readers bothered by the word *soul* might want to think in terms of "soul music" or "soul food."

36. Momaday, *Ancient Child*, 144, 145, 159, 161.

37. Qtd. in Jason W. Stevens, "Bear, Outlaw and Storyteller," 611.

38. Rainwater, "Planes, Lines, Shapes," 831.

39. Momaday, *Man Made of Words*, 169, 2.

40. Momaday, *Ancient Child*, 31.

41. Swan, "Laguna Prototypes of Manhood," 46.

42. Silko, *Ceremony*, 6, 43.

43. Silko, *Ceremony*, 42, 55, 61.

44. Duran and Duran argue that for many Indian men "identification with the aggressor . . . has as a core a desire to gain the aggressor's power and eventually turn that power on the aggressor. . . . Because removal of the colonial forces is not realized, the repressed rage has no place for cathexis except to turn on itself" (*Native American Postcolonial Psychology*, 37).

45. Silko, *Ceremony*, 135.

46. Silko, *Ceremony*, 249.

47. Silko, *Ceremony*, 48.

48. Hultberg, "Shame," 163.

49. Duran and Duran, *Native American Postcolonial Psychology*, 39.

50. Silko, *Ceremony*, 68, 67.

51. As Stuart Cochran remarks, "As a mixed blood, Tayo has internalized the ridicule of the dominant white culture through the hostility of his aunt . . . and the assimiliationist aspirations of his favored cousin Rocky. He will eventually see his own malaise in communal terms as a function of colonialism and Christianity" ("Ethnic Implications of Stories," 76).

52. Woodman, *Ravaged Bridegroom*, 17.

53. Henderson, *Shadow and Self*, 70.

54. Silko, *Ceremony*, 14, 35.

55. Silko, *Ceremony*, 94.

56. Hogan, *Dwellings*, 81.

57. Silko, *Ceremony*, 95, 96.

58. Owens, *Mixedblood Messages*, 227.

59. Linda Tuhiwai Smith, *Decolonizing Methodologies*, 146.

60. Robert Nelson uses the Jungian term *constellation* to suggest how in *Ceremony* Silko's image of the stars "gathers together elements of landscape, story, vision, and the world preceding vision." When Jungians use the verb *to constellate*, the suggestion is that what had seemed independent images have taken on a pattern that gives them meaning. Nelson argues that stories and images in *Ceremony* serve to order Tayo's experience and reorient him to the very specific land of the Laguna people. In the process cultural, personal, and geographic "modes of reality come into constellated congruence so that each mode of reality functions as an exact metaphor for each of the others." See *Place and Vision*, 1, 2.

61. Silko, *Ceremony*, 145.

62. Silko, *Ceremony*, 177, 186.

63. Nelson, *Place and Vision*, 7.

64. Silko, *Ceremony*, 180–81.

65. Henderson, *Shadow and Self*, 65.

66. Silko, *Ceremony*, 192.

67. Silko, *Ceremony*, 194.

68. Silko, *Ceremony*, 195–96.

69. Nelson, *Place and Vision*, 9.

70. Owens, *Other Destinies*, 187.

71. Nelson, *Place and Vision*, 3.

72. Silko, *Ceremony*, 219.

73. Henderson, *Shadow and Self*, 94.

74. Silko, *Ceremony*, 229.

75. Silko, *Ceremony*, 63.

76. As Edith Swan argues, Tayo needs to recover the absent feminine and reconstruct the distorted masculine to become both a hunter and warrior and a nurturer of land and community ("Laguna Symbolic Geography," 236).

77. Silko, *Ceremony*, 191.

78. Silko, *Ceremony*, 242, 246.

79. Silko, *Ceremony*, 247.

80. Silko, *Ceremony*, 247.

81. Silko, *Ceremony*, 246.

82. Henderson, *Shadow and Self*, 93.

83. Henderson, *Shadow and Self*, 103, 107.

84. Owens, "As If," 15, 16.

85. Kingsolver, *Animal Dreams*, 72.

86. Comer, "Sidestepping Environmental Justice," 229, 230.

87. Kingsolver, *Animal Dreams*, 50.

88. Gustafson, "Dark Mother," 5.

89. See Morin, "Professor's Research."

90. Bedi, "Kali," 159–60.

91. Qtd. in Perry, *Backtalk*, 159.

92. Kingsolver, *Animal Dreams*, 52.

93. Kingsolver, *Animal Dreams*, 255, 180.

94. Pratt, "Archetypal Patterns," 368.

95. Kingsolver, *Animal Dreams*, 221.

96. Armstrong, *Short History of Myth*, 53–54.

97. Bedi, "Kali," 178.

98. Robert L. Moore, *Magician and the Analyst*, 19.

99. Kingsolver, *Animal Dreams*, 328.

100. Metzner, "Place and the Story," 2.

101. Plant, "Searching for Common Ground," 159–60.

7. THE CHIPPEWA NOVELS OF LOUISE ERDRICH: TRICKSTER AND RESTORATION

1. Erdrich, *Four Souls*, 127.

2. Mills, *In Service of the Wild*, 2.

3. Qtd. in Coltelli, "Louise Erdrich and Michael Dorris," 21.

4. Peterson, "History, Postmodernism," 987; Perez-Castillo, "Postmodernism," 292.

5. Gunn Allen, *Sacred Hoop*, 2.

6. Erdrich, *Bingo Palace*, 16, 17.

7. Perez-Castillo, "Postmodernism," 293.

8. Rainwater, "Reading between Worlds."

9. Erdrich, *Love Medicine*, 258.

10. Erdrich, *Last Report*, 360–61.

11. Vizenor, *Narrative Chance*, 5.

12. Meeker, "Comic Mode," 157, 159.

13. Erdrich, *Love Medicine*, 320.

14. Erdrich, *Bingo Palace*, 168.

15. Erdrich, *Love Medicine*, 42.

16. Gross, "Trickster and World Maintenance," 49.

17. Erdrich, *Tracks*, 225.

18. Purdy, "Against All Odds," 28.

19. Erdrich, *Love Medicine*, 312.

20. Johnston, *Ojibway Heritage*, 12–15.

21. Erdrich, *Tracks*, 35, 42.

22. Erdrich, *Tracks*, 139.

23. Gross, "Trickster and World Maintenance," 52.

24. Weaver, *That the People Might Live*, 11.

25. Brehm, "Metamorphoses," 682, 684.

26. Brehm, "Metamorphoses," 683.

27. Adamson, *American Indian Literature*, 103.

28. Erdrich, *Tracks*, 177.

29. Erdrich can, however, call on the trickster, who seems active in her composing process as well as in her stories. She describes how, in revising some of the episodes in *Love Medicine*, she and Dorris "realized some of the people who had different names were in fact the same character and that they would unite, very much the same way that this book has now turned into four books" (Coltelli, "Louise Erdrich and Michael Dorris," 21). The writing process Erdrich and Dorris describe here, one in which both of them approved every word after numerous revisions, seems to combine trickster and consciousness fruitfully.

30. Erdrich, *Beet Queen*, 50.

31. This familiar habit—of seeing oneself from outside; regarding one's person as an object of others' gaze; identifying with the images in magazines, fairy tales, or television—afflicts just about all the non-Indian characters in *The Beet Queen*. Such seeing from outside does not promote empathy, since there is no embodiment in the shifting; it only results in shame or inflation. This dynamic is arguably echoed in the name of the town itself. While Argus, North Dakota, is invented (although the *Argus Leader* is the newspaper of Sioux Falls), in Greek mythology Argus Panoptes was the all-seeing, with a hundred eyes. He conquered the dragon Echidna, and Hera made him guardian of the cow into which Io had been transformed. At Zeus's command Hermes put Argus to sleep and then cut off his head, freeing Io. Hera then transferred Argus's eyes to the tail of the peacock. His surname, Panoptes, further suggests the panopticon, Bentham's device for observing prisoners about which Foucault writes. His story seems further to connect to Pete Kozka's cow-eye lens, which Sita covets but which Pete gives to Mary Adare. To look at the world through a cow-eye

lens suggests taking a dairy farmer's view of the land, or perhaps that of his captive animals.

32. Erdrich, *Tracks*, 14, 12.

33. Erdrich, *Tracks*, 69, 68.

34. Erdrich, *Tracks*, 135, 137.

35. Erdrich, *Tracks*, 195.

36. Erdrich, *Tracks*, 205, 140.

37. Vizenor, *People Named the Chippewa*, 3–4.

38. Kerényi, "Trickster," 185.

39. Radin argues that the trickster is both "creator and destroyer, giver and negator, he who dupes others and who is always duped himself. He wills nothing consciously. At all times he is constrained to behave as he does from impulses over which he has no control. He knows neither good nor evil yet he is responsible for both. He possesses no values, moral or social, is at the mercy of his passions and appetites, yet through his actions all values come into being" (*Trickster*, ix).

40. Radin, *Trickster*, 133.

41. Johnston, *Ojibway Heritage*, 19, 20.

42. Erdrich, *Tracks*, 105.

43. Kerényi, "Trickster," 185.

44. Vizenor, *People Named the Chippewa*, 146.

45. Gross, "Trickster and World Maintenance," 63.

46. Jung, "On the Psychology," 196. Jung's essay again raises the troubling question of his use of the word *primitive*. One hypothesis Jung advances regarding the qualities of the trickster is that he represents an "earlier stage of consciousness which existed before the birth of the myth, when the Indian was still groping about in a similar mental darkness. Only when his consciousness reached a higher level could he detach the earlier state from himself and objectify it, that is, say anything about it" ("On the Psychology," 202). That is, the trickster represents a less evolved consciousness, a more instinctual state of awareness, which Jung identifies with the incident in which trickster is caught in an elk's skull. Both a creator and a buffoon, trickster has a "*divine-animal* nature, on the one hand superior to man because of his superhuman qualities, and on the other hand inferior to him because of his unreason and unconsciousness" ("On the Psychology," 204). Trickster represents a stage in the evolution of consciousness that precedes the consciousness capable of telling stories about trickster. Jung argues that some of the contempt and mockery associated with trickster comes from embarrassment at one's own previous ignorance; we can see this dynamic in individual development, where children do not like to be associated with what they think of as "childish." In this developmental sense not only is the figure of trickster a creation of a more evolved consciousness culturally, but he also represents an element of psyche that is perpetually at work, offering generative energy in an unformed state and transforming into something more conscious.

What's troublesome in Jung's expression is the suggestion that trickster stories come out of cultures that are "primitive," with all the negative, supercilious judgment the word implies. Indeed, Jung does from time to time speak of non-European cultures as "primitive," and in this he is bound by European notions of European superiority. What's interesting in his use of the word, however, are its implications of a consciousness or culture that is closer to its natural origins, "primeval," and somehow more authentic. As a student of the psyche, Jung (like everyone else) struggled to find a language to express what precedes language. Believing that the psyche undergoes development and differentiation in an individual, he projected that process onto the cultures he observed. However, sometimes discourse *on* the psyche is also a trickster discourse *of* the psyche, to paraphrase Trevi ("Towards a Critical Approach," 367). Talk *about* psyche is historical, geographical, and biographical. In imagining that his own culture was more fully developed than those of people he called "primitive," Jung was tripped by trickster. Jung saw at least two very different cultural orientations toward both nature and psyche, what we can call in shorthand traditional and European, but his explanatory system wasn't able to embrace the possibility that these were differences of ethics rather than evolution. He knew that one could be technologically advanced and emotionally undeveloped; he remarked that in Europe "outwardly people are more or less civilized but inwardly they are still primitives. Something in man is profoundly disinclined to give up his beginnings, and something else believes it has long since got beyond all that" ("On the Psychology," 208). I think Jung was ambivalent about the notion of the "primitive." At times he uses the term approvingly, to suggest people in closer touch with unconscious energies, less self-divided by an overdeveloped reason. At other times, as here, he seems to use it to suggest that even Europeans go in for superstition, because this sentence is followed by one in which he describes watching a Swiss "witch doctor" removing a spell from a stable located by a then-high-tech railroad line. Jung was bemused by the juxtaposition; that is, he both understood and valued those who live in relation to ritual and shared the assumption of his time that his civilization was "advanced." While Jung had spent time with Africans and with American Indians, he did not understand the culture of either, accepting the standard view of the time that Europe was "more evolved" than these "primitive" cultures. It seems odd to me today that anyone should equate a technology capable of killing across vast distances with cultural evolution, but I know that plenty of people do. In fact, just like the residents of Lake Wobegon, most people believe themselves to be "more evolved" than others (whom they can name) who are "less conscious" or "primitive" in relation to themselves. Personally, I know plenty of people who have ideas I consider Neanderthal. In any culture with power differentials, those with greater power will perceive those with less power as somehow deserving their condition; those with less power will perceive those with greater power either as objects of desire and emulation or as illegitimate and self-indulgent. In either case, let's hope that trickster provides them with a healthy dose of comic energy to counteract the damage such regard can do.

47. Vizenor, *People Named the Chippewa*, 6.

48. Duran and Duran, *Native American Postcolonial Psychology*, 30.

49. Erdrich, *Tracks*, 196, 7, 46, 101, 167.

50. Erdrich, *Tracks*, 114, 121.

51. Polly Elizabeth's narrative is also self-centered. However, she warms to Fleur in

large part through her affection for Fleur and John James Mauser's son, and her point of view becomes larger as her compassion grows. Her narrative dwindles to silence after she falls in love with the war-dumbed Fantan, and Margaret assumes the female voice at the end of *Four Souls*.

52. Vizenor, *Narrative Chance*, 188.

53. "Lipsha" is a Michif version of the French "le petit chou," a term of endearment that indicates Erdrich's fondness for him (Coltelli, "Louise Erdrich and Michael Dorris," 21).

54. Erdrich, *Bingo Palace*, 7.

55. Erdrich, *Bingo Palace*, 37.

56. Erdrich, *Bingo Palace*, 133, 136–37.

57. Erdrich, *Bingo Palace*, 143.

58. Erdrich, *Bingo Palace*, 217.

59. Erdrich, *Bingo Palace*, 218.

60. Erdrich, *Bingo Palace*, 218.

61. Erdrich, *Blue Jay's Dance*, 169, 176, 183.

62. Erdrich, *Bingo Palace*, 219, 221.

63. Erdrich, *Bingo Palace*, 104, 110–11.

64. Erdrich, *Bingo Palace*, 151, 154, 165, 188.

65. Erdrich, *Bingo Palace*, 229–30.

66. Pyne, "Consumed," 83.

67. Erdrich, *Bingo Palace*, 244, 245.

68. Erdrich, *Last Report*, 74.

69. Erdrich, *Last Report*, 41.

70. Erdrich, *Last Report*, 209, 213.

71. Erdrich, *Love Medicine*, 118.

72. Erdrich, *Love Medicine*, 258.

73. Erdrich, *Bingo Palace*, 151.

74. Bacon, "Emissary."

8. AFTERWORD

1. Leopold, *Sand County Almanac*, 251.

2. Walker, "Moral Understanding," 142.

3. Pratt, "Archetypal Patterns," 374, 375.

4. Jordan, "Ghosts in the Forest," 4.

5. Norden, "Ecological Restoration," 104.

6. Meekison and Higgs, "Rites of Spring," 79–80.

7. Leopold, *River of the Mother of God*, 338.

8. Momaday, *Man Made of Words*, 114.

9. Bedi, "Kali," 178.

10. See Spivak, "Can the Subaltern Speak?" 81.

11. Jung, *Psychological Types*, CW, 6.

Bibliography

Abram, David. *The Spell of the Sensuous: Perception and Language in a More-than-Human World.* New York: Pantheon Books, 1996.

Abrams, M. H., and Stephen Greenblatt. *The Norton Anthology of English Literature.* 7th ed. 2 vols. New York: W. W. Norton, 2000.

Achebe, Chinua. "An Image of Africa: Racism in Conrad's Heart of Darkness." In Conrad, *Heart of Darkness*, ed. Kimbrough, 251–62.

———. "Named for Victoria, Queen of England." In Ashcroft, Griffiths, and Tiffin, *The Post-Colonial Studies Reader*, 190–93.

———. *Things Fall Apart.* New York: Fawcett Crest, 1959.

Adam, Ian, and Helen Tiffin. *Past the Last Post: Theorizing Post-Colonialism and Post-Modernism.* Calgary: University of Calgary Press, 1990.

Adams, Michael Vannoy, "The Archetypal School." In Young-Eisendrath and Dawson, *The Cambridge Companion to Jung*, 101–18.

Adamson, Joni. *American Indian Literature, Environmental Justice, and Ecocriticism: The Middle Place.* Tucson: University of Arizona Press, 2001.

Alcoholics Anonymous. New York: Alcoholics Anonymous World Services Inc., 1976.

Aldrich, Marcia. "The Poetics of Transience: Marilynne Robinson's *Housekeeping*." *Essays in Literature* 16, no. 1 (1989): 127–40.

Allen, Chadwick. "Blood (and) Memory." *American Literature* 71, no. 1 (1999): 93–116.

Armbruster, Karla, and Kathleen Wallace. *Beyond Nature Writing: Expanding the Boundaries of Ecocriticism.* Charlottesville: University Press of Virginia, 2001.

Armstrong, Karen. *A Short History of Myth.* New York: Canongate Books, 2005.

Ashcroft, Bill, Gareth Griffiths, and Helen Tiffin. *The Empire Writes Back: Theory and Practice in Post-Colonial Literatures.* London and New York: Routledge, 1989.

———, eds. *The Post-Colonial Studies Reader.* London and New York: Routledge, 1996.

Atwood, Margaret. *Oryx and Crake.* New York: Anchor Books, 2004.

———. *Surfacing*. New York: Anchor Books, 1998. First published 1972 by Doubleday.

———. *Survival: A Thematic Guide to Canadian Literature*. Toronto: Anansi, 1972.

———. *Wilderness Tips*. New York: Doubleday, 1991.

Bacon, Katie. "An Emissary of the Between-World." *Atlantic*, January 17, 2001. http://www.theatlantic.com/doc/200101u/int2001-01-17.

Barash, David P. "Thinking of Biology: Evolutionary Existentialism, Sociobiology, and the Meaning of Life." *BioScience* 50 (November 2000): 1012–17.

Barker, Francis, Peter Hulme, and Margaret Iversen. *Colonial Discourse/Postcolonial Theory*. Manchester: Manchester University Press, 1994.

Barro, Susan C., and Alan D. Bright. "Public Views on Ecological Restoration." *Restoration and Management Notes* 16, no. 1 (1998): 59–65.

Barry, Dwight. "Toward Reconciling the Cultures of Wilderness and Restoration." *Restoration and Management Notes* 16, no. 2 (1998): 125–27.

Bartelt, Guillermo. "American Indian Geopiety in Scott Momaday's Discourse of the Moral Landscape." *Language and Literature* 23 (1998): 19–31.

Barzilai, Shuli. "Who Is He? The Missing Persons behind the Pronoun in Atwood's *Surfacing*." *Canadian Literature* 164 (Spring 2000): 57–79.

Bataille, Gretchen M., ed. *Native American Representations: First Encounters, Distorted Images, and Literary Appropriations*. Lincoln: University of Nebraska Press, 2001.

Bate, Jonathan. *The Song of the Earth*. Cambridge: Harvard University Press, 2000.

Bateson, Gregory. *Mind and Nature*. New York: Bantam Books, 1988. First published 1979 by Dutton.

Bedi, Ashok. "Kali--the Dark Goddess." In Gustafson, *The Moonlit Path*, 157–80.

Bellah, Robert N., Richard Madsen, William M. Sullivan, Ann Swidler, and Steven M. Tipton. *Habits of the Heart: Individualism and Commitment in American Life*. Rev. ed. Berkeley: University of California Press, 1996.

Berg, Peter. "Bioregionalism." 2000. http://www.bioregionalismo.com/analisis/BergBioregionalismoDefinicion.html.

Bernstein, Jerome S. *Living in the Borderland: The Evolution of Consciousness and the Challenge of Healing Trauma*. London: Routledge, 2005.

Berry, Thomas. *The Dream of the Earth*. San Francisco: Sierra Club Books, 1988.

Best, Steven, and Douglas Kellner. *Postmodern Theory: Critical Interrogations*. New York: Guilford Press, 1991.

Bevis, William. "Native American Novels: Homing In." In Fleck, *Critical Perspectives on Native American Fiction*, 15–45.

Bhabha, Homi. "Remembering Fanon." In Williams and Chrisman, *Colonial Discourse and Post-Colonial Theory*, 112–23.

———. "Signs Taken for Wonders." In Ashcroft, Griffiths, and Tiffin, *The Post-Colonial Studies Reader*, 29–35.

Biodiversity Recovery Plan. Chicago: Chicago Region Biodiversity Council, 1999.

Bishop, Peter. *The Greening of Psychology: The Vegetable World in Myth, Dream, and Healing*. Dallas: Spring Publications, 1990.

———. "Wilderness as a Victim of Progress." In Zweig and Abrams, *Meeting the Shadow*, 120–26.

Bloom, Harold, ed. *Native-American Writers*. Philadelphia: Chelsea House, 1998.

Bordo, Susan. "Feminism, Postmodernism, and Gender-Scepticism." In *Feminism/ Postmodernism*, ed. Linda J. Nicholson, 133–56. New York: Routledge, 1990.

Brehm, Victoria. "The Metamorphoses of an Ojibwa Manido." *American Literature* 68, no. 4 (1996): 677–707.

Brown, Joseph Epes. "The Roots of Renewal." In Capps, *Seeing with a Native Eye*, 25–34.

Brydon, Diana. "The White Inuit Speaks: Contamination as Literary Strategy." In Adam and Tiffin, *Past the Last Post*, 191–203.

Bührmann, M. Vera. "Nature, Psyche and a Healing Ceremony of the Xhosa." In *A Testament to the Wilderness*, 75–86.

Burke, William M. "Border Crossings in Marilynne Robinson's *Housekeeping*." *Modern Fiction Studies* 37, no. 4 (1991): 716–24.

Burlingame, Lori. "Empowerment through 'Retroactive Prophecy' in D'Arcy McNickle's *Runner in the Sun: A Story of Indian Maize*, James Welch's *Fools Crow*, and Leslie Marmon Silko's *Ceremony*." *American Indian Quarterly* 24 (Winter 2000): 1–18.

Campbell, SueEllen. "The Land and Language of Desire: Where Deep Ecology and Post Structuralism Meet." In Glotfelty and Fromm, *The Ecocriticism Reader*, 124–36.

Capps, Walter Holden, ed. *Seeing with a Native Eye*. New York: Harper and Row, 1976.

Carson, Rachel. *Silent Spring*. Boston: Houghton Mifflin, 2002. First published 1962 by Houghton Mifflin.

Carter, Anne. "Dark Water Grace: On Transcendence through Transience in *Housekeeping*." 2002. http://athena.english.vt.edu/~exlibris/essays02/Carter1 .html.

Chavkin, Allan, ed. *The Chippewa Landscape of Louise Erdrich*. Tuscaloosa: University of Alabama Press, 1999.

Chavkin, Allan, and Nancy Feyl Chavkin, eds. *Conversations with Louise Erdrich and Michael Dorris*. Jackson: University Press of Mississippi, 1994.

Churchill, Ward. *Fantasies of the Master Race: Literature, Cinema, and the Colonization of American Indians*. San Francisco: City Lights Books, 1998.

Clements, William M. "'Image and Word Cannot be Divided': N. Scott Momaday and Kiowa Ekphrasis." *Western American Literature* 36, no. 2 (2001): 134–52.

Cochran, Stuart. "Ethnic Implications of Stories, Spirits, and the Land in Native American Pueblo and Aztlan Writing." *MELUS* 20, no. 2 (1995): 69–91.

Coltelli, Laura. "Louise Erdrich and Michael Dorris." In Chavkin and Chavkin, *Conversations with Louise Erdrich and Michael Dorris*, 19–29.

Comer, Krista. "Sidestepping Environmental Justice: 'Natural' Landscapes and the Wilderness Plot." In *Breaking Boundaries: New Perspectives on Women's Regional Writing*, ed. Sherrie Inness and Diana Royer, 216–36. Iowa City: University of Iowa Press, 1997.

Conrad, Joseph. *Heart of Darkness: An Authoritative Text, Backgrounds and Sources, Criticism.* Ed. Robert Kimbrough. 3rd ed. New York: W. W. Norton, 1988.

———. *Heart of Darkness: Complete, Authoritative Text with Biographical and Historical Contexts, Critical History, and Essays from Five Contemporary Critical Perspectives.* Ed. Ross C. Murfin. 2nd ed. New York: Bedford Books of St. Martin's Press, 1996.

Cronon, William. *Changes in the Land: Indians, Colonists, and the Ecology of New England.* New York: Hill and Wang, 1983.

———. "The Trouble with Wilderness; or, Getting Back to the Wrong Nature." In *Uncommon Ground: Toward Reinventing Nature,* ed. William Cronon, 69–90. New York: W. W. Norton, 1995.

———, ed. *Uncommon Ground: Toward Reinventing Nature.* New York: W. W. Norton, 1995.

Davis, Randall C, "'Something Other and Irresistible and Wild': Bear in the Work of N. Scott Momaday." *JAISA: The Journal of the Association for the Interdisciplinary Study of the Arts* 1, no. 2 (1996): 79–87.

Deloria, Philip. *Playing Indian.* New Haven: Yale University Press, 1998.

Deloria, Vine, Jr. *C. G. Jung and the Sioux Traditions.* New Orleans: Spring Journal Books, 2008.

———. *God Is Red.* New York: Dell, 1973.

———. *Spirit and Reason.* Golden, CO: Fulcrum Publishing, 1999.

Devall, Bill. "The Deep Ecology Movement." In Merchant, *Ecology,* 125–39.

Devall, Bill, and George Sessions. *Deep Ecology.* Salt Lake City: Peregrine Smith Books, 1985.

Devit, Terry. "Paying Off Mother Nature." 1997. http://whyfiles.org/shorties/cost _nature.html.

Diamond, Irene, and Gloria Feman Orenstein, eds. *Reweaving the World: The Emergence of Ecofeminism.* San Francisco: Sierra Club Books, 1990.

Diffily, Anne Hinman. "My Mother, My Loss." *Brown Alumni Magazine,* May–June, 1998. http://www.brownalumnimagazine.com/storydetail.cfm?ID=1390.

Donovan, Kathleen. "'Menace among the Words': Women in the Novels of N. Scott Momaday." *Studies in American Indian Literatures,* series 2, 6, no. 4 (1994): 51–76.

Driver, Tom F. *The Magic of Ritual.* New York: Harper Collins, 1991.

Duran, Eduardo, and Bonnie Duran. *Native American Postcolonial Psychology.* Albany: State University of New York Press, 1995.

Durning, Alan Thein. "Are We Happy Yet?" In Roszak, Gomes, and Kanner, *Ecopsychology,* 68–76.

Edinger, Edward. *Ego and Archetype.* Boston: Shambhala, 1992.

Eliade, Mircea. *The Myth of the Eternal Return; or, Cosmos and History.* 1954. Reprint, Princeton: Princeton University Press, 1991.

Erdrich, Louise. *The Beet Queen.* New York: Bantam, 1986.

———. *The Bingo Palace.* New York: Harper Collins, 1995.

———. *The Blue Jay's Dance.* New York: Harper Collins, 1995.

———. *Four Souls.* New York: Harper Collins, 2004.

————. *The Last Report on the Miracles at Little No Horse.* New York: Harper Collins, 2001.

————. *Love Medicine.* New York: Harper Collins, 1984.

————. *Tales of Burning Love.* New York: Harper Collins, 1996.

————. *Tracks.* New York: Harper Collins, 1988.

Ezenwa-Ohaeto. *Chinua Achebe: A Biography.* Oxford: James Currey Ltd., 1997.

Ferrari, Rita. "'Where the Maps Stopped': The Aesthetics of Borders in Louise Erdrich's *Love Medicine* and *Tracks.*" *Style* 33, no. 1 (1999): 144–65.

Fiamengo, Janice. "Postcolonial Guilt in Margaret Atwood's *Surfacing.*" *American Review of Canadian Studies* 29, no. 1 (1999): 141–63.

Finch, Robert, and John Elder, eds. *The Norton Book of Nature Writing.* New York: W. W. Norton, 1990.

Fleck, Richard F. *Critical Perspectives on Native American Fiction.* Pueblo, CO: Passeggiata Press, 1997.

Fox, Matthew. *Original Blessings.* Santa Fe: Bear and Co., 1983.

Frantz, Gilda. "Discussion." In Mattoon, *Archetype of Shadow in a Split World,* 174–77.

Frischkorn, Craig. "The Shadow of Tsoai: Autobiographical Bear Power in N. Scott Momaday's *The Ancient Child* (1989)." *Journal of Popular Culture* 33, no. 2 (1999): 23–29.

Fromm, Harold. "From Transcendence to Obsolescence: A Route Map." In Glotfelty and Fromm, *The Ecocriticism Reader,* 30–39.

Galehouse, Maggie. "Their Own Private Idaho: Transience in Marilynne Robinson's *Housekeeping.*" *Contemporary Literature* 41, no. 1 (2000): 117–38.

Gee, Henry. "Costing the Wood for the Trees." *Nature Science Update,* 2000. http://www.nature.com/news/2000/000706/pdf/000706-9.pdf.

Gilligan, Carol. *In a Different Voice: Psychological Theory and Women's Development.* Cambridge: Harvard University Press, 1982.

Gish, Robert F. "Life into Death, Death into Life: Hunting as Metaphor and Motive in *Love Medicine.*" In Chavkin, *The Chippewa Landscape of Louise Erdrich,* 66–83.

Glendinning, Chellis. "Technology, Trauma, and the Wild." In Roszak, Gomes, and Kanner, *Ecopsychology,* 41–54.

Glotfelty, Cheryll. "Introduction." In Glotfelty and Fromm, *The Ecocriticism Reader,* xv–xxxvii.

Glotfelty, Cheryll, and Harold Fromm. *The Ecocriticism Reader: Landmarks in Literary Ecology.* Athens: University of Georgia Press, 1996.

Grassie, William. "Donna Haraway's Metatheory of Science and Religion: Cyborgs, Trickster, and Hermes." *Zygon* 31 (June 1996): 285–304.

Gross, Lawrence W. "The Trickster and World Maintenance: An Anishinaabe Reading of Louise Erdrich's *Tracks.*" *Studies in American Indian Literatures,* series 2, 17, no. 3 (2005): 48–66.

Grossinger, Richard, ed. *Ecology and Consciousness: Traditional Wisdom on the Environment.* Berkeley: North Atlantic Books, 1978.

Guerard, Albert J. "The Journey Within." In Conrad, *Heart of Darkness*, ed. Kimbrough, 243–51.

Guha, Ramachandra. "Radical Environmentalism: A Third-World Critique." In Merchant, *Ecology*, 281–89.

Gunn Allen, Paula. *The Sacred Hoop: Recovering the Feminine in American Indian Traditions*. Boston: Beacon Press, 1986.

Gustafson, Frederick. "The Dark Mother, the Dark Earth, and the Loss of Native Soul." In Gustafson, *The Moonlit Path*, 1–10.

———, ed. *The Moonlit Path: Reflections on the Dark Feminine*. Berwick, ME: Nicolas-Hays, 2003.

Hall, Stuart. "Cultural Identity and Diaspora." In Williams and Chrisman, *Colonial Discourse and Post-Colonial Theory*, 392–403.

Haraway, Donna J. *Simians, Cyborgs, and Women: The Reinvention of Nature*. New York: Routledge, 1991.

Harrison, Robert Pogue. *Forests: The Shadow of Civilization*. Chicago: University of Chicago Press, 1992.

Hauke, Christopher. *Jung and the Postmodern: The Interpretation of Realities*. London: Routledge, 2000.

Held, Virginia. *Justice and Care: Essential Readings in Feminist Ethics*. Boulder: Westview Press, 1995.

Heldrich, Philip. "Constructing the Self through Language and Vision in N. Scott Momaday's *The Ancient Child*." *Southwestern American Literature* 2, no. 2 (1997): 11–19.

Henderson, Joseph L. *Shadow and Self: Selected Papers in Analytical Psychology*. Wilmette, IL: Chiron, 1990.

Hillman, James. *Archetypal Psychology: A Brief Account*. Dallas: Spring Publications, 1983.

———. *Healing Fiction*. Dallas: Spring Publications, 1983.

———. *Insearch: Psychology and Religion*. Woodstock, CT: Spring Publications, 1967.

———. "Justice and Beauty: Foundations of an Ecological Psychology." October 2001. http://www.online.pacifica.edu/alumni/facultyynews/medalhillman.

———. "A Psyche the Size of the Earth: A Psychological Foreword." In Roszak, Gomes, and Kanner, *Ecopsychology*, xvii–xxiii.

———. *The Thought of the Heart and the Soul of the World*. Woodstock, CT: Spring Publications, 1997.

Hochman, Jhan. "Green Cultural Studies: An Introductory Critique of an Emerging Discipline." *Mosaic* 30 (March 1997): 81–96.

Hochschild, Adam. *King Leopold's Ghost*. New York: Houghton Mifflin, 1998.

Hogan, Linda. *Dwellings: A Spiritual History of the Living World*. New York: Simon and Schuster, 1995.

———. "Who Puts Together." In Fleck, *Critical Perspectives on Native American Fiction*, 134–42.

Horkheimer, Max, and Theodor Adorno. "The Concept of Enlightenment." Trans. John Cumming. In Merchant, *Ecology*, 44–50.

House, Freeman. "Learning Home: The Bioregion, the Community, and the University." Talk presented at Cornell University, April 3, 2000.

Howarth, William. "Some Principles of Ecocriticism." In Glotfelty and Fromm, *The Ecocriticism Reader*, 69–91.

Howells, Coral Ann. *Margaret Atwood*. London: Macmillan, 1996.

Hultberg, Peer. "Shame: An Overshadowed Emotion." In Mattoon, *The Archetype of Shadow in a Split World*, 157–73.

Hutcheon, Linda. "Circling the Downspout of Empire." In Adam and Tiffin, *Past the Last Post*, 167–89.

Inness, Sherrie A., and Diana Royer, eds. *Breaking Boundaries: New Perspectives on Women's Regional Writing*. Iowa City: University of Iowa Press, 1997.

Jacoby, Mario. "The Analytical Psychology of C. G. Jung and the Problem of Literary Evaluation." In Sugg, *Jungian Literary Criticism*, 59–75.

Jahner, Elaine. "An Act of Attention: Event Structure in *Ceremony*." In Bloom, *Native-American Writers*, 35–44.

Jameson, Fredric. *The Political Unconscious*. Ithaca: Cornell University Press, 1981.

JanMohamed, Abdul R. *Manichean Aesthetics: The Politics of Literature in Colonial Africa*. Amherst: University of Massachusetts Press, 1983.

Jaskoski, Helen. "The Ancient Child: A Note on Background." *Studies in American Indian Literatures*, series 2, 2, no. 4 (1990): 14–15.

Johnston, Basil. *Ojibway Heritage: The Ceremonies, Rituals, Songs, Dances, Prayers and Legends of the Ojibway*. Toronto: McClelland and Stewart Inc., 1976.

Jordan, William C., III. "The Ghosts in the Forest." *Restoration and Management Notes* 11, no. 1 (1993): 3–4.

Jung, C. G. *Answer to Job*. Trans. R. F. C. Hull. New York: Meridian Books, 1960.

———. *Collected Works*. Trans. R. F. C. Hull. 18 vols. Princeton: Princeton University Press, 1958.

———. *Man and His Symbols*. With Marie-Louise von Franz, Joseph L. Henderson, Jolande Jacobi, and Aniela Jaffe. New York: Dell, 1964.

———. *Memories, Dreams, Reflections*. Ed. Aniela Jaffe. Trans. Richard Winston and Clara Winston. Rev. ed. New York: Vintage Books/Random House, 1989.

———. "On the Psychology of the Trickster Figure." Trans. R. F. C. Hull. In Radin, *The Trickster*, 195–211.

Kaivola, Karen. "The Pleasures and Perils of Merging: Female Subjectivity in Marilynne Robinson's *Housekeeping*." *Contemporary Literature* 34, no. 4 (1993): 670–90.

Kamerling, Jane. "Lilith." In Gustafson, *The Moonlit Path*, 97–110.

Karl, Frederick R. *Joseph Conrad: The Three Lives*. New York: Farrar, Straus and Giroux, 1979.

Kerényi, Karl. "Trickster." In Radin, *The Trickster*, 173–91.

King, Kristin. "Resurfactings of the Deeps: Semiotic Balance in Marilynne Robinson's *Housekeeping*." *Studies in the Novel* 28, no. 4 (96): 565–84.

Kingsolver, Barbara. *Animal Dreams*. New York: Harper Collins, 1990.

Kirkby, Joan. "Is There Life after Art? The Metaphysics of Marilynne Robinson's *Housekeeping.*" *Tulsa Studies in Women's Literature* 4 (1986): 91–109.

Knobloch, Frieda. *The Culture of Wilderness.* Chapel Hill: University of North Carolina Press, 1996.

Kolodny, Annette. *The Lay of the Land: Metaphor as Experience and History in American Life and Letters.* Chapel Hill: University of North Carolina Press, 1975.

Krupat, Arnold. "Postcolonialism, Ideology, and Native American Literature." In *Postcolonial Theory and the United States: Race, Ethnicity, and Literature,* ed. Amarit Singh and Peter Schmidt, 73–94. Jackson: University Press of Mississippi, 2000.

———. *The Turn to the Native: Studies in Criticism and Culture.* Lincoln: University of Nebraska Press, 1996.

LaDuke, Winona. "From Resistance to Regeneration." In Merchant, *Ecology,* 266–71.

———. "Recovering the Land." *Environmental Action* (Fall 1993): 15–16.

Lassman, Ken. "Living on the Prairie—A Bioregional Perspective." http://www .larryville.com/articles/ken_prai.htm.

Lauter, Estella, and Carol Schreier Rupprecht. *Feminist Archetypal Theory: Interdisciplinary Re-visions of Jungian Thought.* Knoxville: University of Tennessee Press, 1985.

Leiss, William. *Under Technology's Thumb.* Montreal: Queen's University Press, 1990.

Leopold, Aldo. *The River of the Mother of God and Other Essays.* Ed. Susan L. Falder and J . Baird Callicott. Madison: University of Wisconsin Press, 1991.

———. *A Sand County Almanac.* San Francisco: Sierra Club/Ballantine, 1970.

Louv, Richard. *Last Child in the Woods: Saving Our Children from Nature-Deficit Disorder.* Chapel Hill: Algonquin Books, 2005.

Love, Glen A. *Practical Ecocriticism: Literature, Biology, and the Environment.* Charlottesville: University of Virginia Press, 2003.

Mackey, Eva. "Death by Landscape: Race, Nature, and Gender in Canadian Nationalist Mythology." *Canadian Women's Studies* 20, no. 2 (2000): 125–30.

Macy, Joanna. "Toward a Healing of Self and World." In Merchant, *Ecology,* 292–98.

Manes, Christopher. "Nature and Silence." In Glotfelty and Fromm, *The Ecocriticism Reader,* 15–29.

Martin, Calvin Luther. *In the Spirit of the Earth: Rethinking History and Time.* Baltimore: Johns Hopkins University Press, 1992.

Marx, Leo. *The Machine in the Garden.* New York: Oxford University Press, 1964.

Matchie, Tom. "Building on the Myth: Recovering Native American Culture in Louise Erdrich's *The Bingo Palace.*" In Morrison, *American Indian Studies,* 299–312.

Mattoon, Mary Ann, ed. *The Archetype of Shadow in a Split World: Proceedings of the Tenth International Congress for Analytical Psychology.* Einsiedeln, Switzerland: Daimon Verlag, 1987.

Meeker, Joseph. "The Comic Mode." In Glotfelty and Fromm, *The Ecocriticism Reader,* 155–69.

Meekison, Lisa, and Eric Higgs. "The Rites of Spring (and Other Seasons): The Ritualizing of Restoration." *Restoration and Management Notes* 16, no. 1 (1998): 79–80.

Meier, C. A. *Healing Dream and Ritual: Ancient Incubation and Modern Psychotherapy.* Einsiedeln, Switzerland: Daimon Verlag, 1989.

Merchant, Carolyn. *The Death of Nature.* New York: Harper and Row, 1983.

———, ed. *Ecology: Key Concepts in Critical Theory.* Atlantic Highlands, NJ: Humanities Press, 1994.

Metzner, Ralph. "The Place and the Story: Where Ecopsychology and Bioregionalism Meet." http://trumpeter.athabascau.ca/index.php/trumpet/article/viewFile/308/463.

———. "The Psychopathology of the Human-Nature Relationship." In Roszak, Gomes, and Kanner, *Ecopsychology,* 55–67.

Mills, Stephanie. *In Service of the Wild: Restoring and Reinhabiting Damaged Land.* Boston: Beacon Press, 1995.

———. "Making Amends to the Myriad Creatures." Great Barrington, MA: E. F. Schumacher Society, 1991.

Mishra, Vijay, and Bob Hodge. "What Is Post(-)Colonialism?" In Williams and Chrisman, *Colonial Discourse and Post-Colonial Theory: A Reader,* 276–90.

Momaday, N. Scott. *The Ancient Child.* New York: Harper Collins, 1990.

———. *House Made of Dawn.* New York: Harper Collins, 1989. First published 1968 by Harper and Row.

———. *The Man Made of Words.* New York: St. Martin's Griffin, 1998.

———. "Native American Attitudes to the Environment." In Capps, *Seeing with a Native Eye,* 79–85.

———. *The Way to Rainy Mountain.* Albuquerque: University of New Mexico Press, 1969.

Moore, David L. "Return of the Buffalo: Cultural Representation as Cultural Property." In Bataille, *Native American Representations,* 52–78.

Moore, Robert L. *The Magician and the Analyst.* Philadelphia: Xlibris, 2002.

Morace, Robert A. "From Sacred Hoops to Bingo Palaces: Louise Erdrich's Carnivalesque Fiction." In Chavkin, *The Chippewa Landscape of Louise Erdrich,* 36–66.

Morin, Richard P. "Professor's Research Breaks the Collective Silence Surrounding Loss of a Mother." *George Street Journal,* November 1996. http://www.brown.edu/Administration/George_Street_Journal/Davidman.html.

Morrison, Dane, ed. *American Indian Studies: An Interdisciplinary Approach to Contemporary Issues.* New York: Peter Lang, 1997.

Moser, Irene. "Native American Imaginative Spaces." In Morrison, *American Indian Studies,* 287–97.

Murphy, Patrick. *Farther Afield in the Study of Nature-Oriented Literature.* Charlottesville: University Press of Virginia, 2000.

Myers, Jeffrey. "The Anxiety of Confluence: Evolution, Ecology, and Imperialism in Conrad's *Heart of Darkness.*" *Interdisciplinary Studies in Literature and the Environment* 8, no. 2 (2001): 97–108.

Nabhan, Gary Paul. "Cultural Parallax in Viewing North American Habitats." In Soule and Lease, *Reinventing Nature?* 87–101.

———. *Cultures of Habitat: On Nature, Culture, and Story.* Washington, DC: Counterpoint, 1997.

Navota, Jason, and Dennis W. Dreher. *Protecting Nature in Your Community.* Chicago: Northwestern Illinois Planning Commission, 2000.

Nelson, Robert M. *Place and Vision: The Function of Landscape in Native American Fiction.* New York: Peter Lang, 1993.

———. "Place, Vision, and Identity in Native American Literatures." In Morrison, *American Indian Studies,* 265–79.

Newman, Lance. "Marxism and Ecocriticism." *Interdisciplinary Studies in Literature and the Environment* 9, no.2 (2002): 1–25.

Ngugi wa Thiong'o, *Decolonising the Mind: The Politics of Language in African Literature.* London: Heinemann, 1987.

Nicholson, Colin, ed. *Margaret Atwood: Writing and Subjectivity.* New York: St. Martin's Press, 1994.

Nicholson, Linda J. *Feminism/Postmodernism.* New York: Routledge, 1990.

Noddings, Nel. *Caring: A Feminine Approach to Ethics and Moral Education.* Berkeley: University of California Press, 1984.

Norden, Christopher. "Ecological Restoration as Post-Colonial Ritual of Community in Three Native American Novels." *Studies in American Indian Literatures,* series 2, 6, no. 4 (1994): 94–106.

Oelschlaeger, Max. *The Wilderness Condition: Essays on Environment and Civilization.* Washington, DC: Island Press, 1992.

Olney, James. *Tell Me Africa: An Approach to African Literature.* Princeton: Princeton University Press, 1973.

Ong, Walter J. *Orality and Literacy: The Technologizing of the Word.* London: Routledge, 1982.

O'Rourke, Meghan. "A Moralist of the Midwest." *New York Times Magazine,* October 24, 2004, 63–67.

Ortiz, Simon J. "The Historical Matrix Towards a National Indian Literature: Cultural Authenticity in Nationalism." In Fleck, *Critical Perspectives on Native American Fiction,* 64–68.

Owens, Louis. "As If an Indian Were Really an Indian: Native American Voices and Postcolonial Theory." In Bataille, *Native American Representations,* 11–24.

———. *Mixedblood Messages: Literature, Film, Family, Place.* Norman: University of Oklahoma Press, 2001.

———. *Other Destinies: Understanding the American Indian Novel.* Norman: University of Oklahoma Press, 1992.

Palmer, Louis H., III, "Articulating the Cyborg: An Impure Model for Environmental Revolution," In *The Greening of Literary Scholarship,* ed. Steven Rosendale, 165–77. Iowa City: University of Iowa Press, 2002.

Papadopoulos, Renos, ed. *Carl Gustav Jung: Critical Assessments.* 4 vols. London: Routledge, 1992.

Parkman, Francis, Jr. *The Oregon Trail*. Ed. David Levin. New York: Penguin, 1982.

Perez-Castillo, Susan. "Postmodernism, Native American Literature and the Real: The Silko-Erdrich Controversy." *Massachusetts Review* 32, no. 2 (1991): 285–94.

Perry, Donna. *Backtalk: Women Writers Speak Out*. New Brunswick: Rutgers University Press, 1993.

Peterson, Nancy J. "History, Postmodernism, and Louise Erdrich's *Tracks*." *PMLA* 109, no. 5 (1994): 982–94.

Philipson, Morris. "Outline of a Jungian Aesthetics." In Sugg, *Jungian Literary Criticism*, 214–27.

Plant, Judith. "Searching for Common Ground: Ecofeminism and Bioregionalism." In Diamond and Orenstein, *Reweaving the World*, 155–61.

Post, Susan L. "Biodiversity Blitz: A Day in the Life of . . ." Chicago: Illinois Steward and Chicago Wilderness, 2002.

Pratt, Annis V. "Archetypal Patterns in Women's Fiction." In Sugg, *Jungian Literary Criticism*, 367–75.

———. "Spinning among Fields: Jung, Frye, Levi-Strauss and Feminist Archetypal Theory." In Lauter and Rupprecht, *Feminist Archetypal Theory*, 94–136.

Purdy, John. "Against All Odds: Games of Chance in the Novels of Louise Erdrich." In Chavkin, *The Chippewa Landscape of Louise Erdrich*, 8–35.

Pyne, Stephen J. "Consumed by Either Fire or Fire: A Prolegomenon to Anthropogenic Fire." In *Earth, Air, Fire, Water: Humanistic Studies of the Environment*, ed. Jill Ker Conway, Kenneth Keniston, and Leo Marx, 78–101. Amherst: University of Massachusetts Press, 1999.

Radin, Paul. *The Trickster: A Study in American Indian Mythology*. With commentaries by Karl Kerényi and C. G. Jung. New York: Philosophical Library, 1956.

Rainwater, Catherine. "Ethnic Signs in Erdrich's *Tracks* and *The Bingo Palace*." In Chavkin, *The Chippewa Landscape of Louise Erdrich*, 144–60.

———. "Planes, Lines, Shapes, and Shadows: N. Scott Momaday's Iconological Imagination." *Texas Studies in Literature and Language* 37, no. 4 (1995): 376–93.

———. "Reading between Worlds: Narrativity in the Fiction of Louise Erdrich." *American Literature* 62, no. 1 (1990): 405–22.

Rappaport, Roy A. "Sanctity and Adaptation." In *Ecology and Consciousness: Traditional Wisdom on the Environment*, ed. Richard Grossinger, 105–34. Berkeley: North Atlantic Books, 1978.

Robinson, Marilynne. *Housekeeping*. New York: Bantam, 1981.

Roemer, Kenneth M. "Ancient Children at Play—Lyric, Petroglyphic, and Ceremonial." In Fleck, *Critical Perspectives on Native American Fiction*, 99–113.

Rosendale, Steven, ed. *The Greening of Literary Scholarship*. Iowa City: University of Iowa Press, 2002.

Roszak, Theodore. *The Voice of the Earth: An Exploration of Ecopsychology*. New York: Touchstone, 1992.

———. "Where Psyche Meets Gaia." In Roszak, Gomes, and Kanner, *Ecopsychology*, 1–20.

Roszak, Theodore, Mary E. Gomes, and Allen D. Kanner, eds. *Ecopsychology: Restoring the Earth, Healing the Mind.* San Francisco: Sierra Club Books, 1995.

Rowland, Susan. *C. G. Jung and Literary Theory: The Challenge from Fiction.* London: Macmillan Press, 1999.

Rubenstein, Roberta. "Homeric Resonances: Longing and Belonging in Barbara Kingsolver's *Animal Dreams.*" In *Homemaking: Women Writers and the Politics and Poetics of Home,* ed. Catherine Wiley and Fiona R. Barnes, 5–21. New York: Garland Publishing, 1996.

Ruddick, Sara. *Maternal Thinking: Towards a Politics of Peace.* Boston: Beacon Press, 1989.

Ruoff, A. Lavonne Brown. *American Indian Literatures.* New York: MLA, 1990.

Rushing, Janice Hocker, and Thomas S. Frentz. *Projecting the Shadow: The Cyborg Hero in American Film.* Chicago: University of Chicago Press, 1995.

Said, Edward. *Culture and Imperialism.* New York: Vintage Books/Random House, 1994.

———. *Orientalism.* New York: Vintage Books, 1979.

Salman, Sherry. "The Creative Psyche: Jung's Major Contributions." In Young-Eisendrath and Dawson, *The Cambridge Companion to Jung,* 52–70.

Samuels, Andrew. "Jung and the Post-Jungians." In Young-Eisendrath and Dawson, *The Cambridge Companion to Jung,* 1–13.

———. *The Political Psyche.* London: Routledge, 1993.

Sanford, John A. "Dr. Jekyll and Mr. Hyde." In Zweig and Abrams, *Meeting the Shadow,* 29–34.

Scarberry-Garcia, Susan. *Landmarks of Healing: A Study of House Made of Dawn.* Albuquerque: University of New Mexico Press, 1971.

Schama, Simon. *Landscape and Memory.* New York: Knopf, 1995.

Schechner, Richard. *The Future of Ritual.* London and New York: Routledge, 1993.

Sessions, George. "Ecocentrism, Wilderness, and Global Ecosystem Protection." In Oelschlaeger, *The Wilderness Condition,* 90–130.

Shanley, Kathryn. "The Indians America Loves to Love and Read: American Indian Identity and Cultural Appropriation." In Bataille, *Native American Representations,* 26–49.

Shepard, Paul. *Man in the Landscape: A Historical View of the Esthetics of Nature.* New York: Knopf, 1967.

———. *Nature and Madness.* San Francisco: Sierra Club Books, 1982.

———. "A Post-Historical Primitivism." In Oelschlaeger, *The Wilderness Condition,* 40–89.

Silko, Leslie Marmon. *Ceremony.* New York: Penguin, 1977.

———. "Landscape, History, and the Pueblo Imagination." In *The Norton Book of Nature Writing,* ed. Robert Finch and John Elder, 883–94. New York: W. W. Norton, 1990.

Singh, Amartjit, and Peter Schmidt. *Postcolonial Theory and the United States: Race, Ethnicity, and Literature.* Jackson: University Press of Mississippi, 2000.

Slemon, Stephen. "Modernism's Last Post." In Adam and Tiffin, *Past the Last Post*, 1–11.

Slovic, Scott. "Nature Writing and Environmental Psychology: The Interiority of Outdoor Experience." In Glotfelty and Fromm, *The Ecocriticism Reader*, 351–70.

Smith, Jeanne Rosier. "Comic Liberators and Word-Healers: The Interwoven Trickster Narratives of Louise Erdrich." In Bloom, *Native-American Writers*, 259–76.

Smith, Johanna M. "'Too Beautiful Altogether': Ideologies of Gender and Empire in *Heart of Darkness*." In *Heart of Darkness: Complete, Authoritative Text with Biographical and Historical Contexts, Critical History, and Essays from Five Contemporary Critical Perspectives*, by Joseph Conrad, ed. Ross C. Murfin, 169–84. New York: St. Martin's/Bedford, 1996.

Smith, Linda Tuhiwai. *Decolonizing Methodologies: Research and Indigenous Peoples*. London: Zed Books Ltd., 1999.

Smith, Ruth L. "Negotiating Homes: Morality as a Scarce Good." *Cultural Critique* 38 (Winter 1997–98): 177–95.

Smyth, Jacqui. "Sheltered Vagrancy in Marilynne Robinson's *Housekeeping*." *Critique Studies in Contemporary Fiction* 40, no. 3 (1999): 281–92.

Snyder, Gary. *The Practice of the Wild*. Berkeley: North Point Press, 1990.

Somé, Malidoma Patrice. *Ritual: Power, Healing and Community*. Portland, OR: Swan/Raven, 1993.

Soule, Michael E., and Gary Lease. *Reinventing Nature? Responses to Postmodern Deconstruction*. Covelo, CA: Island Press, 1995.

Soyinka, Wole. *Myth, Literature and the African World*. Cambridge: Cambridge University Press, 1976.

Spivak, Gayatri Chakravorty. "Can the Subaltern Speak?" In Williams and Chrisman, *Colonial Discourse and Post-Colonial Theory*, 66–111.

Spretnak, Charlene. "Ecofeminism: Our Roots and Flowering." In Diamond and Orenstein, *Reweaving the World*, 3–14.

Staels, Hilde. "The Social Construction of Identity and the Lost Female Imaginary in M. Atwood's *Surfacing*." *Journal of Commonwealth and Postcolonial Studies* 6, no. 2 (1999): 20–35.

States, Bert O. *Dreaming and Storytelling*. Ithaca: Cornell University Press, 1993.

Stein, Murray. *In Midlife: A Jungian Perspective*. Woodstock, CT: Spring Publications, 1983.

Stein, Robert. *Incest and Human Love*. 2nd ed. Dallas: Spring Publications, 1984.

Stevens, Anthony. *Archetype Revisited: An Updated Natural History of the Self*. Toronto: Inner City Books, 2003.

———. *On Jung*. New York: Penguin, 1990.

Stevens, Jason W. "Bear, Outlaw and Storyteller: American Frontier Mythology and the Ethnic Subjectivity of N. Scott Momaday." *American Literature* 73, no. 3 (2001): 599–631.

Stevens, William K. *Miracle under the Oaks: The Revival of Nature in America*. New York: Pocket Books, 1995.

Stevenson, Sheryl. "Trauma and Memory in Kingsolver's *Animal Dreams*." *Literature, Interpretation, Theory* 11, no. 4 (2001): 327–50.

Sugg, Richard P., ed. *Jungian Literary Criticism*. Evanston: Northwestern University Press, 1992.

Sullivan, Jerry. *An Atlas of Biodiversity*. N.p: n.d.

———. *Hunting for Frogs on Elston*. Illus. Bobby Sutton. Chicago: University of Chicago Press, 2004.

Swan, Edith. "Laguna Prototypes of Manhood in *Ceremony*." *MELUS* 17, no. 1 (1991–92): 39–61.

———. "Laguna Symbolic Geography and Silko's *Ceremony*." *American Indian Quarterly* 12 (Summer 1988): 229–49.

Swartz, Patti Capel. "'Saving Grace': Political and Environmental Issues and the Role of Connections in Barbara Kingsolver's *Animal Dreams*." *Interdisciplinary Studies in Literature and the Environment* 1, no. 1 (1993): 65–80.

Swink, Floyd, and Gerould Wilhelm. *Plants of the Chicago Region*. 4th ed. Indianapolis: Indiana Academy of Science, 1994.

Tacey, David. "Negotiating the Numinous: Towards a Taxonomy of Jungian Studies." Talk presented at the Joint Conference of the International Association of Jungian Scholars and the International Association of Analytical Psychology. July 7, 2005. College Station, TX. http://www.jungianstudies.org/conferences/texas/papers/TaceyD.pdf.

Tallmadge, John. "Resistance to Urban Nature." *Michigan Quarterly Review* 40, no. 1 (2001): 178–89.

Testament to the Wilderness, A: Ten Essays on an Address by C. A. Meier. Zurich: Daimon Verlag, 1985.

Thoreau, Henry David. *Walden and Other Writings*. Ed. Brooks Atkinson. New York: Modern Library, 1992.

Tiffin, Helen. "Introduction." In Adam and Tiffin, *Past the Last Post*, vii–xvi.

Todorov, Tzvetan. *The Conquest of America: The Question of the Other*. Trans. Richard Howard. New York: Harper Collins, 1992.

Toelken, Barre. "'Seeing with a Native Eye: How Many Sheep Will It Hold?'" In Capps, *Seeing with a Native Eye*, 9–24.

Trevi, Mario. "Towards a Critical Approach to Jung." In *Carl Gustav Jung: Critical Assessments*, ed. Renos Papadopoulos, 1: 356–75. London: Routledge, 1992.

Turner, Frederick. "Cultivating the American Garden." In Glotfelty and Fromm, *The Ecocriticism Reader*, 40–51.

Turner, Victor. *From Ritual to Theater: The Human Seriousness of Play*. New York: Performing Arts Journal Publications, 1982.

Van der Post, Laurens. "Wilderness—A Way of Truth." In *A Testament to the Wilderness*, 45–58.

Van Dyke, Annette. "Of Vision Quests and Spirit Guardians: Female Power in the

Novels of Louise Erdrich." In Chavkin, *The Chippewa Landscape of Louise Erdrich*, 130–43.

Velie, Alan. "The Indian Historical Novel." In Bloom, *Native-American Writers*, 195–209.

Vizenor, Gerald. *Manifest Manners: Narratives on Postindian Survivance*. Lincoln: University of Nebraska Press, 1999.

———, ed. *Narrative Chance: Postmodern Discourse on Native American Indian Literatures*. Albuquerque: University of New Mexico Press, 1989.

———. *The People Named the Chippewa: Narrative Histories*. Minneapolis: University of Minnesota Press, 1984.

———. "A Postmodern Introduction." In Vizenor, *Narrative Chance*, 3–16.

———, ed. *Summer in the Spring: Ojibwe Lyric Poems and Tribal Stories*. Minneapolis: Nodin Press, 1981.

———, ed. *Touchwood: A Collection of Ojibway Prose*. Minneapolis: New Rivers Press, 1987.

———. "Trickster Discourse: Comic Holotropes and Language Games." In Vizenor, *Narrative Chance*, 187–212.

von Franz, Marie-Louise. "The Process of Individuation." In *Man and His Symbols*, ed. C. G. Jung, 157–254. New York: Dell, 1964.

———. *Shadow and Evil in Fairy Tales*. Rev. ed. Boston: Shambhala, 1995.

Walker, Margaret Urban. "Moral Understanding: Alternative 'Epistemology' for a Feminist Ethics." In *Justice and Care: Essential Readings in Feminist Ethics*, ed. Virginia Held, 139–52. Boulder: Westview Press, 1995.

Wallace, Karen L. "Liminality and Myth in Native American Fiction: *Ceremony* and *The Ancient Child*." *American Indian Culture and Research Journal* 20, no. 4 (1996): 91–119.

Ward, David. "*Surfacing*: Separation, Transition, Incorporation." In *Margaret Atwood: Writing and Subjectivity*, ed. Colin Nicholson, 94–118. New York: St. Martin's Press, 1994.

———. *A Grain of Wheat*. Oxford: Heineman, 1967.

Watkins, Mary. "From Individualism to the Interdependent Self: Changing the Paradigm of the Self in Psychotherapy." *Psychological Perspectives* 27(Fall–Winter 1992):52–69.

Weaver, Jace. *That the People Might Live: Native American Literatures and Native American Community*. New York: Oxford University Press, 1997.

Wehr, Demaris S. "Religious and Social Dimensions of Jung's Concept of the Archetype: A Feminist Perspective." In Lauter and Rupprecht, *Feminist Archetypal Theory*, 23–45.

Welch, James. *Fools Crow*. New York: Penguin Books, 1986.

———. *Winter in the Blood*. New York: Penguin Books, 1974.

Westling, Louise. *The Green Breast of the New World: Landscape, Gender, and American Fiction*. Athens: University of Georgia Press, 1996.

White, Lynn, Jr. "Historical Roots of our Ecological Crisis." In Glotfelty and Fromm, *The Ecocriticism Reader*, 3–14.

Whitmont, Edward C. "The Evolution of the Shadow." In Zweig and Abrams, *Meeting the Shadow*, 12–19.

Whittaker, Robert. *The Mapmaker's Wife: A True Tale of Love, Murder, and Survival in the Amazon*. New York: Bantam Dell, 2004.

Wiley, Catherine, and Fiona R. Barnes, eds. *Homemaking: Women Writers and the Politics and Poetics of Home*. New York: Garland, 1996.

Wilkins, Peter. "Defense of the Realm: Canada's Relationship to the United States in Margaret Atwood's *Surfacing*." *Yearbook of Research in English and American Literature* 14 (1998): 205–22.

Willeford, William. "Feeling, Imagination, and the Self." In Sugg, *Jungian Literary Criticism*, 200–213.

Williams, Patrick, and Laura Chrisman. *Colonial Discourse and Post-Colonial Theory: A Reader*. New York: Columbia University Press, 1994.

Williams, Raymond. *Keywords: A Vocabulary of Culture and Society*. Rev. ed. New York: Oxford University Press, 1983.

Wilson, Edward O. *Biophilia*. Cambridge: Harvard University Press, 1984.

———. *The Diversity of Life*. Cambridge: Harvard University Press, 1992.

Wolke, Howie, "National Wilderness Preservation System under Siege." *Wild Earth* 13, no. 1 (2003): 15–19.

Wong, Hertha. "An Interview with Louise Erdrich and Michael Dorris." In Chavkin and Chavkin, *Conversations with Louise Erdrich and Michael Dorris*, 30–53.

Woodman, Marion. *The Ravaged Bridegroom: Masculinity in Women*. Toronto: Inner City Books, 1990.

Worster, Donald. "Nature and the Disorder of History." In Soule and Lease, *Reinventing Nature?* 65–85.

Young-Eisendrath, Polly, and Terence Dawson, eds. *The Cambridge Companion to Jung*. Cambridge: Cambridge University Press, 1997.

———. "Gender and Contrasexuality: Jung's Contribution and Beyond." In Young-Eisendrath and Dawson, *The Cambridge Companion to Jung*, 223–39.

Zweig, Connie, and Jeremiah Abrams, eds. *Meeting the Shadow: The Hidden Power of the Dark Side of Human Nature*. New York: Putnam's Books, 1991.

Index

Under the Sign of Nature:
Explorations in Ecocriticism